Surveillance of Public Space: CCTV, Street Lighting and Crime Prevention

Kate Painter

and

Nick Tilley

Editors

CRIME PREVENTION STUDIES
Volume 10

◆

Criminal Justice Press
Monsey, New York, U.S.A.
1999

CRIME PREVENTION STUDIES

Ronald V. Clarke, Series Editor

Crime Prevention Studies is an international book series dedicated to research on situational crime prevention and other initiatives to reduce opportunities for crime. Most volumes center on particular topics chosen by expert guest editors. The editors of each volume, in consultation with the series editor, commission the papers to be published and select peer reviewers.

Printed in the United States of America. No part of this book may be reproduced in any manner whatsoever without written permission, except for brief quotations embodied in critical articles and reviews. For information, contact Criminal Justice Press, Willow Tree Press Inc., P.O. Box 249, Monsey, NY 10952 U.S.A.

ISSN (series): 1065-7029
ISBN: 1-881798-18-6 (cloth)
ISBN: 1-881798-22-4 (paper)

Contents

Editors' Introduction: Seeing and Being Seen to Prevent Crime
Kate Painter and Nick Tilley 1

Privatopia on Trial? Property Guardianship in the Suburbs
Tim Hope 15

A Review of Street Lighting Evaluations: Crime
Reduction Effects
Ken Pease 47

Street Lighting and Crime: Diffusion of Benefits in the
Stoke-on-Trent Project
Kate Painter and David P. Farrington 77

A Review of CCTV Evaluations: Crime Reduction Effects and
Attitudes Towards Its Use
Coretta Phillips 123

CCTV and The Social Structuring of Surveillance
Clive Norris and Gary Armstrong 157

Evaluating "Realistic Evaluation": Evidence from a
Study of CCTV
Martin Gill and Vicky Turbin 179

Yes, It Works, No, It Doesn't: Comparing the Effects of Open-
Street CCTV in Two Adjacent Scottish Town Centres
Jason Ditton and Emma Short..201

Burnley CCTV Evaluation
Rachel Armitage, Graham Smyth and Ken Pease.............. 225

Context-Specific Measures of CCTV Effectiveness
in the Retail Sector
Adrian Beck and Andrew Willis 251

EDITORS' INTRODUCTION: SEEING AND BEING SEEN TO PREVENT CRIME

by

Kate Painter
Cambridge University

and

Nick Tilley
Nottingham Trent University

INTRODUCTION

Cohen and Felson (1979) argue that for a direct-contact predatory crime to be committed, one of the three essential conditions that must converge in space and time is "absence of capable guardians," or, more abstractly, "absence of capable guardianship." Surveillance (or the appearance of surveillance) is part of capable guardianship. Clarke (1995) presents 12 "techniques" of situational prevention, organised under three headings: increasing the effort, increasing the risks, and reducing the reward. Three of the four techniques included under "increasing the risks" refer to surveillance: formal surveillance, surveillance by employees, and natural surveillance. This collection, whose contributors are all British, discusses the efficacy, use and social context of varying forms of surveillance.

The weight of attention given to closed circuit television (CCTV; see chapters by Pease; Phillips; Norris and Armstrong; Gill and Turbin; Short and Ditton; and Beck and Willis) reflects the investment in this method of crime prevention in the U.K. over the past few years. There has been a truly dramatic expansion of CCTV in town centres over the past decade. It is estimated that there were two local authorities with CCTV schemes in 1987 (Bulos and Sarno, 1994), 79 town centre schemes in 1994 (U.K. Home Office 1994), and at least 440 schemes specifically in town centres by 1998 (Goodwin et al., 1998).

It is not difficult to understand this growth in CCTV use in the U.K. As Phillips notes, central government through the Home Office made available £37 million between 1994 and 1997 to support over 550 schemes. The money was provided through CCTV Challenge, a competitive bidding process that required local matched funding. Central government contributions thus levered a further substantial funding, primarily from local authorities and the private sector. A further £170 million is being made available by the government in the U.K. over three years, beginning in 1999, for CCTV in town or city centres, car parks, residential areas, other crime hotspots, and to modernise existing systems. This will clearly further extend the reach of CCTV.

Home Office guidance, issued when CCTV Challenge was launched, began by saying,

> It is essential at the outset to assess the crime and other problems to be addressed and to examine a range of responses, which might include CCTV. Avoid falling into the trap of thinking you should use CCTV just because it is available and because neighbouring towns seem to be planning to do so. You need to think through the way in which CCTV will help address **your** problems in **your** circumstances. Remember no two towns are identical: there may be other solutions to particular local problems. Avoid unrealistic expectations. Don't assume that CCTV will *by itself* [emphasis in original] solve your problems. To be successful CCTV needs to be carefully planned, competently managed and generally introduced as part of a package of measures [U.K. Home Office 1994:9.]

In view of this official advice about the need for thought about the appropriateness of CCTV for local problems, consideration of alternative solutions, and the use of packages of measures rather than technological magic bullets, the decision to put so much of a crime prevention budget into this one particular device is surprising. The reasons may well have as much to do with the surface plausibility of the measure, the apparent public popularity of the measures, and the benefits that could be expected by being seen to be doing something visible in response to widespread concerns over crime, as with any serious explanation that CCTV alone would necessarily yield commensurate increases in community safety.

The alacrity with which local areas took up the CCTV Challenge also needs explaining. Cash-strapped local authorities, whose residents typically have crime at or close to the top of their concerns, are quick to take advantage of any funding opportunities offered by central government. As a rule they have been core players in preparing bids. One of the major, if unsurprising, lessons from the extensive installation of CCTV in Britain is the leverage that funding can have in shaping approaches to crime prevention.

Lighting as a crime prevention measure is addressed in two chapters (Pease; and Painter and Farrington), and this reflects the respective attention given to it and to CCTV in Britain in the past few years as a crime prevention measure. As Pease notes, there has been much more official skepticism about the potential of lighting to prevent crime than CCTV. It has certainly not received the same level of cash injection and leverage from central government as a crime prevention measure, though lighting has been upgraded for a range of other reasons: to prevent traffic accidents, to promote social interaction and commercial activity, and as a contribution to an aesthetically improved nighttime environment.

As a general review of street lighting, the chapter by Pease is refreshing in drawing attention to the political context of crime prevention policy. He discusses how the debate about the contribution of street lighting to crime reduction has been bedeviled by dogmatism, wooly thinking, and skepticism, despite generally positive findings from a number of small-scale projects and the "methodological sophistication" and "rigorous analysis" of the two most recent studies. As Pease wryly comments with regard to those accountable for exercising stewardship of public money, "One is tempted to ask where rigorous standards went into the headlong rush for CCTV deployment."

The volume begins with a chapter that is not quite so technique-specific. Hope discusses the context furnished for community property guardianship in suburbia, reminding us of the importance of community context for this.

Surveillance as Crime Prevention

No form of surveillance directly stops crimes from occurring. With improvements in lighting, as Pease notes, some crimes may even become easier to commit: for example, prospective thieves can see what there is to steal, what they are doing in overcoming physical security, and who is coming to stop them from committing their crime, and can more easily find their escape if they are disturbed. Neither CCTV nor lighting constitute physical barriers. If CCTV and lighting do prevent crime it is through some mechanism they trigger, leading to fewer decisions to commit crimes than would otherwise be the case.

Where Clarke (1995) includes surveillance in general, and lighting and CCTV in particular, under "increasing risks" within situational crime prevention, he is indicating how each might have its crime-inhibitive effect. Several of the papers included here discuss in some detail the ways in which lighting and CCTV might lessen crime, and how they might also inadvertently increase it. Not all the mechanisms mentioned are directly risk-related, and even where risk is potentially raised it is not always through the introduction of lighting or CCTV *per se*, but rather through some other surveillance/risk-inducing behaviour triggered by them.

These papers avoid the trap of asking simple-minded and misleading questions about whether or not CCTV or lighting work unconditionally. Earlier research has, sometimes not very helpfully, framed questions about situational crime prevention measures in simple, "does it work?" terms, assuming that if in some case they are found not to have produced a reductive effect this in some sense counts against the measures. What several of these papers bring out is how lighting and CCTV *can* produce decreases in crime in conditions conducive to their efficacy. Pease has noted that in some cases packages of measures will be needed to ensure that conditions are created in which the causal efficacy of measures can be activated. In relation to the two specific measures examined in detail in this volume, lighting may be introduced to create conditions in which CCTV systems can be operated more effectively. At the same time, of course, lighting may have its own effects *sui generis*.

What Painter (1996) has said of lighting improvements in particular — that they might not always reduce crime — would go for almost any crime prevention measure. She says, "One is tempted to ask why anyone ever thought that they would achieve this" (p.333). No one should ever believe that any individual crime prevention measure (including CCTV) will always reduce crime. The potential effectiveness of measures depends on their suitability to the circumstances in which a given crime problem manifests itself.

Solution-led situational crime prevention, where particular situational measures are treated as potential cure-alls are, thus, doomed to disappoint. These measures also risk discrediting situational crime prevention by over-identifying it with the introduction of particular measures, such as bolts, bars and CCTV. A problem-oriented approach to situational crime prevention, in contrast, begins with the presenting crime problem and then tries to figure out ways of triggering mechanisms for reducing opportunities for the offences. There are, of course, by now very many examples of achievements following from this (see Clarke, 1997).

Sadly, in the case of CCTV we see a good deal of funding-inspired, solution-led crime prevention. Equally sadly, in the case of lighting, some previous research seems to have assumed that if it was introduced it must have comprised a solution to a crime problem, or else it has no significance as a situational crime prevention measure. The review by Pease is useful in drawing a line under a sterile debate by concluding that the capacity of street lighting to reduce crime has now been satisfactorily settled. The question now is how policy should move forward to reflect this. Situational crime prevention, as we see it, is about working out how to trigger crime-inhibiting causal powers through the introduction of relevant measures. And what makes sense as a solution will depend on the specific circumstances.

Many of the contributions to this volume are concerned with spelling out how the measures introduced may trigger crime preventive mechanisms in the specific contexts in which they are introduced (Pease; Painter and Farrington; Phillips; Gill and Turbin; Ditton and Short; and Beck and Willis).

There is some evidence that though lighting, CCTV and provision of concierges might look like simple situational measures, because their surface plausibility is associated with the potential they evidently have for triggering direct risk-increasing crime prevention mechanisms, they may operate in more subtle ways. For example, just as Laycock (1997) found that property marking "worked" in small South Wales villages less by the direct consequences of the marking per se and more by the change in perceptions of general crime risks amongst the local offenders, so, too, can lighting have its effects less by the facilitated surveillance through improved illumination and more by the community changes effected by the environmental improvements (see Painter and Farrington).

The Social Significance of and Context for Crime Prevention Measures

There is more to crime prevention measures than their impact on crime rates. They may have other uses, consequences and meanings that are significant in shaping their social acceptability. There are, in this respect, significant differences between lighting and CCTV.

Public-space CCTV can comprise a tool for purposeful, targeted surveillance over what people are doing. It may thereby reduce privacy in public places, by providing the means for people to be watched and recorded as they go about their daily lives. Some feel uncomfortable at the thought that their private out-of-doors actions may be focused on by surveillance specialists, hidden in control rooms, and that their behaviour may in principle be broadcast, or used in evidence. It is not just criminal behaviour, of course, that might be captured, but kissing, scratching, nose-picking, dancing, tripping, colliding, bleeding, panicking, hugging, crying, vomiting, eating, smoking, spilling, quarrelling or dying. Many may feel uneasy about unseen professional watchers being able to look at and tape their private and personal behaviours, even in public places. Goffman (1971) has described the ways in which we preserve our dignity and self by controlling our public presentation in everyday life. CCTV jeopardises our scope for restricting access to public presentational slips.

CCTV can also capture not only what individuals do, but also whom they meet. For a host of innocent reasons, people may not welcome what they might see as intrusive surveillance of their relationships with others. Whether it be with potential business partners, lovers, political allies, or (non-criminal) friendship with offenders, being watched and recorded anonymously may be unwelcome. CCTV may, in addition, be deployed "against" certain persons or types of person who are deemed suspicious. It can thus be used as a means of oppressing those subject to public prejudice. It may even be deployed to exclude people whose face or appearance does not fit (Norris and Armstrong).

Lighting improvements facilitate natural surveillance; unlike CCTV, they are not a means for professional watching. Lighting can, thus, be seen to be less formal and more democratic. It is consonant with Jacobs's concerns about forging conditions for informal mutual control (1961), rather than the development of all-encompassing centrally staffed panopticon[1] of them and us.

There is currently no statutory regulation in Britain for the installation, operation and use of CCTV systems. Most, though, are covered by codes of practice, about whose development the Local Government Information Unit (LGIU) has prepared extensive guidance (LGIU, 1996). The Home Office CCTV Challenge competition called for the formation of codes of practice to effect local regulation of systems. The fact that codes of practice for CCTV are needed reflects the particular issues raised by CCTV as against lighting. In practice, however, policing codes of practice is very difficult.

A further consideration relating to the use of crime prevention measures is their relative cost-effectiveness. This has proved difficult, and relatively few studies have attempted systematically to measure paybacks for investments made. In this volume, pioneering efforts are made by Painter and Farrington in regard to improvements in street lighting, and by Beck and Willis in regard to CCTV in stores. Hope raises interesting questions about the conditions for natural surveillance in (changing) suburbia. He highlights the problems in achieving collective commitments where conditions favour "free-riding," and the consequent fragility of communal efforts. (For an explanation of free-riding, see note 14, page 44.)

The Future of Surveillance in Crime Prevention

Public support or acceptance for CCTV in public spaces in Britain appears to be high (Honess and Charman, 1992; Bennett and Gelsthorpe, 1996). Among a minority, however, there are important concerns about threats to civil liberties (Davies, 1998). Public support is not necessarily robust. While public concerns about crime appear to be enough to elicit acquiescence to the introduction of plausible measures to reduce risk, there has been rather little serious debate. Political parties and the mass media have raised few critical questions. Were the climate to change on the basis of perceived misuse and/or widespread perceptions of CCTV's ineffectiveness in many settings, support could presumably wither quite quickly. Ditton (1998) has entertainingly shown how patterns of answers to a question about support for CCTV can be influenced by the context set by preceding questions (95% versus 56% in favour) within a given research instrument. It is likely that the context set by the debate (or lack of it) outside the interview has a similar conditioning effect on what may be fragile and ephemeral opinions.

There is clearly no point in incurring the costs and other downsides of CCTV where there is no significant crime problem, or in contexts where its installation offers few prospects of triggering direct or indirect crime prevention mechanisms. Equally, opponents of CCTV as a crime prevention measure need to beware of claiming that it can never reduce crime. There is, by now, plenty of evidence that it can. Where there are significant crime problems in contexts where CCTV can plausibly play a part in prevention, presumably a balance has to be drawn between the protective benefits brought and the threats introduced by CCTV. Our hunch is that there will be circumstances where CCTV will be warranted on this basis, but this would probably justify rather fewer schemes than have now been installed in Britain.

Moreover, in these cases, enforceable codes of conduct or statutory regulation will be needed to minimise potential public disquiet and any unintended ill effects.

Technology and crime methods change. Ekblom (1997) has shown how the preventer and the offender are mutually adaptive and innovative. What works as a crime method today may not do so tomorrow as the preventer introduces new initiatives. What worked today as a prevention method may not work tomorrow, as offenders introduce their new initiatives. Both sides are able to take advantage of technological and social developments furnishing new resources and opportunities for crime and its prevention. CCTV and lighting both potentially fit into processes of innovation and adaptation, which can affect both the efficacy and the social significance of measures.

In the case of CCTV, the past decade has seen dramatic improvements in picture quality. From grainy black and white images where it would be quite difficult to recognise an individual, we now have systems where near-broadcast-quality images are relayed to the control room. Moreover, Norris et al. (1998) report the development of automated, "algorithmic" surveillance, using digitised cameras and microcomputers, through which images of scenes plausibly arousing suspicion can be recognised, triggering a response without the interposition of human beings with their perceptual frailties. There are developments towards systems that will hold and begin to match images of particular (known or wanted) individuals. Norris et al. even raise the spectre of a "near national database of all citizens" through which we can all be recognised as we walk the streets (p.268)! These developments will affect both the price and power of CCTV systems, altering at the same time their coverage, potential for detecting and disrupting crime in real time, and implications for civil liberties and possible discriminatory or exclusionary use.

In the case of lighting, developments are rather less dramatic, though the improvements in returns in lighting intensity from a given energy input have meant that the costs of lighting in terms of money and natural resources has dropped dramatically, making more realistic the scope for targeted improvements in lighting levels in the service of crime prevention.

Changes in technology, social arrangements and crime methods mean that fixed answers to effectiveness questions concerning individual surveillance methods cannot be expected. A research and practice agenda is needed to better understand how lighting, CCTV, concierges and residents, as well as combinations of them, can most effectively and economically contribute to public safety and security.

The papers collected here comprise an important start. They certainly show that CCTV, and lighting upgrades can reduce crime, and they begin to tease out some of the conditions needed for preventive effects to be achieved.

THE CONTRIBUTIONS

The opening chapter, by Hope, helps us distinguish between different forms of guardianship, the assumptions behind them, and the conditions needed for their operation. He distinguishes, in particular, the public good-oriented, inclusive, nondemarcatory, natural surveillance stressed by Jacobs (1961), which thrives on unboundaried social and functional heterogeneity, from the "club good"-related, exclusionary, demarcatory, facilitated and sometimes purposive surveillance stressed by Newman (1973), which thrives on boundaried, homogeneous communities of interest. Hope then looks at salient features of the particular physical and social context of the suburbs for the development, operation and maintenance of varying forms of private-property guardianship. He pays particular attention to the problems of free-riding.

The next two chapters examine lighting enhancement as a means of crime prevention. Pease reviews the literature to date and points to potential future uses of lighting to reduce crime. He highlights what is seen as a stale debate between those whose research purports to find that lighting improvements do and those whose research finds that they do not reduce crime. Pease concludes that lighting improvements can, and have, been found in almost all studies to reduce crime, but will not always or necessarily do so. A research agenda, aimed at finding how and in what circumstances changes in lighting levels can affect crime levels, is advocated and some possibilities suggested. Painter and Farrington report the findings of a case study of lighting upgrades in Stoke-on-Trent; the latest evaluation of a continuing programme of work that has been carried out in the United Kingdom over the past decade. Comparing experimental (lighting improved) and surrounding control areas (lighting levels unchanged), they find a significant decrease in crime in the relit area. There was no clear evidence of displacement, but rather diffusion of benefits to adjacent areas. The paper combines qualitative and quantitative data to explain the mechanisms of lighting as a crime prevention measure, and a cost-benefit analysis of reduction in crime is undertaken.

Six chapters focus on the installation of CCTV as a technique for crime prevention. Phillips provides a thorough review of the literature. She concentrates mainly on the effectiveness of CCTV in reducing crime, disorder and fear of crime, but also considers research findings concerning public attitudes towards the use of CCTV in public places and the civil liberties implications raised by its use. Phillips tries to make sense of mixed findings, concluding that CCTV can be effective in deterring property crimes but is less successful in dealing with personal crime, public order problems and fear of crime. Norris and Armstrong examine in detail how CCTV has actually been operated in practice in three sites. They show how operators are inevitably selective in their attention to and direction of cameras. Operators are shown to target surveillance disproportionately on men, the young and blacks, and to more frequently watch these groups for no apparent reason. Suspicions warranting surveillance are shown to be constructed on the basis of cues reflecting operator assumptions, values and stereotypes. Local policies also shape the use of CCTV, for example, to monitor particular crimes such as drug dealing and street robbery, or particular types of people, notably, black youths.

Gill and Turbin's chapter is primarily about methodology, using research on the effectiveness of CCTV in a retail environment as a case study for using "realistic evaluation." Realistic evaluation asks how interventions work to produce their effects according to contextual contingencies. Gill and Turbin highlight realistic evaluation's emphasis on developing and testing theories specifying context-mechanism-outcome configurations (CMOCs) to improve understanding of how measures have varying impacts according to the conditions in which they operate. They identify nine CCTV CMOC conjectures from their two-store study, and try to assemble data to test them. They conclude that whilst it is useful and relatively easy to devise CMOC conjectures, it is much harder to assemble data to test them in the context of research with time and resource limitations.

The chapters by Ditton and Short and by Armitage, Smyth and Pease comprise evaluations of the effectiveness of CCTV in town and city centres. Ditton and Short discuss evaluations they have conducted in two towns in Scotland: Airdrie and Glasgow. Interestingly, very different effects were found in each. In Airdrie, the evidence they adduce suggests that CCTV had been very successful in reducing recorded crime. Moreover, despite efforts to find displacement, they found none. In contrast, in Glasgow the evidence does not show the system to have had the same impact. Ditton and Short try to explain these differences in measured impact. They make a number of suggestions, in part having to do with measurement issues and in part with ways in which CCTV worked very differently in small town Airdrie as opposed to major-city Glasgow. Armitage et al. present findings from their evaluation of the crime prevention effectiveness of the CCTV system installed in Burnley, in the northwest of England. They address the mechanisms through which CCTV may have its impact, and, like Ditton and Short, focus on changes in recorded crimes. Armitage et al. find a significant and sustained reduction in a variety of recorded crimes in the beats covered by the cameras. They find no evidence of displacement to adjoining areas, and some diffusion of benefits. The sustained impact suggests that the effect was not brought about by short-term publicity. They show decreases in some crimes that are not subject to CCTV surveillance, and propose mechanisms through which this may have happened: for example, through disrupting the general-offending behaviour of versatile criminals, releasing the police to attend more fully to crimes committed in private, and/or jogging the memory of potential victims who become aware of their vulnerability.

The final chapter, by Beck and Willis, examines the effects of CCTV as a primary crime prevention measure directed against staff and customer theft in the fashion-retailing sector. They report on a before-and-after study of 15 stores, comparing the impact of CCTV systems with varying levels of sophistication (high, medium, low) on levels of loss, measuring loss through a series of stock takes. The introduction of CCTV was associated with a significant short-term decrease in loss, though effectiveness had largely disappeared after six months. Beck and Willis conjecture that the diminishing impact follows from offenders becoming progressively inured to CCTV's deterrent potential. Beck and Willis also note that relatively easily collected measurements — loss of sales figures and numbers of units lost and their value — function as robust and "good enough" indicators of the likely impact of CCTV. They include useful discussion of and data on the payback from installing CCTV as a loss-reduction measure for stores.

Address correspondence to: Nick Tilley, Crime and Social Research Unit, Nottingham Trent University, Burton Street, Nottingham NG1 4BU, United Kingdom.

REFERENCES

Bennett, T. and L. Gelsthorpe (1996). "Public Attitudes to CCTV in Public Places." *Studies in Crime and Crime Prevention* 5(1):72-90.

Bulos, M. and C. Sarno (1994). *Closed Circuit Television and Local Authority Initiatives: The First National Survey.* London, UK: School of Land Management and Urban Policy, South Bank University.

Clarke, R. (1995) "Situational Crime Prevention." In: M. Tonry and D. Farrington (eds.), *Building a Safer Society: Strategic Approaches to Crime Prevention.* (Crime and Justice: A Review of Research, vol. 19). Chicago, IL: University of Chicago Press.

Clarke, R. (1997). *Situational Crime Prevention: Successful Case Studies* (2nd ed.). New York, NY: Harrow and Heston.

Cohen, L.E. and M. Felson (1979). "Social Change and Crime Trends: A Routine Activities Approach." *American Sociological Review* (44):588-608.

Davies, S. (1998). "CCTV: A New Battlefield for Privacy." In: C. Norris, J. Moran and G. Armstrong (eds.), *Surveillance, Closed Circuit Television and Social Control.* Aldershot, UK: Ashgate.

Ditton, J. (1998). "Public Support for Town Centre CCTV Schemes." In: C. Norris, J. Moran and G. Armstrong (eds.), *Surveillance, Closed Circuit Television and Social Control.* Aldershot, UK: Ashgate.

Ekblom, P. (1997). "Gearing Up against Crime: A Dynamic Framework to Help Designers Keep Up with the Adaptive Criminal in a Changing World." *International Journal of Risk, Security and Crime Prevention* 2:249-265.

Goffman, E. (1971). *The Presentation of Self in Everyday Life.* Harmondsworth, UK: Penguin.

Goodwin, M., C. Johnstone and K. Williams (1998). "New Spaces of Law Enforcement: Closed Circuit Television, Public Behaviour and the Policing of Public Space." Unpublished paper, University of Wales, Aberystwyth, Wales.

Honess, T. and E. Charman (1992). *Closed Circuit Television in Public Places: Its Acceptability and Perceived Effectiveness.* (Crime Prevention Unit Series Paper, #35.) London, UK: Home Office.

Jacobs, J. (1961). *The Life and Death of Great American Cities.* New York, NY: Vintage Books.

Laycock, G. (1997). "Operation Identification or the Power of Publicity?" In: R. Clarke (ed.), *Crime Prevention: Successful Case Studies* (2nd ed.). New York, NY: Harrow and Heston.

Local Government Information Unit (1996). *A Watching Brief: A Code of Practice for CCTV.* London, UK: author.

Newman, O. (1973). *Defensible Space.* London, UK: Architectural Press.

Norris, C., J. Moran and G. Armstrong (1998). "Algorithmic Surveillance: The Future of Automated Visual Surveillance." In: C. Norris, J.

Moran and G. Armstrong (eds.), *Surveillance, Closed Circuit Television and Social Control.* Aldershot, UK: Ashgate.

Painter, K. (1996). "Street Lighting, Crime and Fear of Crime." In: T. Bennett (ed.), *Preventing Crime and Disorder: Targeting Strategies and Responsibilities.* Cambridge, UK: Institute of Criminology.

U.K. Home Office (1994). *CCTV: Looking Out For You.* London, UK: author.

NOTES

1. Jeremy Bentham's 19th century design for a new model prison included a central observation tower from which guards could see all without being seen. He called this a panopticon. Inmates would not know when, or whether, they were being watched.

PRIVATOPIA ON TRIAL? PROPERTY GUARDIANSHIP IN THE SUBURBS

by

Tim Hope
Keele University

Abstract: *This paper explores how distinctions between private and public underpin the concept of guardianship that has been applied to the understanding and control of crime in residential areas. Specifically, it focuses on the guardianship of private property in (affluent) residential suburbs. First, the paper discusses the concept of "natural surveillance" and identifies its role in the crime prevention theories of Jane Jacobs and Oscar Newman, particularly highlighting the issue of boundary maintenance between private and public space. Second, it presents evidence on property crime victimisation in relation to dwelling type and area socioeconomic status, drawn from a multivariate model of British Crime Survey data. Third, the paper discusses the ways in which suburbs deliver guardianship "goods" to their residents, including that collectively provided by, for example, "Neighbourhood Watch." Its broad conclusion is that property guardianship in suburbs is likely to be a zero-sum game for residents unless borders can be maintained; in turn, this implies an underlying logic of converting public security goods into exclusive "club goods."*

INTRODUCTION

Distinctions between public and private permeate thinking about crime control no less than in other spheres of political life. Such distinctions have also played a crucial, if often ambiguous and unacknowledged, role within those "criminologies of everyday life" that have shaped contemporary thought and policy about crime prevention (Garland, 1996). Here, I want to explore how distinctions between the private and the public underpin the concepts of guardianship that have been applied to the understanding and control of crime in residential locales.[1] The substantive focus here will be the guardianship from criminal victimisation of private property in residential suburbs.

There are (at least) three common ways of thinking about the distinction between private and public.[2] First, there is the idea that it is about the privacy of individuals — the (in)visibility to others of individual thought or action. Second, there is the idea that there is a distinction between matters pertaining to, or the property of, individuals as opposed to those to do with collectivities. These two distinctions underpin common-sense and legal definitions, both of property crime victimisation and guardianship against it. However, a third way of distinguishing between the private and the public, which to some extent incorporates the other two and which will be of particular focus here, is the means of enforcement by which the distinction between private and public is maintained. What are the processes, norms or mechanisms that people use or rely upon to exclude others from their property? These various meanings of the distinction are related in their wider consequences to property guardianship in the suburbs. Specifically, they (1) render private domestic property open to victimisation, and (2) lead to private as opposed to collective responses to such vulnerability, which (3) are obtainable through the operation of exclusionary mechanisms.

The rise of "mass private property" — such as shopping malls, educational campuses, condominiums and privately developed residential estates — has been seen as a principal stimulus for the privatised supply and "commodification" of guardianship and security services, particularly leading to increasing demands on the state for additional security and for the right to exercise private guardianship (Shearing and Stenning, 1983). Yet the guardianship needs of large corporate actors and place entrepreneurs (Logan and Molotch, 1987) are perhaps only one element in the development of markets of private property guardianship (Spitzer, 1987). Additionally, the imperatives of private homeownership — of masses of individual private property owners — also affects demands for security. Yet the specific forms that emergent "markets" for guardianship might take are likely to depend upon the spatial and cultural aggregations of the micro-motives of individual homeowners. Since "suburbs" are residential locales composed primarily of privately owned dwellings, then the way in which the surveillance of their shared space, and the guardianship of their private property, is managed — and by whom — will depend upon the outworking of the distinction between public goods and private interests.

RESIDENTIAL GUARDIANSHIP

Suburban homeowners seek guardianship for their property from a mixed economy of impure public and private goods. Typically, they may spend a certain amount of personal resources (including income and time) on home security, mainly of the target-hardening variety, and they take a variety of simple avoidance and risk-protection measures during their everyday lives to protect themselves and their property. Additionally, homeowners pay to defray their losses from property crime victimisation through private insurance which may also provide them with a sense of security. These "goods" comprise self-guardianship, i.e., the kinds of protection and surveillance that individuals can secure by private enterprise and contract, that is, private goods. In contrast, residents also benefit from public guardianship, chiefly, from the property guardianship services supplied publicly by police activity (including detection and patrol). Ideally, the latter takes the form of a public good.[3] Last, but certainly not least, individuals also opt for the collective guardianship of their residential area. They move into, stay and invest in particular locales or neighbourhoods, thereby deriving their security from the trust they hold in their neighbours' conventions, norms, routines as well as their guardianship practices. Such collective guardianship has public-goods qualities, since it is difficult for residents to be excluded. Nevertheless, as nonresidents do not benefit, it more resembles a "club" good — one that remains public to members of the "club" but where nonmembers' access to the good can be denied, controlled or charged (cf. Sandler, 1992).

Guardianship goods are scarce — they require resources and investment in their production. Moreover, the greater the demand for them, the more "congested" their supply becomes.[4] Thus, for example, public good guardianship services provided by police patrols are subject to crowding as a result of increased demand (via calls for service), especially if the capacity of the police to respond is resource-limited but nevertheless predicated on giving universal coverage as a public good. Therefore, congestion in supply occurs, reducing the quality of public police guardianship for any individual the more that aggregate demand for the good increases. Thus, suburban demands for greater public guardianship are likely to be increasingly unmet the more that demand increases. The cost of supplying public guardianship rises at the same time as its effectiveness diminishes; and the means of managing the risk of property crime is displaced to private enterprise.

One of the key public policy responses to this problem has been to seek growth in the supply of guardianship goods through innovation. One course has been to look to technological innovation, for example, closed circuit television, alarms, and other domestic hardware; but these innovations also have public costs. The other course has been to exploit the resource of untapped "natural surveillance" of communities that promises to superficially meet the security deficit for a low rate of additional public investment (Hope, 1995).

NATURAL SURVEILLANCE

The term "natural surveillance" seems to have been coined by Oscar Newman, in his book *Defensible Space* (1973), to describe a form of community self-surveillance that entails the day-to-day supervision by residents of their environment, "...employing the full range of encounter mechanisms to indicate their concerned observation of questionable activity and their control of the situation" (Newman, 1973:4). Superficially, the concept draws upon the ideas of Jane Jacobs in *The Death and Life of Great American Cities* (1965), part of which celebrates the self-policing of the successful "street-neighbourhood." Here, surveillance — in the sense of routine supervision of activity in public — arises from the diversity of public street life (the "intricate sidewalk ballet"). This diversity produces a concerned, though not self-conscious, supervision of behaviour in public places, springing out of the everyday, public, routine activities of those who live, work and play there. Yet although many commentators have seen a broad affinity between Jacobs and Newman by virtue of their common interest in natural surveillance,[5] their respective interpretations of the concept in terms of the public-private distinction are radically opposed.

For Jacobs natural surveillance is collectively produced and publicly inclusive (Berman, 1982): "The first thing to understand is that the public peace — the sidewalk and street peace — of cities is not kept primarily by the police, necessary as the police are. It is kept primarily by an intricate, almost unconscious, network of voluntary controls and standards among the people themselves, and enforced by the people themselves...No number of police can enforce civilisation where the normal, casual enforcement of it has broken down" (Jacobs, 1965:41). Here, a normative urban order emerges spontaneously out of the daily, social life of street neighbourhoods.

The resulting "natural" surveillance is thus a collectively generated public good from which residents cannot be excluded and from which they cannot opt out except by moving away. In this model, individual residents' public participation in the everyday, shared activities of the street would have both a "horizontal" and a "vertical" effect on the street neighbourhood's collective capacity for social control (Hope, 1995). On the one hand, such participation would provide "eyes on the street" — continuous routine opportunities for the mutual surveillance and guardianship of private property (Jacobs, 1965:chapter 2). This routine participation would not only satisfy the needs of residents for sociability but at the same time would provide an arena in which they could subtly negotiate mutually acceptable degrees of privacy through the medium of routine interaction with their neighbours. On the other hand, the street's latent social network would provide a collective resource — over and above the capacity of individuals — which could be mobilised when needed to invoke the wider resources of the city, including policing, to bring added guardianship and security services that neither individuals nor the street could raise themselves.

In contrast, where this public forum for everyday interaction was lacking, people would need to take part in more organised group activities in order to meet their needs for sociability, mutual support and resource mobilisation. Yet, as Jacobs (1965) presciently points out, this kind of organised activity often only works well "for self-selected upper-middle-class people...it solves easy problems for an easy kind of population" (p.76). For more heterogeneous population, the risks to privacy of organised sociability — especially with "strangers" — outweigh the benefits: "...the more common outcome in cities, where people are faced with the choice of sharing much or nothing, is nothing" (Jacobs, 1965:76). And in such circumstances, of course, the street neighbourhood cannot provide natural surveillance.

The solution to this dilemma offered by Newman (1973) is essentially to bring much more of the public arena of the street neighbourhood under the control and surveillance of individual households.[6] While Jacobs seeks to protect constituent individual privacy and property rights by enhancing the shared public arena and social institution of the street — essentially to incorporate the private within the public — Newman's approach is to abolish semipublic street space through privatisation, thereby excluding outsiders. This would be achieved either by extending, via architectural design, residents' ability to supervise and control their proximate public space, or by removing residential space altogether from the sphere of common ownership and use. Yet there are obvious practical limits to the complete abolition of shared public (communal) space. At a minimum, a household's opportunity to enjoy its private space depends upon access that needs to be negotiated around others' private spaces. The crucial issue, then, is where the private-public boundary is drawn in the hierarchy of space that stretches from the individual dwelling to the city itself.

Newman's (1973) approach is to advocate clear, unambiguous boundary demarcations. In one respect, this means clarifying the distinction between private-dwelling space and public space, achieved through the removal of the "confused space" that was neither genuinely private nor purely public (Coleman, 1985). Yet this does not necessarily resolve where the effective boundary between private and public can be drawn. Put differently, to what extent are individuals to derive their security from the privacy of their dwellings or from the public arena of their neighbourhoods? And, in the case of the latter, how is the security of the street neighbourhood itself to be attained?

Jacobs's (1965) preference is to abolish "borders" themselves on the grounds that the more demarcatory they are, the more likely they are to have no purpose other than that of socially sterile border-zones (1965: chapter 14). In contrast, the protection of communities rather lies in their seamless integration into the city as a whole: only continuous networks of street neighbourhoods are able to handle the circulation of strangers, passing them on from one naturally surveyed place to another. Seamlessness also enables neighbourhoods to coalesce into effective political entities if needs be. Thus, city districts can operate as public confederations of street neighbourhoods. This seamlessness points up another fundamental distinction between Jacobs and Newman. Newman (1980) sees neighbourhood disorder arising from the clash of social heterogeneity — and, hence, orderliness deriving from homogeneous "communities of interest." Conversely, Jacobs's (1965) fundamental underpinning of urban order is heterogeneous diversity: the greater a community's diversity of uses and inhabitants, the greater its integration into the wider public economy and civility of cities, and thus the greater the capacity of natural surveillance to preserve order.[7]

The spatial expression of this difference is exemplified in Newman's efforts to demarcate the boundaries of the street neighbourhood itself. His solution lies in collective privatisation of the street neighbourhood in its entirety. Of particular significance is Newman's (1996) interpretation of "The private streets of St. Louis" — city streets not only gated or blocked to through traffic but actually deeded from the city to residents who legally own and maintain them and who agree to be party to a restricted covenant that limits the nature of the use of their homes and property (Newman, 1980). Newman (1973, 1996) sees both the symbolic and real privatisation of the street neighbourhood as not only limiting access to those who have a legitimate presence (i.e., by virtue of private property rights) but also heightening residents' sense of ownership and collective control over their environments — their sense of territoriality. More recently, McKenzie (1994) has dubbed these and similar developments "privatopia" — the growth of self-governing "common-interest developments" that have effectively seceded from the public sphere of city governance, and have thus gained control over the means of membership and exclusion. Thus, while Jacobs's (1965) idea of the organisation of natural surveillance resembles that of a genuine public good, Newman's privatisation of the street neighbourhood more resembles its conversion to a club good.

Yet the question of where boundaries are to be drawn between the private and public spheres is not easily resolved. On the one hand, for example, some have seen the "vernacular" English suburb — especially the development of private, semidetached housing laid down in the interwar period (Coleman, 1985) — as a naturally evolved compromise to the problem of balancing the privacy and guardianship of the dwelling with the need for public access and collective surveillance. For example:

> What seems to be almost unique about the UK suburban housing form is that it combines perimeter security at the rear of the house with a communal social control at the front, derived from implied surveillance by surrounding neighbours...The genius of UK suburban housing is that it combines privacy with just enough mutual surveillance by neighbours to provide a significant social control over potential crime (and no doubt many other aspects of neighbourliness) [Poyner and Webb, 1991:120].

The literal and symbolic "semidetached" nature of such housing seemed to provide a workable balance, first, between the mass provision of housing and the aspirations of the middle classes,[8] and second, between privacy and public accessibility in the guardianship of residential space. Yet, in an urban scenario predicated upon internecine conflict, the tension between public and private solutions to suburban order is only resolved through a radically privatising interest. As Davis (1990:248) notes about suburbs-in-extremis: "On the bad edge of post-modernity...contemporary residential security in Los

Angeles — whether in the fortified mansion or the average suburban bunker — depends upon the voracious consumption of private security services."

What is of interest, then, is the underlying logic of guardianship that operates in the suburbs. From the point of view of prevention, two basic issues remain unresolved: first, where the effective boundaries of guardianship might be drawn — whether around the dwelling or the neighbourhood, or whether, indeed, boundary maintenance itself is necessary at all; and, second, how such boundaries are to be maintained — whether through private (exclusionary) action or public inclusiveness.

HOUSEHOLD CRIME RISK IN THE SUBURBS

What are the contours of insecurity in the suburbs? Table 1 shows the risk for households of becoming a victim of property crime by type of dwelling, estimated from the 1992 British Crime Survey (BCS). The first column shows risks (relative to those of a detached house whose odds are set at unity) weighted only to represent the population. In this estimation, both detached and semidetached dwellings have significantly lower risks than other dwelling types, whose risks do not differ significantly from each other.[9] However, the second column shows the odds re-estimated from a multivariate, logistic regression model that takes into account various characteristics both of the households and of the areas in which they are located. In this context, detached houses and, to a lesser extent, semidetached houses appear to have higher risks than other dwelling types, particularly flats (apartments). The broad reason for this change in the risk-ranking of dwelling types is, of course, the effect of other individual and area-level variables, either amplifying or suppressing risks that might be associated with the dwelling alone. The full model is presented in the Appendix to this paper in Table A.1.[10]

In this model of property crime risk, as with others estimated recently from BCS data, there is a counter-balancing of the risk factors associated with affluence between the individual household and the neighbourhood (Trickett et al., 1995; Ellingworth et al., 1997; Osborn and Tseloni, 1998). Households whose residents are employed in non-manual occupations and have high car ownership also have higher risks of household property crime. A higher risk of victimisation is also associated with the degree of "detachedness" of the dwelling from others adjacent. Thus, our model shows households

Table 1: Likelihood of Property Crime Victimisation by Dwelling

	Unadjusted odds (weighted)	Adjusted odds (multivariate logit regression)
Detached house	1.000	1.000
Semidetached house	1.254	0.845 (.054)
End-terraced (row) house	1.726	0.986 (.901)
Mid-terraced house	1.505	0.763 (.005)
Flats (apartments)	1.569	0.664 (.000)

Source: 1992 British Crime Survey

living in semidetached dwellings to be significantly less at risk than those in fully detached ones; mid-terraced (row) houses less at risk than end-terraced, and households in apartments in multi-occupied buildings less at risk than those in single family buildings. So, in broad terms, "suburban" types of housing and households have higher property crime risks.[11]

The detachedness of dwellings reflects a constellation of values (Hope, 1984). In Britain at least, it represents the cultural value of privacy, expressed as distance and concealment from neighbouring property. In terms of dwelling design, this value is coupled with the amenity of external access to parts of the property and the aesthetic and recreational (i.e., gardening, car parking) facilities of accessible private grounds. In densely populated countries like Britain, land values are high so that the production price of detachedness is also high. Coupled with its use-values of privacy and amenity, dwelling detachedness is highly valued in the housing market and is thus, generally, correlated with the degree of affluence of its occupants, and with the value of domestic private property contained within the dwelling.

There is also a fair degree of research evidence pointing to the greater risk of property crime associated with dwelling detachedness (Hope, 1984). For example, Winchester and Jackson's (1982) study of a relatively affluent area of southern England found marked differences in the annual risk of burglary faced by different types of housing design, with detached houses being five times more vulnerable than other house types. This is a finding supported by Maguire's (1982) study of a similar area. Winchester and Jackson went on to develop and apply an Environmental Risk Index to victimised and non-victimised dwellings, the components of which express various aspects of detachedness in terms of housing plot and environmental setting. This proved to be a powerful discriminator between burgled and non-burgled dwellings, a finding replicated by Litton (cited in Litton, 1997). Moreover, interviews with English burglars have corroborated the view that attributes of dwelling detachedness are attractive as targets primarily through the degree of concealment and access afforded, and the implied value of the property contained within (Maguire, 1982; Bennett and Wright, 1984). In sum, then, dwelling detachedness — the physical expression of individual privacy and affluence — also, ironically, provides the opportunity for burglary.

Yet suburbs themselves suppress the individual risk of property crime. Figure 1 suggests that area affluence — measured here by the proportion of households living in detached dwellings combined with the average number of cars per household — represents a powerful suppressant of household crime risk. This effect is also substantiated in multivariate models of risk (Table A.1; Trickett et al., 1995).[12] Additional area characteristics that seem to reduce property crime risk in our model are also "suburban" — in particular, low child densities, low rates of "disrupted" families, and high rates of home ownership. Despite their individual vulnerability, the typical spatial distribution of dwelling types serves to moderate significantly their risk.[13]

Thus, when the values of privacy, amenity and affluence are attached to the dwelling alone they heighten the risk of property crime. But when such values become the property of neighbourhoods, they reduce risk substantially. Arguably, the "genius" of the English suburb lies in the ability to deliver privacy and amenity in housing to its residents while protecting them from the crime risks that these values might otherwise incur were their owners not fortunate enough to be able to buy into the protection that a better-off suburb seems able to provide.

DEFENDING SUBURBAN BOUNDARIES

Since the real and symbolic boundaries of the dwelling seem to offer insufficient protection, how do the boundaries of the suburbs work to maintain the good of security for their residents? The bulk of

Figure 1: Area Affluence and Property Crime

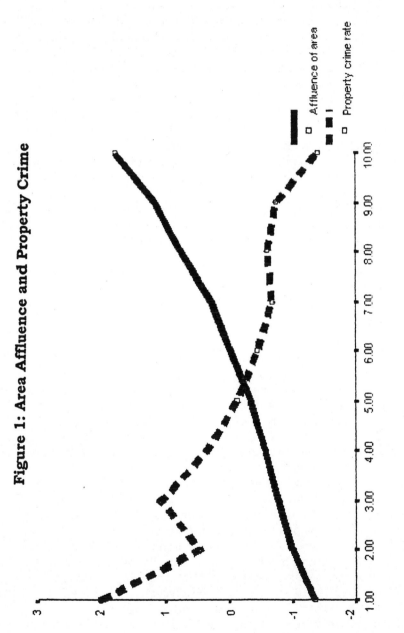

Affluence of area (deciles)

Standardized means per decile

Source: 1992 British Crime Survey (weighted data)

-25-

research into offenders' "journeys to crime" suggests that volume property offending is spatially structured by two broad processes: (1) a fairly sharp "distance decay" from offenders' homes; and (2) a fairly strong degree of routine familiarity that burglars have with the environments in which they offend (Bottoms and Wiles, 1997; Rengert and Wasilcek, 1985; Brantingham and Brantingham, 1984). Additionally, we might make the reasonable supposition that there are two broad classes of offences: those committed amongst familiars; and those amongst strangers. Combining these propositions, the successful low-crime suburb would be one that:

(1) reduced rates of offending amongst proximates and familiars, and created more opportunities for supervising nonresidents (ordering);

(2) maximised its physical and cultural distance from potentially-offending strangers, making it difficult for outsiders to become familiar with the environment of the neighborhood (distancing); and

(3) created buffers between itself and less advantaged outsiders (buffering).

The next three sections will examine each of these elements in detail.

Suburban Ordering

The internal order of residential communities, not least more affluent suburbs, has received less research attention than it deserves (Hope, 1995). We might suppose, however, that there are both compositional and contextual sources of low crime rates in suburbia. On the one hand, suburbs that can attract affluent residents are also attracting people who, for a variety of reasons, have low motivation, or high perception of risk, of committing public criminal acts, particularly of property appropriation. On the other hand, the mores of conduct amongst families, friends and neighbours may resemble what Baumgartner (1988) calls "moral minimalism" — a social order built upon the values of privacy and nonintervention in the lives of others. With greater privacy, mobility and cosmopolitan commitments in work and leisure, strong ties between proximates fail to develop. At the same time, there is an absence of accompanying animosity or grievances that might lead to conflict, including that which could be expressed through property appropriation and destruction.

Yet if moral minimalism and relative affluence reduce opportunities and motivations for property appropriation and destruction amongst proximates in the suburbs, they also have particular consequences for suburban communities' capacities to generate surveillance. If the problem of property guardianship in the suburbs is to prevent offending by outsiders, the more that people value privacy and private lifestyles, the more they become dependent upon specialised institutions — such as police — to maintain the security of the environments in which they wish to pursue their privacy. That is, the more they need agents to provide their public-goods infrastructure of security, including the policing of boundaries, that individual, private action cannot provide. Yet the more overtly supervisory of public space the police become, the more they may intrude on residents' privacy, and the more they become a reminder of the absence of security in the environment (Ericson and Haggerty, 1997).

Still, weak, overlapping ties amongst members of a social group also have strengths for social organisation, providing an extensive network of associations amongst residents through which communication can flow and reciprocities develop. The social strength of these ties is that they provide linkages between sources of power and influence within a community that cannot be achieved by isolated friendship groups, no matter how intrinsically solidaristic these cliques might be (Granovetter, 1973). Extensive networks of social ties provide opportunities for network "closure," creating a reciprocity of social obligation from which "social capital" can be generated (Coleman, 1990). Social capital can also be seen as a collective good that helps in the creation of voluntary community organisations such as residents' associations. These "representative" groups are then able to draw upon the symbolic capital that the neighbourhood holds with extra-communal sources of power, such as public police and local government, to generate resources to preserve neighbourhood amenities and use values, including security (Skogan, 1988).

Those who comprise the social resources that underpin the production of order in suburbs are "socially selected" through the operation of the private free market, primarily in housing. In this respect, the internal production of suburban order, and the process of boundary definition, are apparently seamless — much in the way that Jacobs (1965) envisaged them to be. Yet although weak social ties have strengths for forming associations, they are also weak in sustaining them. As Michael Walzer (1990:15) remarks: "liberalism is distinguished less by the freedom to form groups....than [by] the freedom to leave the groups...behind. Association is always at risk in a liberal society. The boundaries of the group are not policed...that is why liberalism is plagued by free-rider problems." While privacy and affluence may ensure a tranquil internal order in the suburbs — and attract extra-communal resources — they cannot inhibit "exit" from community participation in the form of "free-riding" and outward mobility.[14] Moreover, the availability of incentives to exit continually undermines the production of collective guardianship goods, such as natural surveillance and boundary maintenance.

These effects can be illustrated with reference to resident participation in Neighbourhood Watch (NW), a method favoured in Britain for encouraging growth in the collective guardianship good of natural surveillance. By and large, British NW schemes are initiated and serviced by public police but rely upon individual, voluntary effort to sustain them and to produce and distribute preventive benefits (see Laycock and Tilley, 1995). Importantly, schemes provide club goods for residents — including guardianship through neighbourly natural surveillance, greater security consciousness, property marking, free security advice, and so on — from which households in the area covered by the scheme cannot be excluded. Table 2 is derived from separate multivariate models of the probabilities of a BCS respondent saying that: (a) a NW scheme has been set up in their area; (b) their household actually belongs to such a scheme; and (c) they believe there are reciprocal social relations amongst residents[15] — which we are seeing here as a proxy for social capital (see Appendix for details).

Table 2 shows that although households living in detached houses are more likely to say that a NW scheme exists in their area, they are no more likely than households living in other dwelling types (other than flats) to agree that they actually belonged to a scheme. While respondents' greater access to schemes may indicate that the police have recognised their security needs (see above), their relatively lower likelihood of participating suggests a tendency to free-ride on the collective goods available. Table 2 also suggests that residents of affluent areas are more likely than others to think that reciprocity exists amongst their neighbours (and hence that there is a greater potential for social capital). However, they seem much less likely to have NW schemes set up in their neighbourhoods, and no more likely to belong even when schemes are available. In sum, although the ethos of privacy and weak ties in the suburbs may help sustain "internal" order and create the potential for generating social capital, it also inhibits the transformation of such capital into sustainable social organisation that would provide collective guardianship goods of surveillance and boundary maintenance.

Table 2: Neighbourhood Watch and Community Reciprocity by Dwelling Type and Affluence of Area

	NW scheme set up in area		Household belongs to a NW scheme		Community reciprocity	
	odds	sig	odds	sig	odds	sig
Detached house	1.00		1.000		1.00	
Semidetached house	0.78	.001	1.02	.918	1.03	.640
End-terraced (row) house	0.63	.000	1.01	.953	1.07	.436
Mid-terraced house	0.57	.000	0.80	.194	1.17	.038
Flats/maisonettes	0.45	.000	0.54	.003	1.02	.845
AFFLUENT AREA	0.91	.005	0.95	.509	1.14	.000

Suburb Distancing

Suburbanisation has always meant a search for low housing densities — and their accompanying values of amenity and privacy — at a distance from noxious, high density areas. The theories of the Chicago School provide a framework for predicting the criminogenic outcomes of this dynamic in terms of relatively unregulated competition for urban space between industrial/commercial and residential uses, and between social groups differentiated by income and ethnic and cultural identity (Bursik, 1988). The land and property pricing of the city reflects the outcome of unfettered competition for access to urban resources: inner zones would have high crime rates by virtue of their position in the ecological structure of competition for urban space, a situation that results in a moral vacuum and social disorganisation (Kornhauser 1978; Shaw and McKay 1969). Outer zones would be stable, organised communities reflecting socially homogeneous gradations of income and status. In this context, simple physical distance from areas of offender residence and low spatial mobility would ensure the safety of the suburbs.

Yet such a pattern is ceasing to pertain both in its planned and unplanned forms (Felson, 1994). For example, on the one hand — and perhaps more common in a British context — strict planning controls have limited the capacity for city growth and expansion, in order to hem in suburban sprawl. Additionally, state intervention in housing development, and postwar slum clearance and urban regeneration, has lead to mass social housing developments on the periphery of cities in greater proximity to more affluent suburbs. At the same time, relatively unfettered suburban development and extensive road building, perhaps more common in the American context, have led to a mixing of classes in the suburbs (Logan and Molotch, 1987) and a greater accessibility to a wide-ranging and diverse urban area by a greater range of people (Felson, 1994). In both circumstances, however, the safety of the suburbs can no longer be guaranteed simply by physical distance from areas of offender residence. For would-be ex-urbanites, it takes more resources to achieve distance and maximise amenity, with the costs of counter-urban flight escalating beyond many incomes and occupational needs. Fewer and more affluent people will in future be able to attain the security that distance alone may once have provided.

If sheer distance cannot do the job, other processes may go some of the way towards maintaining suburban boundaries. There are two well-substantiated sets of findings from environmental criminology. Firstly, higher rates of offences are to be found in interstitial or border areas between places that differ in socioeconomic status, with lower rates of offences — especially in better-off neighbourhoods —to be found more towards the social core of these areas. Second, crime rates are higher close to, or in areas with many, through routes and arteries (Brantingham and Brantingham, 1984). Together, it might be inferred that the more a suburb is permeable from the outside, the greater its crime rate (Taylor and Gottfredson, 1986). In this respect, the more that suburban design can be made impermeable to outsiders the greater its internal security: *pace* Jacobs (1965), border zones may well take the blight of diversity but nevertheless benefit the community within; *pace* Newman (1980) the more that borders discourage diverse intrusions, the more safe the community of interest inside.

Finally, studies of the routine activities of property offenders suggest that knowledge and familiarity with a neighbourhood is an important factor in their search behaviour (see Bottoms and Wiles, 1997). Thus, property offenders are likely to commit crimes close to places where they go routinely. To the extent that offenders have similar characteristics — for example, are mostly young men — the less likely are they to go to places where there is little that caters to their lifestyles. Familiarity also cuts the other way: the more socially (or racially) homogeneous the area, the more likely those with non-majority characteristics will stand out. Similarly, the more that strangers differ in obvious and visible ways from residents, the more they will be, and feel, exposed in the public places of the community. Paradoxically, *pace* Jacobs (1965), the fewer people there are in public, the more that those who seem out of place — by virtue of their looks, pedestrianism, car, and so on — will be exposed, provided there is anyone to see and intervene with them. This itself becomes problematic if the routine activities of residents render them less and less likely to spend time in the public places of their community (Felson, 1994). Unless this surveillance deficit can be taken up by other means, for example, public police patrols, even the public-exposure effect of moral minimalism will not suffice.

Suburb Buffering

None of this would matter, however, if suburbs were in a steady state of relations with other parts of their urban areas. Yet even the growth dynamic envisaged by the Chicago School — that is, the process of invasion and succession — implied that there would be periods in which the goods and values of the "outer" suburbs would be threatened, albeit temporarily, by outward growth from the inner core. More contemporary evidence and theory, however, suggests that although the unidirectional, "organic" pattern of growth no longer pertains — nor does its correspondingly stable pattern of relative crime rates (Bursik and Grasmick, 1993) — urban arrangements, nevertheless, are still predicated upon the dynamics and imperatives of growth in capital and rents, and these dynamics affect how places are defined and the meanings they have, especially concerning their boundaries.[16]

Suburban goods, including security, are threatened by crowding. As Hirsch (1977) points out, the amenity (i.e., use) values of suburbs are diminished the more they are overtaken by other suburbs further out from the urban core. The unrestricted dynamic of suburban growth induces congestion in the positional good that once placed the now-engulfed suburb at the edge of the urban area, particularly if it removes residents from proximity to amenity and privacy, for example, when a new road or housing development is built close-by.

Recent ecological analysis of recorded crime rates in Merseyside tends to confirm crowding effects upon the residential security of the more affluent (Hirschfield et al., 1997). In the first place, the highest recorded crime rates in the urban region were found in areas typified by census-based geodemographic methods as "cosmopolitan, multi-racial areas of high population turnover, with a mix of single young professionals, students and young families and over-representations of sub-divided shared dwellings and private renting" (Hirschfield et al., 1997:7). Such "gentrifying" areas are subject to rapid social change and transience, which may itself promote high crime rates

(Bursik and Grasmick, 1993; Taylor and Covington, 1988). These areas are also those that place the poor and the younger segments of the better-off in closest proximity. This proximity may intensify the rate of victimisation, since these areas also had high rates of repeated burglary victimisation; the shortest distance between victims' homes and offence location for assaults and robberies; and high "self-containment" rates for offences (i.e., the extent to which the victim's home and the location of the offence were in the same neighbourhood type).

This study also suggests that as the spatial "width" of relative disadvantage in the areas surrounding an affluent core area increases, the levels of assault and burglary of residents in the affluent core also increases. In addition, the lower the levels of these crimes, the greater the width of relative affluence in the surroundings (Hirschfield et al., 1997). It would seem that social buffering may reduce the crowding of a suburb's security: the more an affluent suburb surrounds itself with other affluent suburbs, and thereby insulates itself from less advantaged neighbours, the more it can resist the crowding of its security.

In sum, then, it would seem that the guardianship goods provided by residence in an affluent suburb, especially those that help control the incursions of nonresidents, are unlikely to be produced through residents' collective actions. Even if public agencies provide affluent suburbs with more free opportunities to organise themselves — as with NW — the values of privacy, mobility, and individualism produce more countervailing incentives for exit than for either political voice within the neighbourhood, or loyalty to its institutions (Walzer, 1990). The property guardianship of the suburbs would seem to reside primarily in border maintenance. As long as suburbanites can distance themselves from offenders — preferably by placing other buffer communities between them so that their positional advantage is not crowded out — the fragility of their internal collective defences, and the vulnerability of their property, need not be tested.

CONCLUSION

Property guardianship in the suburbs is likely to be a zero-sum game unless borders can be maintained. As regards private self-guardianship, the only study of its kind found negligible crime displacement and benefit-diffusion effects between immediate neighbours (Miethe, 1991). It would seem that households cannot usually free-ride on their neighbours' guardianship, nor successfully displace risk to others by taking pre-emptive action. So, when feeling threatened externally, residents may more likely enter into individual zero-sum accumulation of private-security goods, which may indeed become voracious (Davis, 1990). Perhaps only when a certain saturation is reached are collective guardianship goods likely to be generated. Miethe (1991), for instance, also found that there was a clear trend for residents of high-protection areas to benefit from the crime control efforts of their neighbours (supporting free-riding), whereas displacement effects were observed in areas with lower levels of safety precautions. Of course, as the public-goods argument implies, it is difficult to free-ride on others' crime prevention activity if everyone else is free-riding too. Arguably, only when a sufficient aggregation of private self-guardianship is reached does its benefit spill over to the collective advantage of a community as a whole.[17]

An alternative course of private action is move somewhere else, to buy into the total security package offered by another, more secure neighbourhood. But the scarcity of suburbs means that the security of all but the most distant or buffered suburb also becomes devalued (crowded) the more that people seek that option (Hirsch, 1977). Although rising house prices may serve to restrict residential membership of the suburb, they cannot necessarily protect its boundaries other than through market-structured, blighted border zones. The security value of the suburb itself can diminish the more its boundaries are crowded, or its buffers eroded, by encroachment from less advantaged neighbours. Thus, boundary maintenance becomes an important weapon in the preservation of both neighbourhood values and amenities, including security.[18]

Much community action in suburbs is preservationist (Savage et al., 1992), not least with regard to anticrime efforts (Skogan, 1988). Yet suburban communities cannot readily generate organisational resources to take preservative action because private-minded rational action tends towards free-riding and non-contribution. One solution to these public-goods problems is to privatise the street neighbourhood as an exclusive club — "an institutional solution to the collective action problem that internalises an externality through tolls" (Sandler, 1992:64). In this case, if the size and membership of the suburb can be controlled, then crowding effects within the suburb can be prevented and free-riders have an incentive to contribute lest they lose the benefits of club membership. An exclusive club can also police its boundaries by imposing restrictions on who enters the neighbourhood club, whether on a temporary or permanent basis. Thus, taken to its logical conclusion, the public-goods problem of suburban property guardianship lies in the privatopian solutions of Newman (1980). These include the creation of residential club-neighbourhoods that can: deliver boundary-maintenance goods (including additional private guardianship) to residents; generate internal organisational strength and reduce free-riding by virtue of their powers of exclusion; share amongst members the collective benefits of individual security activities; and reduce the costs that their otherwise voracious private consumption of security would incur.

Jacobs's (1965) theory of natural surveillance presupposes an inclusive network of street neighbourhoods. However, this could only come about if every neighbourhood, and each household within it, was seamlessly connected to others within a common, public good that was simultaneously spatial, political and practical. Yet the values of privacy and individualism that suffuse the physical form, cultural life and social position of suburbs within cities militate against this happening. The alternatives for suburbanites to guard their property may be much as Davis (1990) describes them: "fortify your bunker;" support a homeowner politics that preserves the boundaries of the neighbourhood (so that they remain distanced and buffered from the less advantaged); or opt into a privatopian club-neighbourhood where boundary maintenance is part of the service charge.

In Britain and many other countries, these options probably will not need to be put to a serious test for some time; the socio-spatial processes of distancing and buffering still seem likely to provide the main means of suburban protection, unequal and unjust though that may be.[19] To the extent that preservationist homeowner politics are successful, they will continue to distort the distribution of security goods and contribute, indirectly, to the further inequality of the poor. Yet privatopian guardianship may itself be a fugitive utopia unless followed to the logical conclusion of "clubbing" public goods in their entirety. As Jordan points out: "comfortable households in the suburbs ultimately contribute more, through local and national taxes, for their exclusive privileges, because they are required to pay for prisons, reformatories, special schools, psychiatric clinics..[etc.]..many of whose inmates and users could more efficiently be included as members of a heterogeneous and pluralistic community" (1996:181).

Thus, the broader political issue of which the homeowner politics of suburban property guardianship is just a part, is how to control the "secession of the successful,"[20] — how to control opting out and the creation of club-goods, at least so that they do not contribute to distributive injustices in both social harms and the public goods that might be available to remedy them.

Address correspondence to: Professor Tim Hope, Department of Criminology, Keele University, Staffordshire ST5 5BG, United Kingdom. E-mail: t.j.hope@keele.ac.uk.

REFERENCES

Barry, B. and R. Hardin (eds.) (1982). *Rational Man and Irrational Society?* Beverly Hills, CA: Sage.

Baumgartner, M.P. (1988). *The Moral Order of a Suburb*. New York, NY: Oxford University Press.

Bennett, T. and R. Wright (1984). *Burglars on Burglary*. Aldershot, UK: Gower.

Berman, M. (1982). *All That is Solid Melts into Air*. New York, NY: Simon and Schuster.

—— (1995). "In the Forest of Symbols: Some Notes on Modernism in New York." In: P. Kasinitz (ed.), *Metropolis: Centre and Symbol of our Times*. Houndsmill, Hants, UK: Macmillan Press.

Bottoms, A.E. and P. Wiles (1997). "Environmental Criminology." In: M. Maguire, R. Morgan and R. Reiner (eds.), *The Oxford Handbook of Criminology* (2nd ed.). Oxford, UK: Clarendon Press.

Brantingham, P. and P. Brantingham (1984). *Patterns in Crime*. New York, NY: Macmillan.

Bursik, R.J. (1988). "Social Disorganization and Theories of Crime and Delinquency: Problems and Prospects." *Criminology* 26:519-551.

—— and H.G. Grasmick (1993). *Neighborhoods and Crime*. New York, NY: Lexington Books.

Clarke, R.V. (ed.) (1992). *Situational Crime Prevention: Successful Case Studies*. Albany, NY: Harrow and Heston.

Cohen, L. E. and M. Felson (1979). "Social Change and Crime Rate Trends: A Routine Activities Approach." *American Sociological Review* 44:588-608.

Coleman, A. (1985). *Utopia on Trial.* London, UK: Hilary Shipman.

Coleman, J.S. (1990). *Foundations of Social Theory.* Cambridge, MA: Belknap Press.

Davis, M. (1990). *City of Quartz.* London, UK: Verso.

Ekblom, P., M. Sutton and H. Law (1997). *Safer Cities and Residential Burglary: A Summary of Evaluation Results.* (Home Office Research Study #163.) London, UK: Home Office.

Ellingworth, D., T. Hope, D.R. Osborn, A. Trickett and K. Pease (1997). "Prior Victimisation and Crime Risk." *Journal of Crime Prevention and Risk Management* 2:201-214.

Ericson, R.V. and K.D. Haggerty (1997). *Policing the Risk Society.* Oxford, UK: Clarendon Press.

Felson, M. (1994). *Crime and Everyday Life.* Thousand Oaks, CA: Pine Forge Press.

Field, S. and T. Hope (1990). "Economics, the Consumer and Under-Provision in Crime Prevention." In: R. Morgan (ed.), *Policing Organised Crime and Crime Prevention.* (British Criminology Conference 1989, volume 4.) Bristol, UK: Bristol Centre for Criminal Justice.

Garland, D. (1996). "The Limits of the Sovereign State: Strategies of Crime Control in Contemporary Society." *British Journal of Criminology* 36:445-471.

Granovetter M.S. (1973). "The Strength of Weak Ties." *American Journal of Sociology* 78:1360-1380.

Hargreaves Heap, S., M. Hollis, B. Lyons, R. Sugden and A. Weale (1992). *The Theory of Choice: A Critical Guide.* Oxford, UK: Blackwells.

Hirsch, F. (1977). *Social Limits to Growth.* London, UK: Routledge.

Hirschfield, A., K.J. Bowers and P.J.B. Brown (1997) "Neighbourhood Location, Social Cohesion and Disadvantage in Urban Areas: A Merseyside Case Study." Paper presented to the British Criminology Conference, Belfast.

Hope, T. (1984). "Building Design and Burglary." In: R. Clarke and T. Hope (eds.), *Coping with Burglary: Research Perspectives in Policy.* Boston, MA: Kluwer Nijhoff.

—— (1995). "Community Crime Prevention." In: M. Tonry and D.P. Farrington (eds.), *Building a Safer Society: Strategic Approaches to Crime Prevention.* (Crime and Justice, vol. 19.) Chicago, IL: University of Chicago Press.

—— (1997). "Inequality and the Future of Community Crime Prevention." In: S.P. Lab (ed.), *Crime Prevention at a Crossroads.* (Academy of

Criminal Justice Sciences Monograph Series.) Cincinnati, OH: Anderson.

Jacobs, J. (1965). *The Death and Life of Great American Cities.* Harmondsworth, UK: Penguin.

Jordan, B. (1996). *A Theory of Poverty and Social Exclusion.* Cambridge, UK: Polity Press.

Kornhauser, R.R. (1978). *Social Sources of Delinquency.* Chicago, IL: University of Chicago Press.

Laycock, G. and N. Tilley (1995). *Policing and Neighbourhood Watch: Strategic Issues.* (Crime Detection and Prevention Series Paper, #60.) London, UK: Home Office.

Litton, R. A. (1997). "Crime Prevention and the Insurance Industry." In: M. Felson and R.V. Clarke (eds.), *Business and Crime Prevention.* Monsey, NY: Criminal Justice Press.

Logan, J.H. and H. Molotch (1987). *Urban Fortunes: The Political Economy of Place.* Berkeley, CA: University of California Press.

Maguire, M. (1982). *Burglary in a Dwelling.* London, UK: Heinemann.

McKenzie, E. (1994). *Privatopia.* New Haven, CT: Yale University Press.

Miethe, T. (1991). "Citizen-Based Crime Control Activity and Victimisation Risks: An Examination of Displacement and Free-Rider Effects." *Criminology* 29:419-439.

Newman, O. (1973). *Defensible Space.* London, UK: Architectural Press.

—— (1980). *Community of Interest.* Garden City, NY: Anchor Press/Doubleday.

—— (1996). *Creating Defensible Space.* Washington, DC: U.S. Department of Housing and Urban Development.

Osborn, D.R. and A. Tseloni (1998). "The Distribution of Household Property Crimes." *Journal of Quantitative Criminology* 14:307-330.

Poyner, B. and B. Webb (1991). *Crime Free Housing.* Oxford, UK: Butterworth Architecture.

Rengert, G.F. and T. Wasilcek (1985). *Suburban Burglary.* Springfield, IL: Charles C. Thomas.

Sandler, T. (1992). *Collective Action.* New York, NY: Harvester Wheatsheaf.

Savage, M., J. Barlow, P. Dickens and T. Fielding (1992). *Property, Bureaucracy and Culture.* London, UK: Routledge.

Shaw, C.R. and H.D. McKay (1969). *Juvenile Delinquency and Urban Areas.* Chicago, IL: University of Chicago Press.

Shearing, C. and P. Stenning (1983). "Private Security: Implications for Social Control." *Social Problems* 30:493-506.

Skogan, W.G. (1988). "Community Organisations and Crime" In: M. Tonry and N. Morris (eds.,) *Crime and Justice: A Review of Research*, vol. 10. Chicago, IL: University of Chicago Press.

Spitzer, S. (1987). "Security and Control in Capitalist Societies: The Fetishism of Security and the Secret Thereof." In: J. Lowman, R.J. Menzies and T.S. Palys (eds.), *Transcarceration: Essays in the Sociology of Social Control.* Aldershot, Hants, UK: Gower.

Taylor, R.B. and J. Covington (1988). "Neighborhood Changes in Ecology and Violence." *Criminology* 26:553-589.

Taylor, R.B. and S. Gottfredson (1986). "Environmental Design, Crime and Prevention: An Examination of Community Dynamics." In: A.J. Reiss and M. Tonry (eds.), *Communities and Crime.* Chicago, IL: University of Chicago Press.

Trickett, A., D.R. Osborn and D. Ellingworth (1995). "Property Crime Victimisation: The Roles of Individual and Area Influences." *International Review of Victimology* 3:273-295.

Walzer, M. (1990). "The Communitarian Critique of Liberalism." *Political Theory* 18:6-23.

Weintraub, J. (1995). "Varieties and Vicissitudes of Public Space." In: P. Kasinitz (ed.), *Metropolis: Centre and Symbol of our Times.* Houndsmill, Hants, UK: Macmillan.

Winchester, S. and H. Jackson (1982). *Residential Burglary.* (Home Office Research Study, #74.) London, UK: Her Majesty's Stationery Office.

APPENDIX

by Alan Trickett
University Of Manchester

The statistical models in this paper were estimated from data drawn from the 1992 British Crime Survey (England and Wales) combined at the individual-level with data drawn from the 1991 Census. Further details on the data can be found in Ellingworth et al. (1997). Separate logistic regression models were estimated for: (1) property crime victimisation; (2) NW present in the area; (3) membership in a NW scheme; and (4) neighbourhood reciprocity. The full results from these analyses are to be published in forthcoming papers.

Variables Used in the Analysis

Age
AGEHH   Age head of household

Occupation (base: manual occupation)
JOBNONM   Non-manual
JOBOTH   Other

Children in household (base: other)
CHIL1215   Children 12-15 yrs
CHILD511   Children 5-11 yrs
CHILDLT5   Children less than 5yrs

Tenure (base: owner occupied)
RENTC   Rent from local council (public housing)
RENTO   private rental (including Housing associations)
TIED   Rental tied to job

Dwelling type (base: detached)
SEMI   Semidetached
MIDTERR   Mid-terrace
ENDTERR   End-terrace
FLATM   Flat or maisonette
UCACCOM   Unclassified accommodation

Ethnic identity (base: white)
BLACK   Afro-Caribbean
INDIANSC   Indian Sub-Continental
OTHERETH   Other ethnicity
ETHREF   Refused

Mobility (base: other)
MOVED   Household moved in past year

Satisfaction with area (base: not satisfied)
FAIRSATA   Fairly satisfied
VERYSATA   Very satisfied

Neighbourhood reciprocity (base: people go own way)
MIXSOCO   Mixed
GOODSOCO   People help each other

Area-level variables
ZPAGE515   Population aged 5-15 yrs (%)

ZPINDIAN   Population Indian-Sub-Continental identities (%)
ZPOLD1HH   One-pensioner households (%)
ZPSPARHH   Single-parent households (%)
ZRENTED   Privately rented households (%)
AFFLUENT   [Average number of cars per household + proportion of dwelling units in detached houses]
INCITY   Location in an inner-city area

Standard Regions (base: South East [excluding Greater London])

NORTH   North
YORKS   Yorkshire and Humberside
NWEST   North West
WALES   Wales
WMIDS   West Midlands
EMIDS   East Midlands
EANGLIA   East Anglia
SWEST   South West
GLC   Greater London

TABLE A1: Property Crime Victimisation Logit Regression: Victim in Past 12 Months vs. Not Victimised

Variable	Sig	Exp(B)
AGEHH	.0000 .	9868
BASE: Manual		
JOBNONM	.0139	1.1480
JOBOTH	.0167	1.3090
CHIL1215	.3211	1.0821
CHILD511	.0460	1.1458
CHILDLT5	.5200	1.0478
BASE: Owns		
RENTC	' .0015	1.2525
RENTO	.7542	1.0303
TIED	.0451	1.5786
BASE: Detached		
SEMI	.0535	.8449
MIDTERR	.0051	.7627
ENDTERR	.9014	.9859
FLATM	.0003	.6637
UCACCOM	.1986	.8205
BASE: White		
BLACK	.0837	.8459
INDIANSC	.2092	.8726
OTHERETH	.0296	.5853
ETHREF	.4575	1.2405
MOVED	.0021	1.2966
BASE: Not Satis		
FAIRSATA	.0000	.4511
VERYSATA	.0000	.3341
BASE: No SoCo		
MIXSOCO	.1768	.9101
GOODSOCO	.0000	.7638
ZPAGE515	.0357	1.0935
ZPINDIAN	.0000	.8418
ZPOLD1HH	.5085	.9770
ZPSPARHH	.0280	1.0630
ZRENTED	.0003	1.1369
AFFLUENT	.0000	.8456
INCITY	.6047	1.0381
BASE: Seast		

Variable	Sig	Exp(B)
NORTH	.2596	1.1592
YORKS	.0300	1.2718
NWEST	.2662	1.1251
WALES	.1919	.8138
WMIDS	.4133	1.1041
EMIDS	.0010	1.4084
EANGLIA	.1026	.7274
SWEST	.7210	.9585
GLC	.5674	1.0634
Constant	.6368	-.0775

NOTES

1. Cohen and Felson (1979) specifically introduced the term *guardianship* as one of the key components of the routine activity theory of crime occurrence — a term that subsumed not only the notion of natural surveillance but other forms of supervision as well. Clarke et al (1992) had earlier sought, and continues to seek, to distinguish types of surveillance according to the surveying agency, e.g., citizens (natural), employees, or formal agents such as the police.

2. The first two are taken from Weintraub (1995), who suggests that the various meanings of the distinction are "used to distinguish different *kinds* of human action — and beyond that, the different realms of social life, or the different physical and social spaces, in which they occur" (Weintraub, 1995:287).

3. A public good is usually defined as having two characteristics: non-rivalries; and non-excludability (Barry and Hardin, 1982). A good can be thought of as *nonrival* if "one person's enjoying more of the good does not reduce the ability of others to enjoy it" (Hargeaves Heap et al., 1992:345). A good is *nonexcludable* in its provision if access to the good cannot be denied to individuals, even if they have not contributed in some way to its provision. Rarely are goods purely public — air comes close — but, as will be described, these characteristics nevertheless comprise useful criteria for analyzing the nature of particular goods (or bads) and, importantly, how their benefits (or negatives) are produced and distributed.

4. The security that is sought from property guardianship is like a *positional good* (Hirsch, 1977), something that is scarce and diminishes

with extensive demand upon it, and where increased growth in its supply (i.e., through social innovation or cultural change) is slow. Where the supply of positional goods fails to keep pace with demand for them, considerable pressure is placed by consumers upon the *distributional mechanisms* of the positional economy (Hirsch, 1977). Congestion in supply particularly undermines the provision of public goods.

5. Interestingly, Jacobs herself never uses the term as such.

6. As Newman (1973:51) asserts, "...by its very nature, the single-family house is its own statement of territorial claim. It has defined ownership by the very act of its positioning on an integral piece of land buffered from neighbours and [the] public street by intervening grounds."

7. Though as Berman (1953) also notes, the vision was not quite so openly inclusive as it might have seemed — there were "no blacks on her block" (p.153). Indeed, the kind of city from which Jacobs drew her inspiration seems to be one devoid of mass public housing, migration and poverty concentration.

8. "...private ownership, self-determination and social mobility as the keys to personal development" (Savage et al., 1992:94).

9. The one-way analysis of variance test reveals these differences to be highly significant (F=18.01, p.<.00001), while differences between groups are significant according to the least significant difference (multiple range) test at p.<.05.

10. As noted in the Appendix, it should be remembered that the variables used here to estimate the risk of victimisation are only those that also proved significant in the estimation of NW awareness, availability and membership; there are also other risk factors associated with victimisation (see, for example, Ellingworth et al.,1997).

11. In other models of property crime risk estimated from the BCS and census data, we have also found higher household car ownership to be positively correlated with higher risk of *household* property crime, notwithstanding risks of car crime, again suggesting the higher risk of affluent suburban households.

12. This is a highly significant effect (p.<.00001). The model suggests that for a standard unit increase in the probability of a household being located in an "affluent area," the probability of property crime victimisa-

tion is reduced by 15%. Nevertheless, probably as a consequence of collinearities, other models of the 1992 BCS have found that the effect of "area affluence" is derived only from that part of the variable measuring the average number of cars per household (Ellingworth et al., 1997).

13. The BCS data suggest that the relative distributions of household dwelling types — with different risks associated with each — are polarized along the area-affluence variable. Thus, 74% of detached dwellings (at higher individual risk) are located in the top third of these affluent areas (at lowest area risk), while 59% of flats, and 48% of terraced houses (at lower individual risk) are located in the bottom third of the affluence continuum (at higher area risk). The distribution of semi-detached houses is more even, though the largest proportion (44%) can be found in the middle third of areas classified on this variable. On the whole, 96% of detached, and 78% of semidetached dwellings can be found in the top two-thirds of this area-affluence continuum.

14. Free-riders are those who can enjoy the benefits of membership without contributing to the costs of their production, and who cannot be excluded from doing so. It can be shown formally — in a game-theoretic context, with standard rationality assumptions about individual action — that the conditions of nonexcludability and voluntarism attaching to public goods leads to the strategy to free-ride for any participating individual. Even though greater collective benefit would be obtained if everyone contributed to the production of the public good, the individual incentive to free-ride that bears on every participant equally results in the underprovision of public goods that do not carry additional penalties or incentives to participate. That is the public-goods dilemma.

15. Specifically, this was assessed by means of a standard BCS question:

Q.   "In some neighbourhoods people do things together and try to help each other, while in other areas people mostly go their own way. In general, what kind of neighbourhood would you say you live in?"

A.   Help each other, go own way, mixture.

In the logistic regression context, the response variable was coded positive for those agreeing that people mostly helped each other.

16. As Logan and Molotch (1987:43, emphasis in original) note: "places are not simply *affected* by the institutional maneuvers surrounding

them. Places *are* those machinations. A place is defined as much by its position in a particular organizational web — political, economic, and cultural — as by its physical makeup and topographical configuration...the very boundaries of place, as well as the meaning of those boundaries, are a result of intersecting searches for use and exchange values."

17. That is, where significant *externality* benefits are generated for neighbours and the wider community (Field and Hope, 1990). Ekblom's (1997) evaluation of the British Safer Cities Programme, for instance, found greater preventive benefits accruing to areas the greater the amount of expenditure on crime prevention effort.

18. Thus Davis (1990:170, 244) notes: "Homeowner politics have focused on defense of th[e] suburban dream against unwanted development...as well as against unwanted persons...the security-driven logic of urban enclavization finds its most popular expression in the frenetic efforts of Los Angeles's affluent neighbourhoods to insulate home values and lifestyles."

19. As I have pointed out elsewhere, half the communities of England and Wales suffer only 15% of the national amount of property crime; and repeat victimisation is virtually nonexistent in the lowest crime areas (Hope, 1997).

20. Robert Reich quoted in McKenzie (1994).

A REVIEW OF STREET LIGHTING EVALUATIONS: CRIME REDUCTION EFFECTS

by

Ken Pease
University of Huddersfield

Abstract: *Consideration of the literature concerning street lighting effects on crime yields the following conclusions: (1) Precisely targeted increases in street lighting generally have crime reduction effects. (2) More general increases in street lighting seem to have crime prevention effects, but this outcome is not universal. Older and U.S. research yield fewer positive results than more recent U.K. research. (3) Even untargeted increases in crime prevention generally make residents less fearful of crime or more confident of their own safety at night. (4) In the most recent and sophisticated studies, street lighting improvements are associated with crime reductions in the daytime as well as during the hours of darkness. (5) The debate about lighting effects has served to preclude a more refined analysis of the means by and circumstances in which lighting might reduce crime. Our aim should now be to use context-appropriate lighting schemes as part of a full repertoire of crime reduction tactics. Recommendations based upon a strategic view of current crime reduction policy are made about how lighting effects could be clarified and elaborated. The provisions of the British Crime and Disorder Act 1998 constitute a potential vehicle for lighting programmes operating within crime reduction schemes generally.*

INTRODUCTION

After discussions with British Home Office officials and representatives of the lighting industry, a report was commissioned on the relationship between street lighting and crime. For the last 10 years, and in the face of a British research base increasing in both volume and quality, the perception has persisted of a Home Office view that street lighting is not relevant to crime. I have yet to find a Home Office official who admits to believing this in any but a massively qualified way, but the sense of Home Office scepticism is certainly there.

It is possible, on the basis of the content and tone of two publications of the now-defunct Home Office Crime Prevention Unit, in particular its Papers #28 and #29, to see how a sceptical view could have been inferred. Indeed, complex material in memory tend to be reduced to a few simple observations. Anyone reading the publications in question would certainly have to oversimplify to take from those reports the message that street lighting was not helpful in crime control. Equally certainly, the content of those reports would lead that to be the simple conclusion requiring the *least* oversimplification. One of these reports (#29) was a review of research. The other (#28) presented original data later extensively cited as inimical to the cause of lighting as a crime reduction measure.

Reading the research evidence now leads to the inescapable conclusion that street lighting can help in crime control. The sensible question is no longer whether lighting is relevant to crime reduction, but rather how one can identify the circumstances and settings in which it is most helpful and economical in relation to impact, and how one should use lighting in combination with other measures to optimise its effect. Crime reduction has been bedevilled by the tendency to polarise measures into those which will be helpful in all circumstances and those which will not be helpful in any, a process that the evaluative process has often mirrored and accelerated. In recent years in the U.K., closed circuit television (CCTV) has sadly fallen into the first category, and Neighbourhood Watch into the second (see Koch, 1998, for a pertinent discussion).

There is no such thing as an all-purpose crime prevention measure. Recognition of this point is of fundamental importance. The most physically secure house or business can be penetrated if the perpetrator can be sure that fear or indifference means that no one will raise the alarm, however long the crime takes to commit and however much noise is made during its commission. The most insecure house or business may be safe if located in small, watchful and self-confident communities. The most active drug dealer will operate in safety from enforcement if a community and its police tolerate the trade or, alternatively, are paralysed by fear of, or corrupted by money from, the dealers. Safes previously impregnable ceased to be so with the advent of the thermic lance. No security measure on plastic cards, up to and including photographs, will reduce plastic fraud at the point of sale if retail staff fail to look at them. Likewise, no public place, however well lit, will be crime free if offenders have good reason to believe that they will not be recognised, or, if recognised, will not be reported to the police, or, if reported will escape meaningful criminal justice outcomes. While still conditional, some crime control measures will be effective over a broad range of conditions. For example, the presence of large numbers of stewards and police is likely to reduce trouble at all but the most volatile soccer matches. To say that lighting effects are conditional is not to say that they will not be common.

Taking stock of the position of lighting in the repertoire of crime prevention techniques is timely for two reasons. The first of these is unarguable. The second is not, but merits inclusion.

(1)   The recent passage of the Crime and Disorder Act in the U.K. is crucial, with its obligation placed upon locally responsible bodies (comprising local authorities and police) to both develop and implement crime prevention plans, and themselves not to act in ways that facilitate crime and disorder. Since street lighting is a matter under local authority control, it would be extremely sad if the role of lighting in preventing crime were neglected at a time when there is, perhaps for the first time, extrinsic motivation for local bodies to control the levels of crime that their area suffers. Expressing a personal view, locally responsible bodies seem to be in danger of being monopolised by people-processing agencies (like youth justice and probation) to the exclusion of trading standards, environmental health and other local authority functions engaged in the manipulation of places and commerce to render them less criminogenic. The neglect of lighting would be another culpable omission from the crime control armoury alongside the others mentioned.

(2)   The development of Virtual Reality techniques enables a much more complete and sophisticated simulation of lighting effects. If layered alongside crime and disorder data in recognisable and manipulable urban landscapes, lighting can be more precisely deployed for local crime control purposes. The geocoding of crime events and the installation of Geographic Information Systems have advanced only haltingly within the police service. Where it has occurred, the interpretive burden is massively lightened by Virtual Reality, which can depict attributes of frequent crime scenes more satisfactorily than can mapping. Virtual Reality will be mentioned again in the recommendations section of this report.

CRIME AND LIGHTING RESEARCH AND ITS FREQUENT REVIEW

The relationship between lighting and crime is perhaps unique in the number of reviews published per original study carried out. Why is this topic, which is relatively little studied, so thoroughly reviewed? The answer is probably its combination of clear policy relevance, general consensus as to results, but disagreement about what the implications of these results might be. In the light of the rash of reviews, the present offering is an attempt to summarise the data available, the policy conclusions that may safely be based upon them, and the best means by which light may be cast (literally and metaphorically) in the cause of crime prevention.

Perhaps the two most remarkable things about a topic that is generally seen as contentious are:

(1) The relatively high level of agreement to be found in the research.

(2) The lack of research effort expended in establishing the circumstances and conditions in which lighting may become more sophisticated in its crime prevention role.

Given the tensions surrounding this topic, the reader may be surprised to learn that all the reviews seem to agree on three things:

(1) *The bad news*: untargeted general increases in street lighting do not always have overall crime prevention effects, although many do. The division is by epoch and country, with older and U.S. research yielding fewer positive results.

(2) *The good news*: targeted increases in street lighting generally have crime reduction effects.

(3) *The stale news*: even untargeted increases in crime prevention generally make residents less fearful of crime or more confident of their own safety at night.

The first two conclusions have been expressed in terms varying from the optimistic to the decidedly downbeat. Among the more downbeat, Tien et al. (1979:93) concluded "The paucity of reliable and uniform data and the inadequacy of available evaluation studies preclude a definitive statement regarding the relationship between street lighting and crime."

To a large extent, however, the reviewers engineered the paucity they bemoan by taking a narrow and formulaic approach to evaluation, which led them to discard the vast majority of studies that came to their attention. Ramsey and Newton (1991), elaborating on Ramsey (1989), conclude:

> Better lighting by itself has very little effect on crime. There are some limited local 'blackspots' where improved lighting may have a modest impact on crime and perhaps a larger one on incivilities. Also, in conjunction with other measures, better lighting may help to improve an area. Indirectly, this may conceivably assist in reducing crime — although such an outcome is not guaranteed. There is no scope for reducing crime on any broad basis simply by investing in better street lighting [p.24].

Eck (1997:326) opines "Not much has changed since Tien and his colleagues...gave their critical assessment of the impact of lighting on crime." However, Poyner and Webb (1993) generated a rating system for crime control measures, and found lighting (street or otherwise) to be effective as a general crime control measure in most of the studies reviewed, including six of seven studies of residential burglary, two of two studies of commercial burglary, three of four studies of vehicle crime, and three of five measures against robbery. A more recent example (LaVigne, 1994) shows the relevance of illuminating petrol station forecourts, among other variables, to the level of driving off without paying. The La Vigne work is a neat illustration of the relevance of lighting level in *specific* contexts alongside other factors.

The most recent review, that of Painter (1996a), is both the most optimistic and the most complete in terms of research coverage. Painter's own extensive previous work, and work by others that she coordinated, showed *at least* short-term effects in circumscribed areas. The research strategy she adopted, that of showing many localised effects, was very defensible. In aggregate, her work showed many local crime reductions associated with relighting.

As for the "stale news," the effect of lighting upon crime fear, this seems uncontentious (see, for example, Atkins et al., 1991; Vrij and Winkel, 1991; Painter 1996b). "Lighting is still recognised by the Home Office as having an important role, although primarily in terms of the reduction of fear rather than crime" (Ramsey and Newton 1991:22). This may be healthy, insofar as crime fear is greater than the real hazard from crime. It may also be unhealthy, in that crime fear moves one to take prudent avoiding action. To reduce crime fear or perceived safety without reducing crime hazard may not be doing citizens any favours. For that reason, the remainder of this document deals with crime hazard rather than crime fear.

CHILDREN OF LIGHT AND DISCIPLES OF DARKNESS[1]

An understanding of the relationship between lighting and crime has been beset by two problems. Both have the same result in practice. The first has been dogmatism about the effect of lighting in preventing crime. Writing in the highly influential *Handbook of Loss Prevention and Crime Prevention*, edited by Lawrence Fennelly, Girard (1982:96) contends that "good lighting is the single most cost effective deterrent to crime." In the equivalent chapter of the third edition of the same handbook, in a section headed "The Miracle of Light" Girard (1982:253) contends "Police officers are, of course, aware of the effect that lighting has in reducing criminal opportunity. Nonetheless, it is interesting to note that a variety of studies and experiments that have documented this fact. ...[as well as] experience has shown the close relationship between illumination and crime."

Fennelly (1996:38) himself is no less confident:

> What would happen if we switched off all the lights at night? ... Such a foolish act would create an unsafe environment. Senior citizens would never go out and communities would have an immediate outbreak of thefts and vandalism. Commercial areas would be burglarized at an uncontrollable rate. Therefore, lighting and security go hand in hand. The above example may seem to be far-fetched, but in fact installation of improved lighting in a number of cities has resulted in the following:
> 1. Decrease in vandalism;
> 2. Decrease in street crimes;
> 3. Decrease in suspicious persons;
> 4. Decrease in commercial burglaries;
> 5. In general, a reduction in crime.

Fennelly cites no evidence for these assertions. In a similar vein, *The London Times* opined in its 1st September 1989 edition: "Recent research has demonstrated what was obvious to common sense already, that a systematic improvement in street lighting can bring about a substantial reduction in street crime" (p.2).

The dogmatism of the disciples of darkness is of a different kind, and is primarily reactive. It stresses the limitations in method, the area experiencing change and the time scale of demonstrations of lighting effects, rather than seeking to develop a fuller understanding of the mechanisms involved.[2] Although this has never been openly acknowledged to the author, the reactive dogmatism also seems based upon the suspicion that the government is being railroaded by the lighting industry into taking costly measures of uncertain crime-control efficacy.

There is a degree of justification for both extreme positions. For those who, day-to-day, must do something concrete about local crime problems, the installation of lights has obvious face validity. Lighting thus features prominently in security handbooks (e.g., Fennelly, 1982, 1996; Lyons, 1988; Hylton, 1996). Further, attention to lighting parallels the high importance that citizens assign to light as a crime control measure. For example, Bennett and Gelsthorpe (1996) found improved street lighting to be second only to increased police foot patrols and ahead of CCTV and private security patrols among preferred crime prevention measures. By contrast, for those exercising stewardship of public money, good evidence about effects should be necessary before money is spent, although one is tempted to ask where rigorous standards went in the headlong rush to CCTV deployment.

When opinion gets polarised, the sensible questions about the range of application of lighting measures get neglected. For believers, lighting just *does* prevent crime. In the extreme case, whatever the question, the answer involves lighting. In the absence of the believers' specification of how lighting works its magic, sceptics carry out evaluations that believers regard as unrealistic and that indeed could not be otherwise, given the lack of detailed insight into the mechanisms concerned.[3] The effect of combined dogmatism and woolly thinking about how lighting might work in reducing crime has been to preclude the more precise and necessary questions about what kind of lighting, deployed how and under what circumstances, would optimise the cost-efficiency of its crime prevention impact.

The unfortunate consequences of polarised thinking will be illustrated by detailed consideration of the large-scale research project most often cited as indicating the lack of association between lighting and crime. The Home Office's Crime Prevention Unit Paper #28, authored by Stephen Atkins et al., arguably marks the watershed in perceived official thinking about crime and street lighting, and remains the lone major British study to be frequently cited against the crime reduction possibilities of street lighting.

THE ATKINS (1991) CRIME PREVENTION UNIT PAPER

Sceptics of the effects of street lighting on crime rely heavily on a major study conducted by a team at the University of Southampton and published as Home Office Crime Prevention Unit Paper, #28, authored by Atkins et al. (1991). Because of its central role in expressed scepticism, this paper will be dealt with at some length. In 1985, the London borough of Wandsworth began a programme of relighting the borough "to a very high standard, partly with the aim of crime prevention" (Atkins et al., p. viii). An analysis of crime reported to the relevant Metropolitan Police divisional areas contrasted the year before relighting with the year following relighting. The central conclusion was that "[n]o evidence could be found to support the hypothesis that improved street lighting reduces reported crime. Although some areas and some crime types did show reductions in night-time crime relative to the daylight control, the dominant overall pattern, from which this study draws its authority, was of no significant change" (Atkins et al., p. viii).

One must preface comments about the Atkins et al. (1991) report by saying that it was a perfectly competent piece of work, clear about its assumptions, sufficiently detailed to allow further scrutiny of the data, and far more technically detailed than was typical of the research series in which it was published, which was intended primarily for a readership of crime prevention practitioners. The contentious aspect of the study concerns its starting point and assumptions. Its starting point was to examine lighting effects when "relighting is less well-targeted" (p.3) than in the early studies by Kate Painter, to which it was clearly intended as a counterbalance. The central Atkins assumption, enshrined in the analytic approach of the research, was that the effects of lighting were restricted to the hours of darkness. The key results table from Atkins et al. is reproduced below as Table 1. Leaving for the moment the interpretation of Table 1 offered by Atkins et al., let us instead ask the simpler question: did crime fall after new lighting was installed? It did. There were 7,480 crimes recorded in the year preceding relighting, and 6,399 in the year following, a fall of some 15%. This can be calculated from Table 1 above, but is not to be found in the body of the Atkins report. In Appendix E of the report, an example is provided that could well be actual data, but it is not clear to the reader that this is what the Appendix is intended to convey.[4]

The next question, not addressed at all by Atkins et al. (1991), concerns whether crime elsewhere in the Metropolitan Police district fell during a period matched with that of the Wandsworth relighting. It is impossible to answer this rigorously in retrospect, and in particular one cannot precisely match the Atkins figures for the area as a whole without carrying out supplementary research on at least the

Table 1: Reported Crimes in All Relit Zones One Year Before and One Year After Relighting by Crime Type Groupings

Susceptibility	Before			After				
	Day	Dark	DK	Day	Dark	DK	RPC	SIG
Likely	1419 (27%)	2097 (40%)	1722 (33%)	1166 (27%)	1676 (39%)	1446 (34%)	-2.7%	n.s.
Possible	800 (43%)	522 (28%)	542 (29%)	788 (45%)	518 (30%)	447 (25%)	+0.7%	n.s.
Unlikely	192 (51%)	113 (30%)	73 (19%)	192 (54%)	86 (24%)	80 (22%)	-23.9%	n.s.
Total	2411 (32%)	2732 (37%)	2337 (31%)	2146 (34%)	2280 (36%)	1973 (31%)	-6.3%	n.s.

Notes

Susceptibility refers to the Atkins et al. classification of crime types according to whether they are deemed likely to be responsive to lighting effects.
Day, dark and DK are self-explanatory, indicating whether recorded crimes occurred in the hours of daylight or darkness.
RPC indicates relative percentage change in the dark relative to the day.
SIG indicates statistical reliability of difference (in this case no comparison was statistically reliable).

scale of the original study. This is because the introduction of lighting was phased, so a complex process of area matching would be required.

However, a rough reanalysis is possible, whose results cannot be more than suggestive. The crucial years are 1984-89. An ordinary least squares regression of recorded crime by year in the Metropolitan Police district over the period in question shows an average 0.5% annual rise in recorded crime. If that rise is used as the baseline for the Wandsworth decline, i.e., if one expected Wandsworth crime to have increased over the period in line with the force as a whole, then the Wandsworth reduction in crime observed would have been statistically reliable beyond the .001 level. Based on these assumptions, relighting *was* associated with a significant fall in crime.

These are back-of-the-envelope calculations, but they do serve to show that the attribution of failure by Atkins et al. (1991) flowed simply from their use of daytime crime as a comparison for crime in darkness. Looking again at the reduction in total crime in Wandsworth, there was an 11% daytime reduction and a 17% reduction during the hours of darkness. In sum, the reason why the Wandsworth study does not show a lighting effect is because the daylight reduction in crime provides the baseline. This makes the even greater reduction in darkness fall short of statistical reliability.

Looking again at the Atkins et al. (1991) table, the analysis did not show what is evident with log-linear analysis,[5] namely that there is a significant day/darkness * before/after interaction, showing a significant decrease in the proportion of crime committed in the hours of darkness after relighting (p<.001), a result certainly worth reporting. Similarly, there is a significant before/after * crime category interaction (p<.001), which is not easily interpretable given that the increase that generates the result is in the "possibly relevant" class of offences. There is no significant three-way interaction term.

There are two aspects of the Atkins et al. (1991) approach that made it likely to result in scepticism:

(1) A failure to recognise that crime is highly concentrated spatially, and that an overall uprating is a scattergun approach to a series of localised problems.

(2) The assumption that, because lights only shine at night, they only have an effect at night.

WHEN CRIME IS CONCENTRATED, DIFFUSE CRIME CONTROL IS INEFFICIENT

Various analyses of the British Crime Survey (which captures both reported and unreported crime) show that the 10% of areas suffering the most crime experience some 25 to 35 times as much crime as the least victimised 10% (Ellingworth and Pease, unpublished data). Even within the most victimised areas, some individuals and locations suffer disproportionately, and literatures have grown up that detail the phenomena of crime hot spots and repeat victimisation (Pease, 1998; Eck, 1997). This is true for crime as a whole, and for specific crime types such as gun crime (Sherman and Rogan, 1995) and drug dealing (Weisburd et al., 1994). This concentration of crime remains stable over time (Spelman 1995a, 1995b). Failing to reflect crime concentration in the understanding and deployment of crime control measures seems odd, but this is precisely what Atkins et al. (1991) do, in common with many researchers in this area. We already knew from other research that scattergun approaches to crime prevention are inefficient (see Allatt, 1984, for an example and some reasons why). Yet the whole raison d'être of the Atkins study was to test the effect of a scattergun approach to lighting as a crime control measure. Repeatedly in the report, virtue is implicitly (and, to the author, perversely) located by the Atkins study in just such an approach. For example:

> Many factors influence the level of actual crime ... of which lighting may be one. The relative importance of these factors is likely to vary between areas so that, although lighting may be a major influence in certain locations, its influence elsewhere may be minimal compared to other factors [p.3].

> (Previous) study areas included a narrow walkway or railway tunnel, locations that are widely recognised as potential troublespots and where re-lighting would be most likely to be beneficial. The results could well be different when re-lighting is less well-targeted or applied across larger areas [p.3]

> Painter's work is providing useful and consistent information about short-term impacts on particular types of small areas. However, very little is known about longer-term effects or the benefits of re-lighting programmes that are less well-targeted or which are implemented across much wider areas [p.3].

The acknowledgement of localised beneficial effects of lighting on crime is translated in the summary to the conclusion:

> There is a widely held belief that the improvement of street lighting will reduce...crime....[but] there is little firm evidence to support these beliefs. This research aims to fill that gap [p. viii).

The central conclusion is expressed thus:

> ...if street lighting does affect crime, this study should have detected it. The principal conclusion is that no evidence could be found to support the hypothesis that improved street lighting reduces reported crime [p.20].

In the same vein, Malcolm Ramsey's review published as CPU Paper, #29 opined

> Even if one accepted each of the three 'blackspot' projects at face value, it would still be highly misleading to draw from them any sweeping conclusions as to the effects of lighting improvements of crime [p.14].

Thus the prevention of crime by well-targeted deployment of lighting to small areas with big problems. seems not to count as lighting-induced crime control. Only untargeted lighting will do! Painter (1996a:333) comments fairly but perhaps rather acidly:

> The Home Office study suggested that over wide areas, street lighting is unlikely to impact on reported crime. One is tempted to ask why anyone ever thought that it would achieve this.

LIGHTING AND SITUATIONAL CRIME PREVENTION

Before going on to discuss the effects of street lighting that may apply even in the daytime, a brief note is merited on the link between street lighting and the general approach known as situational crime prevention (SCP). The purpose of this slight diversion is to attempt to unlink the literature on street lighting from that background. Had the literature developed within an SCP tradition, the debate would have been less sterile.

SCP involves the modification of environments so that crime involves more effort, more risk and lower reward (see Pease, 1997, for a summary). It is probably not going too far to say that the best strategy for crime control is now clearly a combination of proven techniques for the reduction of individuals' tendency to commit crime through intervention in childhood, and the manipulation of environments to make that more difficult (see Welsh and Farrington, 1999). In combination, we can hope for a country in which fewer people in pubs want to "glass" each other, and those who do find glasses impossible to use because when they break they leave no sharp edges to use as a weapon.

The reason to be specific about the relationship between lighting and SCP is that the former can gain its authority as a crime prevention measure by association with the latter. This conflation of SCP and lighting is evident in the following pronouncement of Atkins et al. (1991:1):

> Does street lighting prevent crime? Making changes to environmental conditions and operational practices to discourage crime has become a well-established part of conventional crime prevention wisdom. These ideas, usually termed 'Situational Crime Prevention' (SCP) underlie a considerable proportion of current crime prevention efforts...Improved street lighting is entirely consistent with SCP concepts; increased visibility

should both reduce opportunities for crime and increase the probability of an offender being caught. But does it really work?

Such an equation of SCP with increased lighting is far too simple. Lighting as a crime prevention tool cannot be justified by reciting the SCP mantra. A defining characteristic of SCP is its close analysis of the situation. There will be circumstances in which extra lighting provides some attackers with an advantage, others with a disadvantage. Try mugging someone in an unlit cave. You don't know what he or she carries that is worth taking, you may not know where the victim is, and if you manage to effect a successful robbery, you don't know which way to go to get out of the cave. In short, a true SCP approach would require a far more detailed and sophisticated analysis of how the situation works for a potential offender and his or her victim. On the basis of the analysis, the situation would then be engineered to:

(1) increase perceived effort in crime commission,

(2) increase received risks, and/or

(3) reduce anticipated rewards.

In these terms, how is street lighting *conventionally* supposed to work to reduce crime? In what follows, for this writer the most plausible (not necessarily the only or most important) account of how lighting might work is discussed, together with its implications. To emphasise, this is not done because this mechanism is a settled fact (the point is made repeatedly that mechanism-based research is conspicuous by its absence), but to illustrate how one could work through the implications of any theoretical position from an SCP standpoint. As an aside, it is noted that the major (albeit now dated) U.S. review explicitly excludes projects that would be among the most effective if the proposed mechanism were important.

Since crime control should not be made to wait 10 years for researchers to make good the omissions of the last decade, practitioners must behave *as if* lighting works by one or another mechanism. Thoughtful practitioners always do this, anyway.

Self-evidently, light is a necessary condition of visual surveillance: if no one notices a crime during daylight, or no one comes to a victim's aid, the light is arguably irrelevant. Lighting is, by this account, the means whereby surveillance becomes achievable in the hours of darkness. However, surveillance — not lighting — is deemed by such reasoning to be an active ingredient, lighting being merely the means by which it becomes possible. Lighting increases surveillance capacity during darkness to daytime levels, by either deterring (by increasing perceived risks) or increasing the probability of apprehension of the offender. Put thus, lighting effects would clearly be contingent on those features of a situation that make surveillance effective or otherwise (see Mayhew, 1981). There is evidence (see, for example, Barker et al., 1993) that offenders are not persuaded that surveillability will be translated into risk for them. The implications of accepting this argument, which will be developed later, are that lighting improvements in pursuit of crime reduction must also seek to translate surveillability into active surveillance or its perception, or be located in areas where such a translation is likely to occur because of the existing community structure.

The contingent nature of lighting effects has one major evaluation consequence, namely, that lighting that is intelligently combined with other measures *probably* stands a better chance of reducing crime. Yet Tien et al. (1979), in the major early review of lighting effects, regarded the combination of lighting with other measures as effectively disqualifying a project evaluation from inclusion on the grounds of its methodological inadequacy. If the Tien et al. view were to prevail, lighting would more often than not be shown to be irrelevant to crime, since measures taken to ensure the salience of lighting improvement would disbar the lighting improvement from consideration.

Some effects of lighting seem to be manifest in daylight, as well as at night. Effects operating in daytime alone, or throughout the 24-hour day, may be the more important.

THE POSSIBLE DAYTIME EFFECTS OF LIGHTING ON CRIME

As noted earlier, Atkins and his colleagues (1991) based their analysis of lighting effects on a set of assumptions about how lighting works to reduce crime. Central to their thinking was the notion that since lights only go on at night, they can have no daytime effect. London-wide data from the same time period suggests that the decline in Wandsworth moved against the citywide trend (see above). Taken at face value, there was a lighting-associated crime decline in Wandsworth, that was more marked during darkness but also present in the daytime. What kind of effect in the daytime might enhanced street lighting have? How might lights work even when they are switched off? A set of varied, but not exhaustive, ways in which lighting may reduce crime appears below.

How Lighting Could Reduce Daytime Crime

(1) The installation of lighting involves increased daytime sur-
     veillance of the streets by workers carrying out the installa-
     tion, subsequent checks and maintenance of lights, and by
     the police oversight of traffic or other problems caused by any
     associated road works.

(2) New lighting offers a demonstration of the serious intent of
     local authorities and police to control crime. This may moti-
     vate citizens to pass on information about street disorder.

(3) New lighting equipment visible in daylight offers potential of-
     fenders cues about area type, leading them to classify an area
     as less conducive to easy criminal activity.

(4) New lighting is a talking point for citizens, leading them to
     spend more daytime hours on the street and hence in infor-
     mal surveillance. Insofar as they get to know others in the
     neighbourhood better, they can recognise strangers in private
     spaces.

(5) Better lighting may increase community pride and cohesive-
     ness, decreasing the motivation to move from an area, and
     thus reducing the opportunities for burglars presented by "for
     sale" signs, decreasing recognition of the legitimacy of visitors
     to the house, etc. (Ellingworth and Pease, 1998).

(6) If offenders commit crime in both light and darkness, arrests
     and subsequent processing during darkness may make of-
     fenders less available to commit crime during the day.

How Lighting Could Reduce Crime in Darkness, Other Than by Deterrence

(1) New lighting may increase the time available for maintenance
     of a front garden and the front of the house, hence increase
     informal surveillance during darkness.

(2) Improved lighting may increase pedestrian traffic (and hence
     informal surveillance), through people walking from their
     homes when otherwise they would not have gone out, or
     taken taxis when they could afford to do so (for a discussion
     of the relationships between pedestrian density and crime,
     see the papers collected in Clarke, 1996).

(3) People may be detected in crime more easily. For serious crime, this may remove them from the area for a while. For less serious crime, they may be deterred from offending in an area now perceived as risky.

(4) The presence of police officers and other authority figures becomes more visible, thus leading to a decision to desist from crime.

How Lighting Could Increase Crime in Daylight

As has often been noted (see, for example Fleming and Burrows, 1986), there are circumstances in which lighting works to an offender's advantage. These might include the following:

(1) Masquerading as electricity board or contracted workers making checks, burglars by deception could gain entrance to homes.

(2) Residents developing social lives after dark may find these extending into daylight. For example, attending a midweek evening soccer match may prove so enjoyable that matches are also attended on Saturday afternoons.

(3) Disorderly activities focused upon a newly illuminated area may spill over into the use of the well-illuminated place as a daylight meeting point.

How Lighting Could Increase Crime in Darkness

(1) Increased social activity outside the home in the evenings may increase the number of unoccupied homes available for burglary.

(2) Increased visibility of potential victims allows better judgement of their vulnerability and the value of what they carry.

(3) Increased visibility allows better judgement of the proximity of "capable guardians," i.e., those people who may observe and intervene in crime.

(4) Increased illumination of an area reduces visibility from the area into contiguous areas with unenhanced lighting (imagine looking into the street from a well-lit room compared with a dark room). This enhances the possibilities for escape of those offending.

(5) Increased illumination facilitates activities like drug dealing and other problematic forms of "street life."

Given the range of mechanisms through which lighting could influence crime, it would be unwise and simplistic to make statements of general application. To restate, projects incorporating lighting have been convincingly shown to reduce problems at points of particular crime and disorder. Our aim should be to develop imaginative context-appropriate lighting schemes, and to derive from them a repertoire of tactics. Before developing this point, we will briefly discuss the Dudley Project, the most recent and methodologically sophisticated demonstration of the reduction of crime by the enhancement of street lighting.

THE DUDLEY PROJECT

This initiative (whose evaluation is published as Painter and Farrington, 1997) is probably the most rigorously analysed study of general lighting effects on crime carried out to date. Victimisation surveys (in which people are asked about crimes they have suffered in the previous six months or one year) were employed, covering a 12-month before period and an equivalent 12-month follow-up period. This avoids the primary problem associated with data based on crime reported to the police, namely, that crime suffered is conflated with the tendency to report it to the police (see Painter, 1991). Sample size was decided so as to be confident of detecting a crime reduction of 10% or more. The year before and after lighting enhancement was the time frame for interviews in order to avoid the criticism that the effects were short-term. A comparison area was chosen to establish that the effect was specific to the lighting-enhanced zone, and that crime was apparently not displaced. Detailed checks were made about variables like weather, to minimise the possibility that any effects were attributable to something other than lighting.

The results clearly demonstrated that:

(1) The incidence of crime in the lighting-enhanced area fell by 41%, in contrast to a 15% reduction in the comparison area.

(2) The prevalence of crime (i.e., the proportion of people victimised) fell by 23% in the lighting-enhanced area, in contrast to a 3% reduction in the comparison area.

(3) Incidence and prevalence fell in all crime categories.

(4) The proportion of people who personally knew a victim of crime fell in the lighting-enhanced area relative to the comparison area.

(5) People in the lighting-enhanced area became somewhat more satisfied with their area, whereas those in the comparison area became somewhat less satisfied.

Importantly, the decline in daytime crime was similar to the decline of crime after dark. The interpretation of results that the study's authors prefer is in terms of resident confidence, optimism, and community pride, translating itself into informal surveillance. This is of interest because an often overlooked feature of crime control measures is that their effects are almost too speedy, i.e., that the effects exhibit themselves from the commencement of a project rather than at some later point where they may reasonably kick in. To my knowledge, this feature has not been scrutinised formally, although it is evident but unremarked on many projects. For example, a programme of changes to public transport systems in Victoria, Australia had its peak effect on train window breakages within two months of its introduction (see Carr and Spring, 1993). If confidence were to increase with the installation of the first lampost, the decline in crime would be precipitous.

The Dudley Project establishes, as completely as any single study could, the relevance of lighting to crime reduction. It rises to the challenge presented by the Atkins et al. (1991) study to demonstrate a lighting effect using a more refined design and techniques of analysis. A rearguard action could still be mounted by the disciples of darkness against the results. It would probably make reference to the demand characteristics of the post-illumination interview, where residents may think it churlish to continue to complain about crime when high-quality crime prevention measures had been taken. Also, it may be objected that events may be interpreted as accidents or horseplay by the confident respondent which may be interpreted as crime by the fearful. In this way, the same events occur, but lose their emotional charge and hence are not reported as crime. However tendentious such objections, there will always be the inevitable residuum of uncertainty in the wake of evaluative research. However, the Dudley study is now the benchmark. The comments of Clarke (1997:209) on the project merit quotation:

> Until recently, the received wisdom on improved street lighting was that it might reduce fear, but it has little effect on crime...This view is now changing, largely due to the work of

Kate Painter in Britain. In the face of much scepticism...she has produced a series of studies suggesting that the crime prevention benefits of street lighting have been underestimated. Each of her studies has sought to improve on the methodology of earlier ones. ...[T]his study produces clear evidence that crime of all kinds decreased significantly in the re-lit estate compared with the control.

THE STOKE-ON-TRENT STUDY

Painter and Farrington (this volume) extend the work of the Dudley Project using essentially the same methods. The results are substantially the same as those found at Dudley. The following additional points are worth making about the Stoke-on-Trent enterprise.

(1) Three areas were studied: the area of enhanced lighting, a contiguous area to which crime would have been displaced had displacement occurred, and a comparison area to which displacement would not have been expected. It was found that the incidence of crime declined in the relit area, and in the contiguous (displacement) area, albeit to a lesser extent. This seems to be an example of diffusion of benefits, whereby crime reduction measures taken in one area sometimes spill over into beneficial effects in adjacent areas.

(2) The cost of prevented crime in the relit area suggested it covered the full capital expenses incurred in lighting enhancement and some £215,000 more, when reductions in relit and adjacent areas were included.

(3) Unlike the Dudley project, the proportion of crimes committed in darkness fell relative to the comparison area.

The proposed account of the reduction is Stoke was somewhat more complex than that offered for Dudley:

...the effects of improved street lighting on crime operated via two different causal pathways. In the first pathway, improved street lighting caused increased visibility, street use and surveillance after dark, which in turn led to decreased perceived opportunities and rewards of crime and increased perceived risks by potential offenders, which in turn led to decreased crime. The pathway would especially explain a decrease in crime outside after dark. In the second pathway, improved street lighting led to increased community pride,

increased community cohesion and increased informal social control, which deterred potential offenders. This pathway would explain decreases in crime at all times of the
day. The operation of both pathways simultaneously would
lead to large decreases in crime after dark and to smaller
decreases in crime in the light. This prediction, and the hy-
pothesised pathways, are concordant with the quantitative
and qualitative results obtained in the Stoke-on-Trent project [Painter and Farrington, this volume, pp. 116-117].

In the face of such a technical tour de force as represented by the
combined Dudley and Stoke projects, the debate must surely and
belatedly move from the (now settled) question of whether street
lighting can reduce crime (it can), to how it can best be used to do so.
As recently as 1996, Painter commented "The Home Office study suggested that over wide areas, street lighting is unlikely to impact on
reported crime. One is tempted to ask why anyone ever thought that
it would achieve this" (1996a:333).

One cannot help but feel that Painter has spent years trying to
combat scepticism of the general principle of lighting-induced crime
change when she would rather have been detailing how it happens.
The Dudley and Stoke projects are impressive demonstrations of the
possibility of lighting-induced change, but they are general rather
than mechanism-oriented. They are the last word in a debate whose
terms were set by others, from Tien et al. (1979) to Atkins et al.
(1991).

Painter and Farrington (1997) orient their specification of future
research towards the detailing of boundary conditions and dose-
response relationships in lighting effects on crime, i.e., give close attention to the circumstances in which lighting works. It is almost
with a sense of regret that one perceives how Painter and Farrington
were forced by studies such as the Dudley Project to settle the general point, before they and others could move on to these crucial
questions. What if conditions in Dudley and Stoke had lain outside
the boundaries in which the general improvement of lighting showed
crime reduction benefits? It would have put back for a long time the
application of focused lighting changes. Yet Painter's early research
and some other work had shown that targeted lighting of small,
crime-prone areas was beneficial. That body of research would, as a
basis to work from in crime control, probably have been disregarded.

One aspect of the Dudley and Stoke studies to which attention is
not drawn in their written accounts is that of crime concentration.
Earlier in this report, the highly concentrated nature of crime victimi-

sation was noted, together with the implications this must have for lighting strategies. Is there any clue from these studies about the effect of lighting on crime concentration in the areas covered?

The two preferred measures of crime used by Painter and Farrington (1997) — and almost everyone else — are prevalence and incidence. Prevalence counts the number of people victimised in relation to the population. Incidence counts the number of crime events in relation to the population. Thus, in a village of 100 people, if 20 people are victimised twice each, the prevalence is 0.2 (20/100), and the incidence is 0.4 ((20*2)/100). There is a third measure, concentration, which relates to the number of victimisations per victim, measured as incidence/prevalence (0.4/0.2). The reason why this is both theoretically and practically important is that one aim of crime reduction is to reduce the impact of crime on those most heavily victimised. Measuring concentration in the way described above is crude. More sophisticated methods are available, but cannot be applied to the Dudley and Stoke data available to the present writer. However, one can ask whether the crime reduction achieved through lighting serves to help the most victimised more than the less victimised, i.e., does it reduce crime concentration? One would hypothesise that it should. Insofar as the darkest areas offer the richest crime opportunities during the hours of darkness, those are the areas on which crime in darkness would be concentrated, and also in which the introduction of lighting would have its greatest proportional impact.

In recognition of the crudity of the measures at hand, Table 2 below shows the change of concentration measures for total crime in Dudley and Stoke in relit, adjacent and comparison areas. It will be seen that in both towns, the lighting-enhanced area experienced the greatest reduction in crime concentration. In Stoke, the reduction in concentration was limited to the lighting-enhanced area, i.e., the "diffusion of benefit" effect did not extend to the reduction in crime concentration in the adjacent area. This is important because it *suggests* that diffusion of benefits does not extend to the benefit of reduced concentration of victimisation on certain victims. However, the central message of Table 2 is that lighting changes confer the most help on those most frequently victimised by crime. The benefits of street lighting for the most heavily victimised are consistent with the early Painter work, which shows the effects of lighting in crime hot spots.

Table 2: Changes in Crime Concentration, Stoke and Dudley Study Areas

Area	Change in crime concentration
Dudley lighting-enhanced area	-23%
Dudley comparison area	-13%
Stoke lighting-enhanced area	-33%
Stoke contiguous (displacement) area	- 9%
Stoke comparison area	-13%

WHAT NEXT?

Given that the capacity of street lighting to influence crime has now been satisfactorily settled, how should policy move forward to reflect this, and how should formal research and practical experience be combined most helpfully? The writer's *personal* view is detailed below.

Movement is necessary on two fronts:

- the incorporation of lighting issues in local plans under the Crime and Disorder Act 1998; and
- the eschewal of a formulaic approach to lighting as crime control, and the gathering, dissemination and evaluation of case studies of innovative use of lighting and other crime control measures.

The Crime and Disorder Act 1998

In the short term, it is suggested that the Home Office advise local authorities and police of the desirability of having lighting expertise at least available to community safety organisers, and possibly actually sitting on "responsible authority" groups locally.

In the middle term, it is suggested that crime audits and resulting plans be scrutinised in terms of the presence or absence in them of the whole repertoire of crime control techniques, including the deployment of lighting. A review of such audits and plans should then be available to inform the second three-year planning cycle envisaged under the Crime and Disorder Act 1998. Local community safety organisers would not be averse to such a process, since the first round, now being completed, can politely be described as approximate! Incorporated in this process should be the dissemination of innovative schemes currently operating elsewhere, including those involving lighting.

In the longer term, the Virtual Reality capacity of local authorities should be enhanced to the point at which illumination and other effects can be modeled alongside crime and disorder data. This will allow a tool for community consultation and provide the basis for a reasoned choice about lighting and other priorities.

LITERAL AND LATERAL THINKING ABOUT LIGHTING AND CRIME

Bathing an area in light to reduce crime in parts of it may be as crude as bathing a body in radiation to shrink a tumour in one organ. The changes in crime concentration in Dudley and Stoke-on-Trent suggest that lighting may have its greatest effect in small areas. Economy and the avoidance of light pollution, along with the need to optimise crime control efforts, argue for a more reasoned and possibly more selective approach to lighting. There is a trade-off here. Clearly one should not stigmatise a localised hot spot by supplementing lighting *only* there. Likewise, one should not relight large areas with little crime on the grounds of crime reduction. One should think of areal units that are large enough not to stigmatise, but small enough not to protect areas that do not need such protection.

Concretely, what is recommended is a trawl for (and stimulation into existence, if necessary, of) innovative targeted uses of lighting and other crime reduction techniques, to be fed into the second three-year cycle of local crime audits and plans instituted by the Crime and Disorder Act 1998 and due in 2001. This trawl may allow limited retrospective analysis of effects, and some resources should be put into such evaluation. However, the purpose is hypothesis generation about the diverse ways in which light might work, not hypothesis testing about the effects of their installation. In what areas may innovative thinking about lighting effects be particularly welcome?

Change and Stasis in Lighting

There is a noteworthy contrast between the use of street lighting for crime control on the one hand, and the private market in security lighting on the other. Specifically, street lighting is simply on during the hours of darkness. Security lighting comes on only when a sensor detects movement. The reason for street lighting to be generally constant is clear.

> ... in the United Kingdom, central government funds for promoting street lighting projects comes under the jurisdiction of the Department of Transport and the Department of the Environment rather than the Home Office, which has most interest in crime prevention. This arrangement tends to marginalise the crime-related aspects of street lighting projects. Street lighting programmes are funded out of the highway budgets of local authorities, primarily on the basis of traffic safety and traffic flow [Painter 1996a:318].

The particular virtues of lighting change rather than lighting per se in crime reduction is clear. Change elicits attention, hence (potentially) surveillance. Is there scope on streets and in other public areas for movement-triggered lighting? Clearly there is. Multistorey car parks typically have small areas in which crime is more frequent. Lighting triggered by the movements of motorists leaving or returning to their cars, and those engaged in car crime, may be more effective attention-getters than constant enhanced lighting.

Movement-triggered change may be from darkness to light, or from light to darkness. Are there circumstances in which the sudden removal of light may be helpful? Imagine commercial robbery in which movement triggers an alarm and makes internal lights inoperable, thus making the choice of things to take, and leaving, more difficult. This may or may not be undesirable for staff and legitimate customers. In a bank, for example, would plunging the staff area into darkness and increasing the illumination of the customer area be feasible? It would make staff invisible to the robbers, yet would not put customers in a more difficult position than they would otherwise be in.

It may be apparent, after full discussion, that movement-triggered lights (or darkness) are of limited application in crime control in public spaces. However, the fact that locations where lighting is marketed for security purposes are triggered by change suggests that this may not be the case. What is advocated is the exploration of a variety of lighting styles in the public arena. As with the suggestions made later, it may be that there are projects already under way that use lighting in this way. If so, all that needs to be done is to create a trawl for local studies, some evaluation, and the publication of the most promising research.

Lighting Plus...

If we can discard the view that a crime reduction measure must be administered alone to be evaluated, and encourage a substitute view that intelligent combinations should be evaluated, we can revisit the literature to find *sparse and as yet inconclusive evidence* that lighting improvements may be particularly valuable in combination with other measures, such as increases in police patrol (Wheeler 1967; Tyrpak 1975), commercial security surveys (Griswold 1984, 1992), and rearrangement of available space (Poyner and Webb 1992). An obvious combination would be movement-triggered lighting and closed circuit television (CCTV) surveillance. If movement-triggered lighting were an overt symbol of CCTV surveillance, with posters advertising the fact, that would constitute a visible token of being watched and recorded. As noted by Baldrey and Painter (1998), lighting enhancement often accompanies CCTV installation, so there may already be the makings of a natural experiment to determine whether the measures combined seem particularly successful.

Lighting Change and Gradients

An intriguing study links day-to-day variation in illumination levels with fear of crime (Vrij and Winkel, 1991). It is intriguing because it focuses on the variation of illumination, rather than its absolute level, as a tool.

Insofar as it is technically possible, we can think of:

- The effects of day-to-day variations in lighting in crime-prone areas. There is evidence (Kelling and Coles, 1996; Pease, 1998) that change in itself may reduce crime. The original and highly influential "broken windows" hypothesis of Kelling and Wilson (1982) suggests that the absence of change (instantially the non-repair of a building's broken windows) suggests area indifference to crime, and, hence, its probable recurrence. Could more subtle changes, e.g., of lighting, have crime-reductive effects?

- Brighter lighting is often installed at major road inter-
  sections. Could illumination levels be increased locally
  and routinely in the wake of a rash of recorded crimes?
  Alternatively, could behaviour be shaped by gradients of
  illumination that subtly move people away from where
  they could cause disorder, e.g., by having slightly higher
  illumination levels in those sections of the street in
  which fewest problems would result?[6]

- Could street lighting be integrated with the 999 (911)
  telephone system, so that street illumination increases
  immediately following an emergency call, hopefully
  alerting people living around to look out or help more
  actively?

If the reconsideration of the lighting-crime nexus helps to liberate
the debate from the sterile "does it work or doesn't it?" to the more
productive "how can I flexibly and imaginatively incorporate lighting
in crime reduction strategy and tactics?" it will have been worth the
effort. Lighting is only one element in the armoury of situational reduction, and does not merit any special consideration because of its
recent neglect. However, it does deserve consideration as one more
tool, to be used with intelligence and possibly in combination with
other methods, in the perpetual "arms race" between the resourceful
criminal and the resourceful preventer of crime.

◆

Address correspondence to: Ken Pease, Applied Criminology Group,
University of Huddersfield, Queensgate, Huddersfield HD1 3DH, United
Kingdom

REFERENCES

Allatt, P. (1984). "Residential Security: Containment and Displacement of
Burglary." *Howard Journal of Criminal Justice* 23:99-116.

Atkins S., S. Husain and A. Storey (1991). *The Influence of Street Lighting on Crime and Fear of Crime.* (Crime Prevention Unit Paper,
#28.) London, UK: Home Office.

Baldrey, P. and K. Painter (1998). "Watching Them Watching Us." *Surveyor*, April 30, pp. 14-16.

Barker, M., J. Geraghty and B. Webb (1993). *The Prevention of Street Robbery*. (Crime Prevention Unit Paper, #44.) London, UK: Home Office.

Bennett, T. and L. Gelsthorpe (1996). "Public Attitudes Towards CCTV in Public Places." *Studies on Crime and Crime Prevention* 5:72-90.

Carr, K. and G. Spring (1993). Public Transport Safety: A Community Right and A Communal Responsibility. In: R.V. Clarke (ed.), *Crime Prevention Studies*, vol. 1. Monsey, NY: Criminal Justice Press.

Clarke, R.V, (ed.) (1996). *Preventing Mass Transit Crime*. (Crime Prevention Studies, vol. 6.) Monsey, NY: Criminal Justice Press.

—— (1997). *Situational Crime Prevention: Successful Case Studies* (2nd ed.). Albany, NY: Harrow and Heston.

Demuth, C. (1989). *Community Safety in Brighton*. Brighton, UK: Brighton Borough Council Police and Public Safety Unit.

Eck, J. (1997). "Preventing Crime at Places." In: L. Sherman et al. (eds.), *Preventing Crime: What Works, What Doesn't, What's Promising*. (Report to U.S. Congress.) Washington, DC: National Institute of Justice.

Ellingworth, D.M. and K. Pease (1998). "Movers and Breakers: Household Property Crime Against Those Moving Home." *International Journal of Risk, Security and Crime Prevention* 3:35-42.

Fennelly, L.J. (1982). *Handbook of Loss Prevention and Crime Prevention*. London, UK: Butterworth.

—— (1996). "Security Surveys." In: L.J. Fennelly (ed.), *Handbook of Loss Prevention and Crime Prevention* (3rd ed). London, UK: Butterworth.

Fleming, R. and J. Burrows (1986). "The Case for Lighting as a Means for Preventing Crime." *Home Office Research Bulletin* 22:14-17.

Girard, C.M. (1982). "Security Lighting." In: L.J. Fennelly (ed.), *Handbook of Loss Prevention and Crime Prevention*. London, UK: Butterworth.

Griswold, D.B. (1984). "Crime Prevention and Commercial Burglary: A Time Series Analysis." *Journal of Criminal Justice* 12:493-501.

—— (1992). "Crime Prevention and Commercial Burglary: A Time Series Analysis." In: R.V. Clarke (ed.), *Situational Crime Prevention: Successful Case Studies*. Albany, NY: Harrow and Heston.

Hylton, J.B (1996). *Safe Schools: A Security and Loss Prevention Plan* London, UK: Butterworth.

Kelling, G.L. and C.M. Coles (1996). *Fixing Broken Windows.* New York, NY: Free Press.

Koch, B.C.M. (1998). *The Politics of Crime Prevention.* Aldershot, UK: Ashgate.

LaVigne, N. (1994). "Gasoline Drive-Offs: Designing a Less Convenient Environment." In: R.V. Clarke (ed.), *Crime Prevention Studies,* vol. 2. Monsey, NY: Criminal Justice Press.

Lyons, S.L. (1988). *Security of Premises: A Manual for Managers.* London, UK: Butterworth.

Mayhew, P.M. (1981). "Crime in Public View: Surveillance and Crime Prevention." In: P.J. Brantingham and P.L. Brantingham (eds.), *Environmental Criminology.* Prospect Heights, IL: Waveland.

Painter, K. (1991). *The West Park Estate Survey: An Evaluation of Public Lighting as a Crime Prevention Strategy.* Cambridge, UK: Institute of Criminology.

—— (1996a). "Street Lighting, Crime and Fear of Crime." In: T. Bennett (ed.), *Preventing Crime and Disorder: Targeting Strategies and Responsibilities.* Cambridge, UK: Institute of Criminology.

—— (1996b). "The Influence of Street Lighting Improvements on Crime, Fear and Pedestrian Street Use, After Dark." *Landscape and Urban Planning* 35:193-201.

—— and D.P. Farrington (1997). "The Crime Reducing Effect of Improved Street Lighting: The Dudley Project." In: R.V. Clarke (ed.), *Situational Crime Prevention: Successful Case Studies* (2nd ed). Albany, NY: Harrow and Heston.

Pease, K. (1997). "Crime Prevention." In: M. Maguire et al. (eds.), *Oxford Handbook of Criminology.* Oxford, UK: Clarendon.

—— (1998). *Repeat Victimisation: Taking Stock.* (Crime Detection and Prevention Paper, #92.) London, UK: Police Research Group, Home Office.

Poyner, B. and B. Webb (1992). "Reducing Theft from Shopping Bags in City Centre Markets." In: R.V. Clarke (ed.), *Situational Crime Prevention: Successful Case Studies.* Albany, NY: Harrow and Heston.

—— (1993). "What Works in Crime Prevention: An Overview of Evaluations." In: R.V. Clarke (ed.), *Crime Prevention Studies,* vol. 1. Monsey, NY: Criminal Justice Press.

Ramsey, M. (1989). "Crime Prevention: Lighting the Way Ahead." *Home Office Research Bulletin* 27:18-20.

—— and R. Newton (1991). *The Influence of Street Lighting on Crime and Fear of Crime.* (Crime Prevention Unit Paper, #29.) London, UK: Home Office.

Sherman, L. and D.P. Rogan (1995). "Effects of Gun Seizure on Gun Violence: Hot Spots Patrol in Kansas City." *Justice Quarterly* 12:755-781.

Spelman, W. (1995a). "Criminal Careers of Public Places." In: J.E. Eck and D. Weisburd (eds.), *Crime and Place.* (Crime Prevention Studies, vol. 4.) Monsey, NY: Criminal Justice Press and Police Executive Forum.

—— (1995b). "Once Bitten, Then What? Cross-Sectional and Time Course Explanations of Repeat Victimisation." *British Journal of Criminology* 35:366-383.

Tien, J., V.F. O'Donnell, A. Barnett and P.B. Mirchandani (1979). *Street Lighting Projects. National Evaluation Programme Phase 1 Report.* Washington, DC: National Institute of Law Enforcement and Criminal Justice.

Tyrpak, S. (1975). *Newark High-Impact Anti-Crime Program: Street Lighting Project Interim Evaluation Report.* Newark, NJ: Office of Criminal Justice Planning.

Vrij, A. and F.W. Winkel (1991). "Characteristics of the Built Environment and Fear of Crime: A Research Note on Interventions in Unsafe Locations." *Deviant Behavior* 12:203-215.

Weisburd D., L. Green and D. Ross (1994). "Crime in Street Level Drug Markets: A Spatial Analysis." *Criminology* 27:49-67.

Welsh, B. and D.P. Farrington (1999). "Value for Money? A Review of the Costs and Benefits of Situational Crime Prevention." *British Journal of Criminology* 39:345-368.

Wheeler, S. (1967). *The Challenge of Crime in a Free Society. Presidential Commission on Law Enforcement and Administration of Justice.* Washington, DC: U.S. Government Printing Office.

Wilson, J.Q. and G.L. Kelling (1982). "Broken Windows." *Atlantic Monthly* (Mar):29-38.

NOTES

1. No offense is intended to those yet to be persuaded of lighting effects on crime. I just couldn't think of a more succinct way of describing the protagonists in the debate.

2. Sometimes the results of preconceptions are amusing. Demuth (1989) asked Brighton citizens about areas they avoided, and found that only 9% cited poor lighting as a reason for avoidance. Few of the streets avoided were also regarded as being poorly lit. This is like asking those who avoid soccer matches about the quality of lighting in soccer stadia. If you avoid the stadium, how are you supposed to make a sensible judgement about the quality of its illumination?

3. This is not to say that believers are indifferent as to mechanism, merely that research has not yet been carried out to elaborate such mechanisms.

4. Painter (1996a) seems to think the example reflects real data, but this writer thinks they do not since the reductions there illustrated are somewhat different from those calculable from Table 2 of the Atkins report.

5. Using Glim, with Poisson error and log link, probabilities derived from G^2 with appropriate df.

6. Please allow the writer one moment of nostalgia. Forty years ago he was a "youth causing annoyance," as the police report would have it, in an estate in North Cheshire. The cricket stumps were the foot of a lamppost, which doubled as one of the goalposts during winter. One lady rang the police about us often. If the lamppost three further down the street had been brighter, we would have gone there and either annoyed no one or spread the misery of our presence along the street. This would also have made the chances of our survival to adulthood greater, given the closeness of a road turning.

STREET LIGHTING AND CRIME: DIFFUSION OF BENEFITS IN THE STOKE-ON-TRENT PROJECT

by

Kate Painter

and

David P. Farrington
Institute of Criminology, University of Cambridge

Abstract: *Using a victim survey, the prevalence and incidence of crime were measured 12 months before and 12 months after the installation of improved street lighting in an experimental area of Stoke-on-Trent, U.K.; and at the same times in adjacent and control areas where the street lighting remained unchanged. The prevalence of crime decreased by 26% in the experimental area and by 21% in the adjacent area, but increased by 12% in the control area. The incidence of crime decreased by 43% in the experimental area and by 45% in the adjacent area, but decreased by only 2% in the control area. Police-recorded crimes in the whole police area also decreased by only 2%. It is concluded that the improved street lighting caused a substantial decrease in crime in the experimental area, and that there was a diffusion of these benefits to the adjacent area (which was not clearly delimited from the experimental area). Furthermore, the benefits of improved street lighting, in terms of the savings to the public from crimes prevented, greatly outweighed its costs.*

The main aim of the present research was to assess the effect of improved street lighting on crime, using before and after victimization surveys in experimental, adjacent and control areas. This quasi-experimental design makes it possible to control for many threats to valid inference. It also permits the investigation of displacement and diffusion of benefits from experimental to adjacent areas. In many ways, the study resembles a "double-blind" clinical trial, since neither respondents nor interviewers knew about its purpose.

INTRODUCTION

Previous Research on Street Lighting and Crime

Contemporary interest in the relationship between street lighting and crime began in North America during the dramatic rise in crime that took place in the 1960s. Many towns and cities embarked upon major street lighting programmes as a means of reducing crime, and initial results were encouraging (Wright et al., 1974).

The proliferation of positive results across North America led to Tien et al.'s (1979) detailed review of the effect of street lighting on crime funded by the federal Law Enforcement Assistance Agency. The final report describes how 103 street lighting projects originally identified were eventually reduced to a final sample of only 15 that were considered by the review team to contain sufficiently rigorous evaluative information. With regard to the impact of street lighting on crime, the authors found that as many projects reported an increase or no change as a reduction in crime. However, each project was considered to be seriously flawed because of such problems as: weak project designs; misuse or complete absence of sound analytic techniques; inadequate measures of street lighting; poor measures of crime (all were based on police records); insufficient appreciation of the impact of lighting on different types of crime; and inadequate measures of public attitudes and behaviour.

Obviously, the Tien et al. (1979) review should have led to attempts to measure the effects of improved street lighting using alternative measures of crime, such as victim surveys, self-reports or systematic observation. Unfortunately, it was interpreted as showing that street lighting had no effect on crime and, thereafter, the topic was neglected.

In the United Kingdom, very little research was carried out on street lighting and crime until the late 1980s. There was a resurgence of interest in the issue between 1988 and 1990, when three small-scale street lighting projects were implemented and evaluated in different areas of London: Edmonton, Tower Hamlets and Hammersmith/Fulham (Painter, 1994). In each location, crime, disorder, and fear of crime declined and pedestrian street use increased dramatically after the lighting improvements (see Painter, 1996, for a review of U.K. projects).

In contrast to these generally positive results, a major Home Office-funded evaluation in Wandsworth (Atkins et al., 1991) concluded that improved street lighting had no effect on crime, and a Home Office review, publicised simultaneously, also asserted that "better lighting by itself has very little effect on crime" (Ramsey and Newton, 1991:24). The Atkins et al. (1991) evaluation appeared to be well-designed, since it was based on before and after measures of police statistics and victimization reports in relit (experimental) and control areas. However, in analyzing police statistics, crimes were dubiously classified into those "likely" or "unlikely" to be affected by street lighting. For example, robbery and violence, which decreased significantly in the Wright et al. (1974) project, were thought *unlikely* to be affected by street lighting (Atkins et al., 1991:10). Interestingly, while the "likely" crimes decreased by only 3% after the improved lighting, the "unlikely" crimes decreased by 24% (Atkins et al., 1991). Unfortunately, the response rates in the victimization surveys were very low (37% before and 29% after). Only 39 crimes were reported in the before survey in the experimental area and only 13 in the control area, suggesting that the research had insufficient statistical power to detect changes in crime rates.

The best-designed previous evaluation of the effect of improved street lighting on crime was the Dudley project (Painter and Farrington, 1997), which was the forerunner of the present project. Before and after victimization surveys were carried out in experimental and control areas. The areas were adjacent to each other but clearly defined and physically separated. Large samples were interviewed (about 440 before and 370 after in each area). In general, the experimental and control respondents were closely comparable, except that more of the control respondents were aged over 60 and more of them in the before survey said that they had seen a police officer on foot on their estate in the previous month.

The prevalence and incidence of crime decreased significantly on the experimental estate after the relighting compared with the control estate. This result held not only after controlling for initial levels of crime, but also after controlling for the respondent's age and for the visibility of police officers on the estate. There was no sign of crime displacement from the experimental to the control estate. The percentage of crimes committed after dark was about 70% before and after in both estates. Therefore, the reduction in crime in the experimental estate applied equally to crimes committed in the day or night.

The experimental sample noticed that the lighting had improved and became more satisfied with their estate afterwards. Also, they were more likely than the control sample to say that their estate was safe after dark in the after survey. Pedestrian counts showed that the number of women out on the streets after dark increased significantly in the experimental area compared with the control area; the number of men also increased in the experimental area, but less markedly. It was concluded that the improved street lighting had caused a decrease in crime, and that this was probably mediated by increased community pride and informal social control deterring potential offenders.

Street Lighting: Mechanisms of Crime Reduction

Explanations of the way street lighting improvements could prevent crime can be found in "situational" approaches which focus on reducing opportunity and increasing perceived risk through modification of the physical environment (Clarke, 1992). Explanations can also be found in perspectives that stress the importance of strengthening informal social control and community cohesion through more effective street use (Jacobs, 1961; Angel, 1968), and investment in neighbourhood conditions (Taub et al., 1984; Fowler and Mangione, 1986; Lavrakas and Kushmuk, 1986; Taylor and Gottfredson, 1986). The situational approach to crime prevention suggests that crime can be prevented by environmental measures that directly affect offenders' perceptions of increased risks and decreased rewards. This approach is also supported by theories that emphasize natural, informal surveillance as a key to crime prevention. For example, Jacobs (1961) drew attention to the role of good visibility combined with natural surveillance as a deterrent to crime. She emphasized the association between levels of crime and public street use, suggesting that less crime would be committed in areas with an abundance of potential witnesses.

Other theoretical perspectives have emphasised the importance of investment to improve neighbourhood conditions as a means of strengthening community confidence, cohesion and social control (Wilson and Kelling, 1982; Taub et al., 1984; Taylor and Gottfredson, 1986; Skogan, 1990). As a highly visible sign of positive investment, improved street lighting might reduce crime if it physically improved the environment and signalled to residents that efforts were being made to invest in and improve their neighbourhood. In turn, this might lead them to have a more positive image of the area and increased community pride, optimism and cohesion. It should be noted that this theoretical perspective predicts a reduction in both daytime and nighttime crime. Consequently, attempts to measure the effects of improved lighting should not concentrate purely on nighttime crime.

The relationship between visibility, social surveillance and criminal opportunities is a consistently strong theme to emerge from the literature. A core assumption of both opportunity and informal social control models of prevention is that criminal opportunities and risks are influenced by environmental conditions, in interaction with resident and offender characteristics. Street lighting is a tangible alteration of the built environment but it does not constitute a physical barrier to crime. However, it can act as a catalyst to stimulate crime reduction through a change in the perceptions, attitudes and behaviour of residents and potential offenders.

There are several possible ways in which improved lighting might reduce crime:

(1) Lighting reduces crime by improving visibility. This deters potential offenders by increasing the risks that they will be recognized or interrupted in the course of their activities (Mayhew et al., 1979).

(2) Lighting improvements encourage increased street usage, which intensifies natural surveillance. The change in routine activity patterns works to reduce crime because it increases the flow of potentially capable guardians. From the offender's perspective, the proximity of other pedestrians acts as a deterrent increasing the risks of being recognised or interrupted when attacking personal or property targets (Cohen and Felson, 1979). From the potential victim's perspective, perceived risks and fears of crime are reduced.

(3) Enhanced visibility and increased street usage combine to heighten possibilities for informal surveillance. Pedestrian density and flow and surveillance have long been regarded as crucial for crime control since they can influence offenders' perceptions of the likely risks of being caught (Jacobs, 1961; Newman, 1972; Bennett and Wright, 1984).

(4) The renovation of a highly noticeable component of the physical environment, combined with changed social dynamics, acts as a psychological deterrent. Offenders judge that the image of the location is improving and that social control, or-

der, and surveillance have increased (Taylor and Gottfredson, 1986). They may deduce that crime in the relit location is riskier than elsewhere, and this can influence behaviour in two ways. First, offenders living in the area will be deterred from committing offences or escalating their activities. Second, potential offenders from outside the area will be deterred from entering it (Wilson and Kelling, 1982). Crime in the relit area is reduced though it may be displaced elsewhere.

(5)   Lighting improves community confidence. It provides a highly noticeable sign that local authorities are investing in the fabric of the area. This offsets any previous feelings of neglect and stimulates a general "feel-good" factor. Fear is reduced.

(6)   Improved illumination reduces fear of crime because it physically improves the environment and alters public perceptions of it. People sense that a well-lit environment is less dangerous than one that is dark (Warr, 1990). The positive image of the nighttime environment in the relit area is shared by residents and pedestrians. As actual and perceived risks of victimization lessen, the area becomes used by a wider cross-section of the community. The changed social mix and activity patterns within the locality reduce risks of crime and reduce fear.

It is feasible that lighting improvements could, in certain circumstances, increase opportunities for crime by bringing greater numbers of potential victims and potential offenders into the same physical space. It is also likely that more than one of the preventive mechanisms may operate simultaneously or interact.

The Stoke-on-Trent and Dudley projects represent the most thorough attempts to develop a coherent theory linking street lighting, the urban environment and resident dynamics with the incidence of crime. The methods of measurement were designed empirically to test whether street lighting could facilitate informal surveillance and pedestrian use of an area in ways that promote the capacity and willingness of residents to protect the community from potential offenders. These are theory-based evaluations.

Crime Displacement

The main theoretical criticism of Crime Prevention Through Environmental Design (Jeffery, 1971) and situational approaches is that blocking opportunities for crime in one place will merely result in it being displaced to a different time, place or target, or cause the offender to change tactics or commit different types of offences (Reppetto, 1976; Gabor, 1983). The assumption underpinning the displacement hypothesis is that making one offence more difficult to accomplish does not eliminate the motivation to offend, and that the rational criminal will simply seek out alternative opportunities.

Rational choice theory, while accepting the possibility that displacement occurs, holds that it will only happen to the extent that alternative crimes offer the same reward without greater costs in terms of risk or effort. From this perspective, displacement is not seen as an inevitable outcome of situational measures but as conditional upon the offender's assessment of the ease, risk and appeal of other criminal opportunities.

Recent reviews of the evidence on crime displacement suggest that empirical evidence in support of the phenomenon is hard to come by (Bannister, 1991; Barr and Pease, 1992; Clarke, 1992, 1995; Hesseling, 1994). Nonetheless, displacement has been found in a number of studies. For example, evidence of spatial displacement of burglary was noted in a study of Neighbourhood Watch in Vancouver, Canada (Lowman, 1983); spatial and functional displacement occurred following a target-hardening project in Newcastle, UK (Allatt, 1984) and spatial displacement has been observed following property marking schemes in Ottawa, Canada (Gabor, 1983, 1990).

There are so many methodological difficulties associated with measuring displacement that Barr and Pease (1990) questioned whether the issue could ever be resolved by empirical research. A recent study of the use of slugs (false coins) on the London underground demonstrated how an uncritical acceptance of displacement could mean that increases in crime, which might have occurred in the absence of any preventive measure, might be wrongly interpreted as evidence of displacement (Clarke et al., 1994).

Clarke (1992, 1995) cites numerous examples of successful situational measures that did not lead to displacement, and other research has shown that, depending on the nature of the offence, there may be no point in looking for displacement effects. For example, the likelihood of crime displacement occurring from the introduction of random breath testing (Homel, 1993) or of speed cameras in Australia (Bourne and Cook, 1993) is minimal because people are not normally predisposed and determined to commit drunk driving and speeding offences.

Research focussing on the "choice structuring properties" of different offence types has demonstrated the contingent nature of crime displacement and explained why it is not an inevitable outcome of situational preventive measures (Clarke and Mayhew, 1988; Mayhew et al., 1989; Clarke and Harris, 1992a, 1992b). Even where displacement has been observed, it has rarely been total (Gabor, 1990). It might be benign if offenders were deflected from more serious to less serious offences, or from offending against a repeatedly victimized vulnerable group of the population to offending against a group that is better able to resist and withstand antisocial and criminal events (Painter, 1991; Pease, 1991; Barr and Pease, 1992). Arguing that displacement symbolises pessimism about crime prevention, Barr and Pease (1990) prefer the term "deflection," which indicates success in moving a crime from its intended target.

Diffusion of Benefits

A considerable number of studies have observed the reverse of displacement, whereby the effects of a preventive action led to a reduction in crimes not directly targeted by the measure (see Clarke, 1992, 1995, for a summary). For example, Miethe (1991) used the term "free-rider" effect to refer to the benefits to unprotected residents whose neighbours had taken preventive actions. Sherman (1990) noted the "bonus effects" of prolonged preventive effects after the period during which police crackdowns took place. Scherdin (1986) observed a "halo" effect, when a library book detection system prevented not only electronically protected material from being stolen but also unprotected items.

Poyner and Webb (1992) noticed that measures designed to reduce thefts in indoor markets in the Birmingham city centre also appeared to reduce thefts in other markets. Poyner (1991) found that a closed circuit television (CCTV) system, aimed at reducing thefts of cars in a university car park, also led to a reduction in a nearby car park not covered by the cameras. Poyner (1992) showed that CCTV on buses not only reduced vandalism on the five targeted vehicles but extended to the entire fleet of 80 buses, simply because schoolchildren were unsure which buses did, or did not, have cameras. Painter (1991) also found a reduction in crime in two unlit roads adjacent to a relit area following a street lighting initiative, and Pease (1991) noted a "drip-feed" effect to other households that were not targeted by a burglary prevention scheme, so that the burglary rate across the entire estate declined.

This phenomenon has been termed "diffusion of benefits." This is defined as the "spread of the beneficial influence of an intervention beyond the places which are directly targeted, the individuals who are the subject of control, the crimes which are the focus of the intervention or the time periods in which an intervention is brought" (Clarke and Weisburd, 1994:169). Diffusion through deterrence works by affecting offenders' perceptions of risk, as illustrated by Poyner's (1992) study of CCTV on buses, which appeared to bring a widespread benefit because the children were unsure about which buses had cameras. Diffusion through discouragement works by changing offenders' assessments of the relative effort and reward involved in committing offences. For example, Pease (1991) explained the "drip-feed" effect in the Kirkholt burglary project as a consequence of the removal of prepayment meters from burgled households, which meant that burglars could no longer count on finding a meter containing cash in a house. Ekblom (1988) also noted that the introduction of anti-bandit screens in London post offices brought about a reduction not only in over-the-counter robberies but also in other robberies of staff and customers. He considered that potential robbers had been discouraged by the general message that something was being done to increase security at post offices.

Possible displacement and diffusion effects have implications for evaluation designs. On the one hand, displacement of crime from the target area to a nearby control area may lead to "double counting" and an exaggeration of the impact of the intervention. On the other hand, as Ekblom and Pease observed (1995:9): "...diffusion of benefits from the action to the control area (occasioned, for example by offenders giving the action area a wider berth than strictly necessary) may lead to an underestimate of impact. In effect, the more successful a programme is in spreading benefits beyond its boundaries, the less success may be attributed to it." Clarke (1995:42) commented that it was likely that in the 1990s, diffusion of benefits might supersede displacement as "the principal focus of theoretical debate about the value of situational measures."

RESEARCH DESIGN

The Stoke-on-Trent evaluation employed a non-equivalent control group design with before and after measures of crime in experimental (relit), adjacent and control areas. Using a victim survey, the prevalence and incidence of crime were measured 12 months before and 12 months after the installation of improved street lighting in the experimental area and, at the same times, in adjacent and control areas where the street lighting remained unchanged. The questions on crime were identical in all surveys. The adjacent and control areas selected were located near the experimental area for two reasons.

First, it was envisaged that the people living in them would be similar in many respects to those in the experimental area, and second, to facilitate the investigation of spatial and temporal displacement of crime or diffusion of benefits. Hence, demographic factors that might influence crime rates should be equivalent in all areas at the outset. It becomes more plausible, therefore, that any change in crime between the relit and non-relit areas can be attributed to the street lighting programme rather than to preexisting differences between the samples. This design controls for the major threats to internal validity (history, maturation, testing, instrumentation, regression and mortality).

Research Hypotheses

The main research hypotheses were as follows:

(1) Improved street lighting will decrease crime after dark in the experimental area (e.g., either because the increased risk of offenders being seen and identified acts as a deterrent, potential victims can more easily avoid potential offenders, or it is harder for potential offenders to hide and surprise their victims).

(2) Improved street lighting will decrease crime both in the dark and the light in the experimental area (e.g., because the improved lighting signals an improving neighbourhood and leads to increased community confidence and community pride, which, in turn, leads to increased informal social control, which then deters potential offenders).

(3) Improved street lighting will displace crime to the adjacent area, so that crime in the adjacent area increases.

(4) Improved street lighting will cause a diffusion of benefits to the adjacent area (e.g., because potential offenders are deterred not only from the experimental area but also from adjacent areas), so that crime in the adjacent area decreases.

(5) Improved street lighting will lead to a decreased fear of crime after dark.

(6) Improved street lighting will lead to an increased number of people outside on the streets after dark.

(7) Improved street lighting will lead to a more favourable assessment of the quality of the neighbourhood.

Selection and Description of the Experimental Area

Stoke-on-Trent is a city in the North Midlands of England, which has been formed around the six towns of Burslem, Fenton, Hanley, Longton, Stoke and Tunstall. The towns lie in close proximity to one another, within a single metropolitan area about eight miles in diameter. The city has been dominated by two industries, mining and pottery. Though the area was badly hit by unemployment throughout the 1980s, Stoke-on-Trent remains a flourishing and vibrant place. The large project area lies to the north of the city, and is surrounded by open land. It offers few social amenities. The northern part is bounded by a main arterial road, which contains the usual mixture of neighbourhood public houses, small shops, a snooker (pool) club, a church, fish-and-chip shops, and take-away food outlets. Within the large project area, experimental, adjacent and control areas were studied.

The experimental area comprises what was originally a council estate containing 365 properties. The majority of houses are still rented from the council, although approximately 17% have been sold to tenants. The estate is characteristic of many others built in the early 1950s. It is made up of low-rise, short-terraced and semi-detached houses that have gardens back and front. The adjacent areas were located to the west and east of the experimental area, and were not clearly differentiated from it. Some roads continued from the experimental area into the adjacent areas with no obvious boundary, making it difficult for respondents to know where one area ended and another began. The adjacent area to the east was primarily council-owned property, whereas the adjacent area to the west was primarily privately owned property. The control areas were located further away from the experimental area, to the north and south. They were physically separate from and clearly demarcated from the experimental and adjacent areas, and were primarily council-owned property.

The Nature and Implementation of the Street Lighting Programme

Details of the street lighting programme and the way and the time it was implemented are important; the type, level and uniformity of lighting will affect the likelihood of preventing crime. If, for instance, the level or uniformity of the lighting is inadequate, or if the lighting is obscured by other environmental features such as shrubbery, then the potential mechanisms suggested earlier may not be induced. Each of the improved lighting schemes in the programme was designed to meet British Standard, BS 5489, Part 3. This lists three categories of lighting levels — from 3/1 (the best) to 3/3 (the worst). These categories are based on levels of traffic, pedestrian use and perceived levels of crime. Thus, an area with high traffic flow, high pedestrian flow and high crime should be illuminated to the 3/1 standard. The preexisting street lighting in the experimental, adjacent and control areas did not even achieve the minimum standard of 3/3. Consequently, the lighting upgrade constituted a very noticeable alteration of the nighttime environment in the experimental area.

The experimental area was chosen for relighting by the council on the basis of its perceived need. Between mid-December 1992 and mid-January 1993, 110 high-pressure sodium (white) street lights (lantern type) were installed over 1,000 metres of roadway. These lights replaced the older, domestic-type tungsten lamps. Detached footpaths that were previously unlit were also illuminated. The area was illuminated in accordance with category 3/2 of BS 5489, giving an average illuminance of 6 lux and a minimum of 2.5 lux. Maintenance and energy costs doubled as a consequence of reducing the large spacing of up to 50 metres pre-test to approximately 38 metres post-test. However, the amount of useful light increased fivefold and the efficient use of electricity doubled.

THE BEFORE AND AFTER VICTIMIZATION SURVEYS

The timing of data collection was the same in all the areas. The before survey was carried out from the last two weeks of October to mid-November 1992. The lighting installation commenced in December 1992 and was completed by the second week in January 1993. The after surveys were undertaken 12 months later, from mid-November to mid-December 1993. In investigating the impact of street lighting on crime, the 12-month period prior to street lighting installation (November 1991-November 1992) was compared with the 12 month period after, including the installation period (December 1992-December 1993).

The before and after surveys measured household victimization and respondents' perceptions, attitudes and behaviour. The majority of questions on victimization, fear of crime and quality of life were similar to those used in successive British Crime Surveys (e.g., Mayhew et al., 1993; Mirrlees-Black et al., 1996). Respondents were only asked about crimes that had occurred on their estate during the previous 12 months, and supplementary questions ensured that the same criminal event did not generate reports of two categories of crime. Additional questions on public reactions to the new lighting and travel behaviour after dark were included at the end of the after survey, as part of a process evaluation of programme implementation. Other crime prevention strategies, such as Neighbourhood Watch and policing strategies, were monitored through closed and open-ended questions and interviewer fieldwork sheets, as were other possible extraneous historical influences that might have caused a change in outcomes within and between the project areas.

Interviewing Procedures

The household face-to-face interviews took between 45 and 90 minutes, depending on the extent of victimization. Prior to an interviewer calling, households were sent a leaflet explaining that a crime survey was taking place, but no mention was made of the proposed street lighting initiative. To minimize any unwitting interviewer bias, interviewers were *not* told about the true purpose of the survey, and were therefore unaware of the lighting improvements that were to take place. They were also unaware that there were experimental and control areas. The same interviewing team, consisting of 19 interviewers, was employed in each of the study areas, both before and after the initiative. For the after survey, every effort was made to match interviewers to their before respondents. The research was carried out by a company with previous experience in undertaking community surveys. A 20% quality control check was undertaken. Each week the fieldwork supervisor visited 10% of respondents to check that interviews had been conducted, and a further 10% of respondents were mailed a self-completion questionnaire that asked whether the interview had been conducted in a satisfactory manner.

The type of local authority dwelling ensured that only one household lived at each address. A "household" was defined as "people who are catered for by the same adult(s) and share the same meals." An individual over the age of 18 years was selected for interview by a random procedure, which involved the interviewer listing, in alphabetical order, the first names of household members. Selection of the interviewee was based on a pre-assigned random number between one and nine, depending on the number of persons living in the household. The initial cross-sectional target samples can therefore be considered as representative of people living in the areas.

In the before survey, interviewers were instructed to make unlimited callbacks to contact the selected individual and no substitution was allowed. In the after survey, interviewers were instructed to contact the same individual from the same household. After six callbacks, another member of the household could be selected for interview, using the same randomized procedures described above. New tenants who had moved in were interviewed in the after survey, but no attempt was made to trace individuals who had moved from one address on the estate to another.

Selection of Samples

The electoral register was used as the sampling frame for the experimental, adjacent and control areas. Field enumeration was used to identify missing addresses and void properties. It would be more accurate to describe the Stoke-on-Trent survey, carried out in the experimental area, as a census because every household on the electoral register was included. The reason for this was to ensure that there were sufficient numbers of criminal incidents for statistical analysis. In the adjacent and control areas, every third household on the electoral register was selected for inclusion. The intention was to produce a sample size approximately comparable to that in the experimental area.

Of the issued sample of 756 addresses (drawn from a sampling frame of 1,580 addresses in all areas), 79 were void (vacant). The response rate in the before survey was 89% in the experimental area (317 completed interviews from 357 addresses) and 80% in the adjacent and control areas (255 completed interviews from 320 addresses). There were originally three control areas, but one was dropped from the design because it was being extensively renovated by the council, and many of the houses were boarded up because tenants had temporarily moved out during the renovation. Many of the void addresses were in this area. Excluding this area, there were 88 completed interviews in the before survey in the two remaining control areas, and 135 completed interviews in the two adjacent areas. For ease of exposition, the two adjacent areas will in future be termed the adjacent area, and the two control areas will be termed the control area.

In the after survey, the aim was to complete interviews only at houses where interviews had been completed in the before survey. The follow-up response rates were 88% (278 out of 317) in the experimental area, 90% (121 out of 135) in the adjacent area, and 92% (81 out of 88) in the control area. In 92% of cases, the respondent was the same in the after survey as in the before survey; in 6% of cases, a different respondent from the same household was interviewed in the after survey; and in 2% of cases, a different respondent from a different household living at the same address was interviewed in the after survey. Unfortunately, it was not possible to link up before addresses with after addresses in order to carry out longitudinal analyses, with each address acting as its own control. Hence, the before and after surveys had to be treated as repeated cross-sectional surveys.

In the Dudley project, it was estimated that samples of 325-400 people before and after were required to have sufficient statistical power to detect a reasonably likely and practically important magnitude of change in crime rates, from a 50% to a 40% overall victimization rate (Painter and Farrington, 1997). Hence, the small sample sizes in the adjacent and control areas are a limitation of the Stoke-on-Trent project. These small sample sizes mean that changes in crime rates (or in other variables) between the before and after surveys would have to be quite large in the adjacent and control areas in order to be statistically significant. Roughly speaking, a reduction in the victimization rate from 50% to 40% in the experimental area would be significant, but the reduction would have to be from 50% to 35% in the adjacent and control areas in order to be significant.

Victimization surveys have many limitations. Respondents may experience memory decay, especially in relation to less important events that have occurred within the previous 12 months. "Telescoping" is also a possible distorting factor, in that respondents may recall events from outside this 12-month period as occurring within it. However, the comparison of experimental, adjacent and control areas, and before and after surveys, largely controls for these kinds of measurement limitations, which should be similar in all surveys and all areas.

QUANTITATIVE RESULTS

Comparability of the Experimental, Adjacent and Control Areas

Table 1 shows the extent to which the experimental, adjacent and control areas were comparable in the before surveys. For example, 55.2% of respondents in the experimental area were female, compared with 63.7% of those in the adjacent area and 56.8% of those in the control area, a non-significant variation on the 3 x 2 chi-squared test. The variation in age was nearly significant (p=.061). The local authority did not permit a question about ethnic origin, but the vast majority of respondents were white. Most had lived in the area for 10

Table 1: Comparability of Experimental, Adjacent and Control Areas Before Improved Lighting

	Experi-mental % (N=317)	Adjacent % (N=135)	Control % (N=88)	p value
Demographics				
Female	55.2	63.7	56.8	ns
Age 45+	54.9	64.4	65.9	ns
On Estate 10+ years	56.5	61.5	58.0	ns
Employed	28.4	31.1	25.0	ns
Opinion of Estate				
Talk to most/all neighbours	72.6	80.0	71.6	ns
Friendly area	74.1	75.6	73.9	ns
Well kept	39.1	50.4	46.6	ns
Unsafe to walk in dark	66.2	68.9	60.2	ns
Risks for women alone after dark	88.1	90.3	88.9	ns
Risks for elderly alone after dark	93.7	94.6	88.2	ns
Youth hang around	81.1	76.3	68.2	.033
Quality of life worse last year	60.3	56.3	44.3	.028
Quality of life better last year	3.5	4.4	17.0	.0001
Saw police in last month	21.1	25.9	58.0	.0001
Estate Lighting				
Badly lit	73.5	57.0	62.5	.002
Too dull	72.2	64.4	64.8	ns
Creates shadows	55.2	51.9	46.6	ns
Worry about Crime				
Burglary	75.7	80.0	68.2	ns
Street robbery	30.5	37.0	36.4	ns
Street assault	36.2	38.5	34.5	ns
Vandalism to home	63.4	67.4	59.1	ns
Car stolen/damaged	53.3	68.4	59.5	.020
Avoid going out after dark	33.1	38.6	34.1	ns
Feel unsafe in own home	52.7	53.3	46.6	ns
High fear of crime	54.3	58.5	48.9	ns
Prevalence of Crime				
Burglary	24.3	20.0	12.5	ns
Outside theft/vandalism	20.5	30.4	17.0	.030
Vehicle crime	25.9	18.5	11.4	.008
Property crime	53.0	52.6	31.8	.001
Personal crime	12.6	16.3	6.8	ns
All crime	57.7	55.6	34.1	.0004
Increased last year	83.0	87.4	65.9	.0002
% Outside in dark	70.3	72.3	48.9	.009
% Reported to police	56.7	48.1	59.6	ns

p values based on chi-squared from 3 x 2 tables

or more years, and over 40% had lived in the area for 20 or more years. Less than one-third of respondents were employed full-time or part-time. Generally, the respondents in the different areas were comparable on these demographic factors.

About three-quarters of respondents in all areas said that they talked to most or all of their neighbours, and about three-quarters said that their area was friendly. The experimental respondents were somewhat less likely than the remainder to say that their area was well kept, but this was not quite statistically significant (p=.067). About two-thirds of all respondents said that it was unsafe to walk in the dark in their area, and about 90% in all areas said that there were risks for women and elderly people out alone after dark.

Respondents in the control area were somewhat less likely to say that groups of youths hung around their area. They were also less likely to say that their environment and quality of life had become worse, and more likely to say that things had become better, in the last year (although very few respondents thought that their environment and quality of life had improved). Respondents in the control area were also much more likely to say that they had seen a police officer on foot in their area in the last month.

In response to questions about street lighting, most people said that their area was badly lit, and those in the experimental area were most likely to say this. However, there was no significant variation among area respondents in saying that the street lighting was too dull or that it created shadows. About three-quarters of respondents in all areas worried "a lot" or "quite a bit" about burglary. There was no significant variation among the areas in worries about burglary, being robbed in the street, being attacked in the street, or having one's home damaged by vandals. However, respondents in the adjacent area were most worried about having their car stolen or damaged. There were no significant differences among the areas in avoiding going out after dark (always or often), feeling unsafe in one's own home, or having a very or fairly high fear of crime.

Crimes were divided into four types:

(1) burglary (including attempts),

(2) theft from outside the home, vandalism of the home or bicycle theft,

(3) theft of or from vehicles or damage to vehicles, and

(4) personal crime against any member of the household, including street robbery, snatch theft, assault, threatening behaviour or sexual pestering of females.

Categories (1), (2) and (3) together constitute property crime. Table 1 shows that the experimental and adjacent area were generally comparable on the reported prevalence of victimization in the last year, but the control area had a lower victimization rate. Similarly, whereas 83% of those in the experimental area and 87.4% of those in the adjacent area thought that crime had increased in the last year, this was true of only 65.9% of those in the control area. About 70% of all crimes were committed during the hours of darkness outside or in a public place in the experimental and adjacent areas, but this was true of only about 50% of crimes committed in the control area. There was no significant variation among the areas in the probability of reporting a crime to the police.

None of the variables measured in this project and shown in Table 1 can explain the significant before differences in crime among the experimental, control and adjacent areas. The variations in youths hanging around and in the perceived quality of life are similar to the variations in crime. It is possible that more police on foot in an area might correlate with lower crime rates. However, as also found in the Dudley project, there was no correlation whatever between seeing police on foot in the area and the prevalence of any type of crime. The non-comparability of the before crime rates in the three areas will be controlled in regression analyses.

Changes in the Prevalence of Crime

Table 2 shows changes in the prevalence of crime (the percentage of households victimized in the last year) between the before and after surveys. For all crime categories except burglary, prevalence decreased significantly in the experimental area after the street lighting was improved. For example, the percentage who were victims of any crime decreased by a quarter, from 57.7% to 42.8%. The greatest percentage decreases were in personal crime (52%), outside theft/vandalism (40%) and vehicle crime (37%).

The prevalence of crime also decreased in the adjacent area. None of the decreases was statistically significant, but the decreases in all crime (p=.080) and in property crime (p=.070) were not far off. The decreases in vehicle crime (37%), personal crime (34%) and outside theft/vandalism (27%) were substantial. Crime did not change consistently in the control area. Overall, the prevalence of all crime increased slightly, from 34.1% before to 38.3% after.

The extent to which changes in prevalence in one area were significantly different from changes in prevalence in another was tested using the interaction term in a logistic regression equation (Farrington, 1997):

$$LOG [P/(1-P)] = b_0 + b_1 PREPOST + b_2 CONEXP + b_3 PREPOST*CONEXP$$

Where

LOG = Natural logarithm
P = Probability of crime
PREPOST = Dichotomous before/after variable
CONEXP = Dichotomous control/experimental variable
PREPOST*CONEXP = Interaction term

This method of analysis controls for preexisting differences in crime rates between areas. It showed that the change in all crime in the experimental area was significantly different from the change in all crime in the control area (LRCS=4.69, p=.030). Similarly, the change in property crime in the experimental area was significantly different from the change in property crime in the control area (p=.044). It can be concluded that the prevalence of crime decreased significantly in the experimental area compared with the control area, but decreased similarly in the experimental and adjacent areas.

Changes in the Incidence of Crime

Table 3 shows changes in the incidence of crime (the average number of victimizations per 100 households, allowing a maximum of 10 per household in each crime category). For all crime categories except burglary and outside theft/vandalism, incidence decreased significantly in the experimental area after the street lighting was improved. For example, the incidence of all crimes decreased by 43%, from 173.8 to 99.3 crimes per 100 households. The greatest percentage decreases were for personal crime (68%) and vehicle crime (46%).

The incidence of crime also decreased in the adjacent area, and the decreases were significant for property crime (38%), personal crime (66%) and all crime (45%). However, crime did not change consistently in the control area. Overall, the incidence of all crime decreased marginally, from 69.3 to 67.9 crimes per 100 households.

The extent to which changes in incidence in one area were significantly different from changes in incidence in another was tested using the interaction term in a Poisson regression equation. (This was carried out using the GLIM computer package to specify a Poisson distribution of incidence and a logarithmic link to the right hand side

Table 2: Changes in the Prevalence of Victimization

	Experimental			Adjacent			Control		
	Before (317)	After (278)	% Change	Before (135)	After (121)	% Change	Before (88)	After (81)	% Change
Burglary	24.3	21.2	-13	20.0	18.2	-9	12.5	16.0	+28
Outside theft/vandalism	20.5	12.2	-40*	30.4	22.3	-27	17.0	16.0	-6
Vehicle crime	25.9	16.2	-37*	18.5	11.6	-37	11.4	8.6	-25
Property crime	53.0	39.2	-26*	52.6	40.5	-23	31.8	35.8	+13
Personal crime	12.6	6.1	-52*	16.3	10.7	-34	6.8	4.9	-28
All crime	57.7	42.8	-26*	55.6	43.8	-21	34.1	38.3	+12

* Change significant on chi-squared test (p<.05, two-tailed)
Change in experimental area significantly different from change in control area:
  Property crime, LRCS=4.05, p=.044
  All crime, LRCS=4.69, p=.030
  LRCS = Likelihood Ratio Chi-Squared = Interaction term in logistic regression

Table 3: Changes in the Incidence of Victimization

	Experimental			Adjacent			Control		
	Before (317)	After (278)	% Change	Before (135)	After (121)	% Change	Before (88)	After (81)	% Change
Burglary	38.5	32.7	-15	31.1	24.8	-20	15.9	16.0	+1
Outside theft/vandalism	43.8	27.0	-38	65.2	38.8	-40	26.1	34.6	+33
Vehicle crime	47.6	25.5	-46*	34.8	18.2	-48	17.0	11.1	-35
Property crime	130.0	85.3	-34*	131.1	81.8	-38*	59.1	61.7	+4
Personal crime	43.8	14.0	-68*	48.9	16.5	-66*	10.2	6.2	-39
All crime	173.8	99.3	-43*	180.0	98.3	-45*	69.3	67.9	-2

Note: Mean offence rate per 100 households
*Change significant on t-test (p<.05, two-tailed)
Change in Experimental area significantly different from change in Control area:
   Outside theft, LRCS=5.91, p=.015
   Property crime, LRCS=4.69, p=.030
   All crime, LRCS=7.17, p=.007
Change in Adjacent area significantly different from change in Control area:
   Outside theft, LRCS=5.74, p=.017
   Property crime, LRCS=4.82, p=.028
   All crime, LRCS=7.19, p=.007
LRCS = Likelihood Ratio Chi-Squared = Interaction term in Poisson regression

of the equation.) This showed that the change in all crime in the experimental area was significantly different from the change in all crime in the control area (LRCS=7.17, p=.007). Similarly, the changes in outside theft/vandalism and property crime were significantly different in the experimental and control areas. Also, the changes in outside theft/vandalism, property crime and all crime in the adjacent area were significantly different from the corresponding changes in the control area. Once again, these tests show that crime decreased in the experimental and adjacent areas compared to the control area.

Changes in the Prevalence of Known Victims

Respondents were asked whether they, personally, knew anyone else from their estate who had been a victim of specified crimes in the last year. Table 4, modelled on Table 2, shows changes in the prevalence of known victims in the experimental, adjacent and control areas. For all crime categories except vandalism to the home (outside theft and bicycle theft were not asked), prevalence decreased significantly in the experimental area after the street lighting was improved. For example, the prevalence of known victims of any crime decreased from 86.8% to 78.4%. The greatest percentage decreases were in personal crime (33%) and vehicle crime (27%).

In the adjacent area, the prevalence of known victims also decreased for vehicle crime (by 20%, significantly) and personal crime (by 26%). The prevalence of known victims generally increased in the control area. The increases were greatest, and almost significant, for vandalism (by 42%, p=.060) and vehicle crime (by 51%, p=.065).
Changes in known victims in the experimental area were significantly different (according to the interaction term in logistic regressions) from changes in known victims in the control area for burglary, vandalism, vehicle crime and property crime. Also, differences were nearly significant for all crime (p=.079). In all cases, the prevalence of known victims decreased in the experimental area and increased in the control area. For vehicle crime, changes in known victims in the adjacent area were significantly different from changes in known victims in the control area. Also, differences were not far off significance for property crime (p=.094). For burglary, changes in the experimental area were not far off statistically different from changes in the adjacent area (p=.098). Generally, the prevalence of known victims decreased in the experimental area, decreased less in the adjacent area, and increased in the control area.

Table 4: Changes in the Prevalence of Known Victims on Estate

	Experimental			Adjacent			Control		
	Before (317)	After (278)	% Change	Before (135)	After (121)	% Change	Before (88)	After (81)	% Change
Burglary	77.9	66.2	-15*	76.3	76.0	0	62.5	69.1	+11
Vandalism	49.5	42.8	-14	50.4	50.4	0	37.5	53.1	+42
Vehicle crime	57.5	42.1	-27*	65.9	52.9	-20*	29.5	44.4	+51
Property crime	86.4	76.3	-12*	88.1	81.8	-7	72.7	79.0	+9
Personal crime	27.4	18.3	-33*	28.9	21.5	-26	34.1	27.2	-20
All crime	86.8	78.4	-10*	88.1	82.6	-6	76.1	79.0	+4

* Change significant on chi-squared test (p<.05, two-tailed)
Change in experimental area significantly different from change in control area:
    Burglary, LRCS=5.60, p=.018
    Vandalism, LRCS=6.61, p=.010
    Vehicle crime, LRCS=12.50, p=.0004
    Property crime, LRCS=6.02, p=.014
Change in adjacent area significantly different from change in control area:
    Vehicle crime, LRCS=8.39, p=.004
LRCS = Likelihood Ratio Chi-Squared = Interaction term in logistic regression

Changes in the Prevalence of Witnessed Crimes

Respondents were also asked whether they, personally, had seen or heard specified incidents happening on their estate in the last year. Interviewers were asked to check that these incidents were different from those reported elsewhere on the questionnaire. Incidents were classified as vandalism or vehicle crime (which together comprised property crime; burglary was not asked about here), personal crime, and a further category of "incivilities" (drunk, rowdy or abusive people, or someone vomiting or urinating).

Table 5 shows changes in the prevalence of crime witnesses in the experimental, adjacent and control areas. The prevalence of crime witnesses decreased significantly in the experimental area after the street lighting was improved, for all crime categories. For example, 77.3% of respondents witnessed a crime in the before period, compared with 59.7% in the after period, a decrease of 23%. The greatest percentage decreases were in personal crime (51%), incivilities (34%) and vehicle crime (31%).

The prevalence of crime witnesses also decreased in the adjacent area. These decreases were significant for vehicle crime (29%) and property crime (23%) and not far off significance (p=.090) for vandalism (24%). The prevalence of crime witnesses increased in the control area for vandalism (22%) and incivilities (25%), but decreased for personal crime (31%). For all crime, the prevalence of crime witnesses' increased in the control area from 63.6% to 70.4%.

Changes in crime witnesses in the experimental area were significantly different from changes in the control area, for vandalism, property crime, incivilities and all crime. Also, the comparison was not far off significance for vehicle crime (p=.091). Changes in crime witnesses in the adjacent area were significantly different from changes in the control area for vandalism, and nearly significantly different (p=.076) for property crime. Changes in crime witnesses in the experimental area were significantly different from changes in the adjacent area for personal crime, and nearly significantly different for incivilities (p=.084) and all crime (p=.064). Generally, the prevalence of crime witnesses decreased in the experimental area, decreased less in the adjacent area, and increased in the control area.

Table 5: Changes in the Prevalence of Crime Witnesses

	Experimental			Adjacent			Control		
	Before (317)	After (278)	% Change	Before (135)	After (121)	% Change	Before (88)	After (81)	% Change
Vandalism	50.2	37.8	-25*	45.9	34.7	-24	46.6	56.8	+22
Vehicle crime	61.8	42.8	-31*	58.5	41.3	-29*	48.9	44.4	-9
Property crime	68.1	52.5	-23*	64.4	49.6	-23*	58.0	60.5	+4
Personal crime	27.8	13.7	-51*	24.4	23.1	-5	25.0	17.3	-31
Incivilities	49.5	32.7	-34*	43.0	38.8	-10	30.7	38.3	+25
All crime	77.3	59.7	-23*	68.9	63.6	-8	63.6	70.4	+11

* Change significant on chi-squared test (p <.05, two-tailed)
Change in experimental area significantly different from change in control area:
  Vandalism, LRCS=6.81, p=.009
  Property crime, LRCS=4.60, p=.032
  Incivilities, LRCS=8.03, p=.005
  All crime, LRCS=9.23, p=.002
Change in adjacent area significantly different from change in control area:
  Vandalism, LRCS=4.79, p=.029
Change in experimental area significantly different from change in adjacent area:
  Personal crime, LRCS=4.99, p=.025
LRCS = Likelihood Ratio Chi-Squared = Interaction term in logistic regression

Comparison of the Estates after the Intervention

Table 6, modelled on Table 1, shows differences between the estates after the improved street lighting on the experimental estate. Not surprisingly (in light of the high response rates), the demographic characteristics of the respondents in the after survey were similar to those in the before survey, and there were no significant differences among the estates on gender, age, length of tenure or employment.

As in the before survey, about three-quarters of respondents in each area said that their estate was friendly. However, there was a significant increase in the experimental area in the percentage who said that their estate was well kept (from 39.1% to 57.2%; p<.0001). This large increase in the experimental area was almost significantly greater (p=.061) than the small increase (from 50.4% to 54.5%) in the adjacent area, and was significantly different (p=.002) from the decrease (from 46.6% to 37.0%) in the control area.

As in the before survey, most respondents in all areas said that it was unsafe to walk in the dark in their area, and that there were risks for women and elderly people out alone after dark. There were no significant differences between the areas in these statements. However, there was a significant change over time: respondents in the experimental area were less likely to say that it was unsafe to walk in the dark in the after survey (66.2% before, 56.5% after; p=.018).

Respondents in all areas were equally likely to say that groups of youths hung around their area. However, there was a significant decrease in the percentage of respondents saying this in all areas in the after survey compared with the before survey. Similarly, although there was no significant difference among the areas in the after survey in saying that the environment and quality of life had become worse in the last year, significantly fewer respondents said this in all areas in the after survey compared with the before survey. Unlike the adjacent and control areas, there was a significant increase in the experimental area in the percentage of respondents saying that the environment and quality of life had become better in the last year (from 3.5% to 22.7%; p<.0001). Respondents in all areas were equally unlikely to say that they had seen a police officer on foot in their area in the last month. The probability of this decreased significantly in all areas between the before and after surveys.

Table 6: Comparisons of Experimental, Adjacent and Control Areas After Improved Lighting

	Experi-mental % (N = 278)	Adjacent % (N = 121)	Control % (N=81)	p value
Demographics				
Female	54.0	65.3	58.0	ns
Age 45+	59.4	62.8	66.7	ns
On estate 10+ years	60.8	62.0	64.2	ns
Employed	29.9	34.7	23.5	ns
Opinion of Estate				
Friendly area	78.8	81.0	77.8	ns
Well kept	57.2	54.5	37.0	.006
Unsafe to walk in dark	56.5	61.2	59.3	ns
Risks for women alone after dark	86.4	83.6	81.3	ns
Risks for elderly alone after dark	92.1	89.0	87.0	ns
Youths hang around	63.3	61.2	51.9	ns
Quality of life worse last year	22.7	24.8	13.6	ns
Quality of life better last year	22.7	9.9	21.0	.011
Saw police in last month	9.7	12.4	11.1	ns
Estate Lighting				
Badly lit	4.0	61.2	65.4	.0001
Too dull	5.8	62.8	54.3	.0001
Creates shadows	3.6	55.4	45.7	.0001
Experimental estate brighter	98.9	100.0	100.0	ns
Worry about Crime				
Burglary	73.4	74.4	71.6	ns
Street robbery	33.5	33.9	28.4	ns
Street assault	35.3	37.2	32.1	ns
Vandalism to home	67.3	66.1	66.7	ns
Car stolen/damaged	47.5	53.7	45.7	ns
Avoid going out after dark	33.1	35.9	37.0	ns
Feel unsafe in own home	49.3	43.0	34.6	ns
High fear of crime	51.4	47.1	39.5	ns
Prevalence of Crime				
Burglary	21.2	18.2	16.0	ns
Outside theft/vandalism	12.2	22.3	16.0	.037
Vehicle crime	16.2	11.6	8.6	ns
Property crime	39.2	40.5	35.8	ns
Personal crime	6.1	10.7	4.9	ns
All crime	42.8	43.8	38.3	ns
Increased last year	33.5	49.6	25.9	.0009
% Outside in dark	71.4	71.9	63.2	ns
% Reported to police	68.1	51.7	68.4	.024

p values based on chi-squared from 3 x 2 tables

There was no doubt that the improvement in street lighting was noticed by respondents in the experimental area. In the after survey, 96% of experimental respondents said that their area was well lit, and only 4% said that it was badly lit; in the before survey, 73.5% said that the experimental area was badly lit, compared with 26.5% who said that it was well lit (see Table 1). Of course, the percentage of experimental respondents who said that their area was badly lit decreased significantly (p<.0001). There was no significant change in the percentage of respondents in the adjacent area who said that their area was badly lit (from 57.0% before to 61.2% after), or in the corresponding percentage in the control area (from 62.5% before to 65.4% after). Similarly, there were dramatic decreases in the experimental area in the percentages who said that the street lighting was too dull or that it created shadows.

In the after survey, respondents in the adjacent and control areas were asked if they had walked through the experimental area after dark. Of those in the adjacent area, 25% said that they had walked through the experimental area very often or regularly, and a further 21% said that they had walked through the experimental area occasionally (not shown in Table 6). Of those in the control area, 12% had walked through the experimental area very often or regularly, and a further 6% had walked through the experimental area occasionally. Virtually all respondents in all areas noticed that the lighting on the experimental estate had become brighter (Table 6).

On most questions on worries about crime, there were no significant differences among respondents in the three areas in the after survey and no significant changes over time. However, there was a significant decrease in the percentage who said that they worried about their car being stolen or damaged in the adjacent area (from 68.4% to 53.7%; p=.029) and the difference was not far off significance in the control area (from 59.5% to 45.7%; p=.10). The decrease was less in the experimental area (from 53.3% to 47.5%). Similarly, there were marked (and in some cases near-significant) decreases in the adjacent and control areas in the percentages feeling unsafe in their own homes and the percentages with a high fear of crime. It seemed that fear of crime did not change in the experimental area but decreased in some cases in the adjacent and control areas.

In most cases, the prevalence of victimization did not differ significantly among the three areas in the after survey. However, outside theft/vandalism was lowest in the experimental area and highest in the adjacent area. There were significant (p<.0001) decreases in all three areas in the percentages of those who thought that crime had increased in the last year. The decreases in this percentage were not significantly greater in any area compared with any other area. The percentage of crimes committed outside in the dark was very similar in the experimental and adjacent areas and in the before and after surveys. It increased significantly in the control area (from 48.9% to 63.2%; p=.005). The percentage of crimes reported to the police increased significantly in the experimental area (from 56.7% to 68.1%; p=.015) and increased non-significantly in the control area (from 59.6% to 68.4%).

Changes in Police-Recorded Crimes

The Staffordshire Police agreed to provide recorded crime figures for the police area that included the experimental, adjacent and control areas. Unfortunately, police force areas in Staffordshire were restructured in March 1992, making data before and after this date non-comparable. In comparing police-recorded crime before and after the improved street lighting, the most valid comparison is between April -December 1992 and April - December 1993 in police area JC22 (a wide geographical area including the project areas).

Table 7: Crimes Recorded in Police Area JC22

	Included Crimes	Excluded Crimes	Total Crimes
April - June 1992	177	42	219
July - September 1992	198	43	241
October - December 1992	210	59	269
Total 1992	585	144	729
April - June 1993	209	53	262
July - September 1993	159	34	193
October - December 1993	203	48	251
Total 1993	571	135	706
Change 1992 - 1993	-2%	-6%	-3%

Note: Excluded crimes: Non-residential burglary, going equipped to steal, shoplifting, fraud, receiving stolen property, drugs.

Table 7 shows that the total number of police-recorded crimes decreased by 3% between 1992 and 1993 in this police area. However, not all of these crimes would have been reported in the before and after victimization surveys, which focussed on offences against households and persons. In particular, non-residential burglaries, being equipped to steal, shoplifting, fraud, receiving and drug offences would not have been reported. When these crimes were excluded, comparable police-recorded crimes decreased by 2% between 1992 and 1993 in this police area. This was a negligible decrease.

Pedestrian Street Use

The number of pedestrians using the streets after dark was counted in the experimental, adjacent and control areas. Pedestrians were counted on a Thursday and Friday evening between 7:00 p.m. and 9:30 p.m. during the first week of December in 1992 and in 1993.

In both years the weather conditions were similar (cold but dry). Table 8 shows that the number of male pedestrians increased by 72% in the experimental area and by 27% in the adjacent and control areas, a significant difference (chi-squared = 7.85, p= .005). The number of female pedestrians increased by 70% in the experimental area and by 41% in the adjacent and control areas, a non-significant difference.

Table 8: Nighttime Pedestrian Counts

	Before	After	% Change
Experimental Area			
Men	199	343	+72
Women	160	272	+70
All	359	615	+71
Adjacent Area			
Men	279	360	+29
Women	165	234	+42
All	444	594	+34
Control Area			
Men	255	320	+25
Women	196	276	+41
All	451	596	+32

QUALITATIVE RESULTS

Statements from Respondents

Respondents were asked a general question about whether their quality of life had improved, gotten worse or remained the same over the previous 12 months. They were not asked specifically about the effects of the improved lighting. Nevertheless, statements from respondents in the experimental area suggested that they thought the improved street lighting had decreased crime rates and improved their quality of life, especially because the improved illumination led to increased surveillance. Respondents' observations included:

"You can see everything that moves outside now."

"You can see more. It's like Blackpool Illuminations — they're the best I've seen — these lights."

"It's much brighter now than before and you can even see people coming to your door."

"You can see people more clearly. The lighting is just great. It was terrible before."

"If you hear a noise outside and you look outside, you can recognise who they are."

"Stronger light means less people hang around to be seen."

"It's safer because you can now recognise who is walking towards you."

"You can see where you are walking. You can see anybody. All the little walkways are lit up."

"You can see more of the area in the dark alleyways. Nobody can hide. You can see where you are walking now. You can see if anybody is loitering about."

"You can see people from a distance now and recognise them as well."

"Everywhere is illuminated. It's good. It's so bright and there's no shadows."

And finally, as one 69-year-old man commented: "It's cut out shadows, it deters people from lurking. There is less chance of being pounced on from dark corners and hedges. I've been out in the early hours to get into my car at my garage. Because of the lighting I felt quite safe. We feel happier to go out now."

Local Hearsay and Community Confidence as a Means of Diffusing Benefits

The qualitative data also indicated that the relighting scheme was a topic of general discussion throughout the project area, and this may be an important mechanism of diffusion. The area most affected was the adjacent area, where respondents showed a general optimism about the future of their neighbourhood. The proposition that the benefits of relighting increased optimism about future investment, and reduced crime and fear in the adjacent area untouched by lighting improvements, can be illustrated by remarks made by residents. A councillor in the adjacent area commented: "We are targeting this area for improvements, and as the local councillor I feel optimistic and confident that the area is about to improve even further."

Another respondent in the adjacent area observed: "We need better lighting. People in [the experimental] area have now a greater respect for the area they live in... getting it more done up."

It also appeared that residents in the adjacent area, especially those closest to the new lighting scheme, felt resentful that their roads had not been lit, and this galvanised them into lobbying for improvements. As one interviewer put it, "This respondent [in the adjacent area] complained that the street lights are not continued up...Road. Have got up a petition with other residents...for the new lighting to come further up."

There were also indications that the effects of relighting one part of the neighbourhood had an effect on perceptions of crime and safety in the adjacent and control areas. The following comments are indicative of this process.

"Since the new lighting was put in it's been very quiet around here [adjacent area]... there used to be loads of trouble but now it's quietened down."

"I think the street lighting improvements should be carried on throughout this area. This would greatly improve things, along with more police patrols." [adjacent area]

"People would feel safer with lights, like in the [experimental] area. A lot more people feel safer. My mum does who lives there, and there's been less break-ins." [control area]

"The general quality of life around here has improved. Why? The street lighting. Things have quietened down recently with crime." [control area]

"I feel safer because of the new street lights further up the road." [adjacent area]

Though not conclusive, these personal accounts support the idea that relighting the experimental area was taken as a sign that the adjacent area was about to improve. If so, the relighting served to promote community confidence in the adjacent area because residents detected that the local authority was willing to invest in the physical environment. It certainly led to an increase in nighttime street use. These attitudinal and behavioural changes in themselves may have had an impact on offender and resident perceptions of the neighbourhood, in ways that reduced actual and perceived opportunities for crime and increased actual and perceived risk.

Street Lighting and Crime from a Police Perspective

In addition to household surveys and pedestrian traffic counts, an in-depth survey of local police patrol officers was undertaken. Seven officers who regularly patrolled the area were interviewed, and they generally thought that relighting had reduced fear of crime in the experimental area. One officer said: "People have commented on the lighting and they feel safer, especially the elderly. They are glad it's been put in." From talking to people in the area about the lighting, these officers said that the locals were "over the moon about it." The officers thought that the lighting had reduced crime because the visibility was so much better on the streets. As one officer put it: "Street lighting has reduced crime, fear of crime, improved visibility in the back alleys and improved the confidence of those using the area. The police can patrol slowly in cars and get a good view of who is around, and recognise them. The locals also say the lighting [has] improved their sense of security."

The three beat officers believed that the street lighting had "warned off the villains" because the police were getting increased calls from the public about prowlers, to which they were responding. This finding is consistent with the increased reporting of crime noted in the household survey. The officers welcomed this increase and said that a partnership between them and the community was developing. One officer said that he was much more willing to get out of his car and patrol on foot. Another officer commented: "The burglars don't need to carry torches now. If they do, they stick out like a sore thumb and if they don't their activities are highly visible."

The sergeant thought that the street lighting made the work of the police easier after dark. When called to suspicious events, officers now drove to a nearby point and got out of the cars and approached on foot. This was quieter and gave them the element of surprise.

All seven officers were convinced of the deterrent effects of good lighting. One commented: "Improved lighting is viewed positively from a police perspective. The [experimental] area is very well lit now but we need to get the same standard of street lighting throughout the [project] area. Criminals are deterred by good street lights."

There was also support for the proposition that street lighting improved community confidence through aesthetically enhancing the environment: "The lighting is very pleasing to look at and the young people are less willing to climb up the columns. It has greatly increased the sense of pride in the area and has encouraged public respect for the place. The improved lighting has increased people's confidence in using the area due to the decrease in crime."

This was a small sample, yet all seven police officers surveyed were very supportive of the view that street lighting deterred crime, improved the quality of life, increased police efficiency when patrolling the area after dark, and increased the willingness of the public to report offences to the police.

ESTIMATING BENEFITS AND COSTS OF IMPROVED STREET LIGHTING

The capital cost of the improved street lighting scheme on the experimental estate was £77,071. The annual maintenance costs of the lighting increased from £286 to £443, and the annual cost of electrical energy increased from £935 to £1,880. Hence, the annual costs were £1,102 greater after the improvement. As the improved street lighting was expected to last at least 20 years, it would be reasonable to pay off the capital cost over a 20-year period (Safe Neighbourhoods

Unit, 1993). Assuming an annual interest rate of 8%, annual payments at the end of each year of £7,850 would clear the debt in 20 years. Therefore, it would be reasonable to translate the cost of the improved street lighting into an annual cost of £8,952.

In attempting to assess whether these increased annual costs might be outweighed by the benefits of reduced crimes, what is needed is an estimate of the cost of each type of crime. This is available, for the U.S., in 1993 dollars. Miller et al. (1996) took account of property loss and damage, medical and mental health costs, police and fire services (but not other criminal justice) costs, social and victim services costs, and lost productivity in estimating the tangible costs of different types of crimes. They also attempted to calculate intangible costs such as pain, suffering and a reduced quality of life, but these costs are more controversial. For example, it was estimated that each U.S. robbery, on average, involved tangible costs of $2,300 and intangible quality-of-life costs of $5,700, making the total cost $8,000. Because of the controversial nature of intangible quality-of-life costs, we will not consider them.

Unfortunately, no estimates of the costs of all types of crimes are available for the U.K. Indeed, there have only been seven previous attempts to assess costs and benefits of U.K. situational crime prevention programmes where the primary victim was a person or a household (see Welsh and Farrington, 1999, for a review). Since we wanted 1993 estimates of the costs of different types of crimes, we began with the average value of stolen property published in the 1993 Criminal Statistics (U.K. Home Office, 1994). For example, its Table 2.18 shows a total value of stolen property in residential burglaries of £537 million, with £50.8 million recovered, and a total number of residential burglaries (including attempts) of 727,276. Dividing £486.2 million of stolen (and not recovered) property by the total number of offences reveals an average property loss in each burglary of £668.

Of course, burglaries recorded by the police may involve a greater property loss than unrecorded burglaries. Based on the British Crime Survey, Mirrlees-Black et al. (1996, Table A5.5) estimated the average net loss in each 1995 burglary (including attempts) as £370. However, this figure was net of insurance repayments, which might be excluded in assessing the cost of a burglary to the victim but should surely be included in assessing the cost of a burglary to society (which is our interest). The gross loss per burglary in 1995 was £676 (Mayhew, 1998), a number very similar to the Criminal Statistics figure for 1993.

Of course, property loss is only one of many types of costs of crime. For example, Ekblom et al. (1996) estimated that each completed residential burglary cost victims about £900 and caused criminal justice (e.g., police, courts and prisons) costs of about £300, making the total (property loss plus criminal justice) cost of a completed burglary £1,200. We estimated the tangible costs of each crime using the figures of Miller et al. (1996, Table 2). Unfortunately, these exclude criminal justice costs other than the police. Nevertheless, they show that the average U.S. burglary (including attempts) in 1993 involved property loss or damage of $970 and total tangible losses of $1,100 (13.4% greater). In order to estimate the average tangible loss of a 1993 U.K. burglary, we scaled up the Criminal Statistics property loss figure of £668 by 13.4% (to £758).

All other estimates of the cost of different property crimes were obtained in the same way, by obtaining a property loss figure from the 1993 Criminal Statistics and scaling it up to a tangible loss figure using the estimates of Miller et al. (1996). There were two main exceptions. First, to estimate the cost of outside theft/vandalism, we combined the average loss in household vandalism of £116 according to the 1993 British Crime Survey (Budd, 1998) with the average loss in theft from vehicles of £239 according to the 1993 Criminal Statistics. Second, because we had no available costs for personal crimes, we had to use the U.S. costs of Miller et al. (1996). For example, they estimated the total tangible loss of an assault as $1,550 (principally caused by lost productivity of $950 and medical costs of $425), and we translated this into £939 at the current rate of exchange of 1.65 dollars to the pound.

Table 9 shows the results of the calculations. Beginning with the Stoke experimental area, the total number of before burglaries (including attempts) of 122 reported by 317 respondents was scaled up to an estimate of 137.4 for the 357 occupied houses. This assumes that the non-respondents had the same burglary rate as the respondents. Similarly, the total number of after burglaries of 91 reported by 278 respondents was scaled up to an estimate of 116.8 for the 357 occupied houses. This led to the estimate that 20.6 burglaries had been prevented by the improved street lighting. At £668 per burglary, this yielded a total savings of £13,761 in property loss alone, or a total savings of £15,615 when all tangible losses were included.

The total savings in the Stoke experimental area in one year from 266 prevented crimes came to £65,892 in property loss alone and to £103,495 when all tangible losses were included. Thus, the tangible savings from crimes prevented paid for the full capital cost of the improved street lighting (£77,071) and for the increased annual costs (£1,102) within one year. Including the full capital cost, the benefit-to-cost ratio was 1.3 to 1 after one year. More reasonably paying off the capital cost over 20 years, the benefit-to-cost ratio was 12 to 1 after one year (£103,495 divided by £8,952).

This calculation does not take account of crimes reduced in the adjacent area, which are calculated in Table 9 on the same basis as those in the experimental area. More crimes were prevented in the adjacent area because it was larger than the experimental area; thus, 42 before burglaries reported by 135 respondents in the adjacent area was scaled up to an estimate of 163.3 for the 525 occupied houses. The total savings in the adjacent area from 428.8 prevented crimes came to £77,003 in property loss alone and to £125,272 when all tangible losses were included.

The total tangible savings in the experimental and adjacent areas came to £228,747. Assuming that both were attributable entirely to the improved lighting, these savings more than paid for the full capital costs of the improved lighting in one year. Including the full capital cost, the benefit-to-cost ratio after one year was 2.9 to 1. More reasonably paying off the capital cost over 20 years, the benefit-to-cost ratio was 26 to 1 after one year. The control area was not included in these analyses because the incidence of crime did not change in it.

Clearly, better estimates of the costs of different types of crime are needed. Our estimates, based on national police-recorded crimes, may not apply very accurately to the particular housing estates studied. Nevertheless, even if our estimates were double or triple the true costs (which seems unlikely, especially since they do not include quality of life costs), it would still be clear that the crime-reduction benefits of the improved street lighting greatly outweighed the costs.

This is essentially because improving street lighting is relatively cheap compared with other environmental improvements. For example, Osborn (1994) reported that £856,000 was spent on putting fences all over the Kirkholt estate of 2,288 dwellings in Rochdale in 1986-90. Davidson and Farr (1994) reported that £1,400,000 was spent on improving security (to lifts, foyers, entrance doors and landings) in the Mitchellhill estate of 570 dwellings in Glasgow in 1989. Compared with many estate improvement projects funded by the Department of the Environment (Safe Neighbourhoods Unit, 1993, 1994) street lighting is inexpensive. Under any reasonable assumptions about the costs of crime, the benefits exceeded the costs in the Stoke project.

Table 9: Estimated Cost Savings from Reductions in Crime

	Estimated No. of Crimes			Property Savings		Tangible Savings	
	Before	After	Reduced	Per Crime £	Total £	Per Crime £	Total £
Experimental							
Burglary/attempts	137.4	116.8	20.6	668	13,761	758	15,615
Outside theft/vandalism	135.1	86.0	49.1	178	8,740	244	11,980
Cycle theft	21.4	10.3	11.1	213	2,364	292	3,241
Theft of vehicle	24.8	3.9	20.9	1,328	27,755	1,408	29,427
Theft from vehicle	145.3	87.4	57.9	239	13,838	328	18,991
Robbery/snatch theft	1.1	3.9	-2.8	202	-566	619	-1,733
Assault	16.9	1.3	15.6	0	0	939	14,648
Threats/pestered	138.5	44.9	93.6	0	0	121	11,326
Total	**620.5**	**354.5**	**266.0**	**248**	**65,892**	**389**	**103,495**
Adjacent							
Burglary/attempts	163.3	130.2	33.1	668	22,111	758	25,090
Outside theft/vandalism	318.9	173.5	145.4	178	25,881	244	35,478
Cycle theft	23.3	30.4	-7.1	213	-1,512	292	-2,073
Theft of vehicle	11.7	4.3	7.4	1,328	9,827	1,408	10,419
Theft from vehicle	171.1	91.1	80.0	239	19,120	328	26,240
Robbery/snatch theft	7.8	0	7.8	202	1,576	619	4,828
Assault	15.6	8.7	6.9	0	0	939	6,479
Threats/pestered	233.4	78.1	155.3	0	0	121	18,791
Total	**945.1**	**516.3**	**428.8**	**180**	**77,003**	**292**	**125,252**

CONCLUSIONS

Four measures of crime were derived from the before and after surveys: the prevalence and incidence of victimization, the prevalence of known victims, and the prevalence of witnesses of crime. Taking the results from all four measures together, there was a marked and significant decrease in crime in the experimental area, a somewhat lesser decrease in crime in the adjacent area, and no decrease or a slight increase in crime in the control area. The crime decreases in the experimental area were often significantly greater than in the control area but rarely significantly different from the decreases in the adjacent area. The benefits of improved street lighting, in terms of the savings to the public from crimes prevented, greatly outweighed the costs.

The percentage of crimes committed outside after dark was similar (about 70%) in the experimental and adjacent areas, and in the before and after surveys. It increased significantly in the control area. Hence, the number of crimes committed outside after dark decreased considerably in the experimental and adjacent areas compared with the control area, while the number of crimes committed at other times decreased somewhat in the experimental and adjacent areas compared with the control area. According to police statistics, there was no change in recorded household crime in the large police area that included the project areas. The probability of victims reporting crimes to the police increased significantly in the experimental area and non-significantly in the control area.

Respondents in all areas noticed the improvement in lighting in the experimental area. This was partly because respondents in the adjacent and control areas had heard about the improvement in lighting, and partly because they had walked through the experimental area themselves. People in the experimental area became more likely to say that their estate was well kept, and that their environment and quality of life had improved in the last year. Pedestrian counts showed that there were increased numbers of people on the streets after dark in the experimental area compared with the adjacent and control areas (which showed lower increases). Respondents in the experimental area became less likely to say that it was unsafe to walk after dark in their area. However, experimental respondents also said that they had the greatest fear of crime, and they were the most likely to say that they felt unsafe in their own homes in the after survey.

Qualitative data suggested that residents of the experimental area and police officers thought that the improved lighting had reduced crime and the fear of crime after dark, and that potential offenders were deterred by the increased visibility and surveillance. They also thought that it had increased community pride and the perceived quality of life, and had increased police effectiveness and the willingness of the public to report crimes to the police.

What is the most plausible explanation of these results? The null hypothesis that improved street lighting had no effect on crime seems implausible because of the marked decreases in crime in the experimental area after the improved lighting. Any argument in favour of the null hypothesis would have to suggest that some other factor, occurring at about the same time as the improved lighting, caused the decrease in crime in the experimental area. However, we are confident that no other factor could have influenced the experimental area but not the control area or the larger police area containing the project areas. A decrease in crime might conceivably have been caused by decreased unemployment, decreased poverty, increased prosperity, decreased police cautioning, tougher sentences, decreased drug and alcohol use, etc., but to the extent that any of these factors was important it would have affected not only the experimental area but also the control and wider police areas.

The most plausible explanation is that improved street lighting caused a decrease in crime in the experimental area. In absolute terms, the decrease in crime outside after dark was the same as the decrease in other types of crimes. However, relative to changes in crime rates in the control area, the decrease in crime outside after dark was greater than the decrease in other types of crimes.

It is plausible, therefore, to suggest that the effects of improved street lighting on crime operated via two different causal pathways. In the first pathway, improved street lighting caused increased visibility, street use and surveillance after dark, which, in turn, led to decreased perceived opportunities and rewards of crime and increased perceived risks by potential offenders, which in turn led to decreased crime. This pathway would especially explain a decrease in crime outside after dark. In the second pathway, improved street lighting led to increased community pride, community cohesion and informal social control, which deterred potential offenders. This pathway would explain decreases in crime at all times of the day. The operation of both pathways simultaneously would lead to large decreases in crime after dark and to smaller decreases in crime in the light. This prediction, and the hypothesized pathways, are concordant with the quantitative and qualitative results obtained in the Stoke-on-Trent project. However, surveys of potential offenders are needed to verify the proposed causal pathways.

The research hypothesis that improved street lighting leads to an increased number of people outside on the streets after dark was also supported, as was the hypothesis that improved street lighting leads to a more favourable assessment of the quality of the area. However, the hypothesis that improved street lighting leads to a decreased fear of crime was supported only by the qualitative data. Apart from respondents in the experimental area saying that it became more safe to walk in the dark, no other quantitative results supported this hypothesis.

Interestingly, decreases in crime in the adjacent area were almost as great as in the experimental area. This suggests that there was no displacement of crime, but rather a diffusion of the benefits of improved street lighting. Conceivably, the improved lighting in the experimental area deterred potential offenders not only in this area but in the adjacent area as well, since the areas were not clearly delimited. The qualitative data showing how information about the areas was communicated, and how relighting led to increased community pride in the adjacent area, supported this hypothesis.

Summarizing, our main conclusion is that improved street lighting led to substantial and cost-effective decreases in crime in the experimental area, and that there was a diffusion of these benefits to the adjacent area.

Acknowledgements: We are particularly grateful to Patrick Baldrey, Managing Director of Urbis Lighting, and the Midlands Electricity Board, for generously funding the research. We are also grateful to Wyn Cridland for expert fieldwork supervision, to Alan and Jacqueline Pate for computerization of the data, to the Staffordshire Police for cooperation and for providing recorded crime figures, and to Stoke-on-Trent City Council street lighting engineers. We are also grateful to Pat Mayhew and Tracey Budd for providing unpublished data from the British Crime Survey, and to Nick Tilley for helpful comments on an earlier version of this chapter.

Address correspondence to: Kate Painter, Institute of Criminology, University of Cambridge, 7 West Road, Cambridge CB3 9DT, United Kingdom.

REFERENCES

Allatt, P. (1984). "Residential Security: Containment and Displacement of Burglary." *Howard Journal of Criminal Justice* 23:99-116.

Angel, S. (1968). *Discouraging Crime Through City Planning* (Working Paper, #5.) Berkeley, CA: University of California Press.

Atkins, S., S. Husain and A. Storey (1991). *The Influence of Street Lighting on Crime.* (Crime Prevention Paper, #28). London, UK: Home Office.

Bannister, J. (1991). *The Impact of Environmental Design upon the Incidence and Type of Crime.* Edinburgh, SCOT: Scottish Office Central Research Unit.

Barr, R. and K. Pease (1990). "Crime Placement, Displacement and Deflection." In: M. Tonry and N. Morris (eds.), *Crime and Justice,* vol. #12. Chicago, IL: University of Chicago Press.

—— (1992). "A Place for Every Crime and Every Crime in its Place." In: D.J. Evans, N.R. Fyfe and D.T. Herbert (eds.), *Crime, Policing and Place: Essays in Environmental Criminology.* London, UK: Routledge.

Bennett, T. and R. Wright (1984). *Burglars on Burglary.* Hants, UK: Gower.

Bourne, M.G. and R.C. Cooke (1993). "Victoria's Speed Camera Program." In: R.V. Clarke (ed.), *Crime Prevention Studies,* vol. 1. Monsey, NY: Criminal Justice Press.

Budd, T. (1998). Personal communication to the author from Home Office.

Clarke, R.V. (ed.) (1992). *Situational Crime Prevention: Successful Case Studies.* Albany, NY: Harrow and Heston.

—— (1995). "Situational Crime Prevention." In: M. Tonry and D.P. Farrington (eds.), *Building a Safer Society: Strategic Approaches to Crime Prevention.* (Crime and Justice, vol. 19.) Chicago, IL: University of Chicago Press.

—— R.P. Cody and M. Natarajan (1994). "Subway Slugs: Tracking Displacement on the London Underground." *British Journal of Criminology* 34:122-138.

—— and P.M. Harris (1992a). "Auto Theft and its Prevention." In: M. Tonry (ed.), *Crime and Justice*, vol. 16. Chicago, IL: University of Chicago Press.

—— (1992b)."A Rational Choice Perspective on the Targets of Automobile Theft." *Criminal Behaviour and Mental Health* 2:25-42.

—— and P. Mayhew (1988). "The British Gas Suicide Story and its Criminological Implications." In: M. Tonry and N. Morris (eds.), *Crime and Justice*, vol. 10. Chicago, IL: University of Chicago Press.

—— and D. Weisburd (1994). "Diffusion of Crime Control Benefits: Observations on the Reverse of Displacement." In: R.V. Clarke (ed.), *Crime Prevention Studies*, vol. 2. Monsey, NY: Criminal Justice Press.

Cohen, L.E. and M. Felson (1979). "Social Change and Crime Rate Trends: A Routine Activity Approach." *American Sociological Review* 44:588-608.

Davidson, J. and J. Farr (1994). "Mitchellhill Estate — Estate Based Management (Concierge) Initiative." In: Safe Neighbourhoods Unit (ed.), *Housing Safe Communities*. London, UK: Safe Neighbourhoods Unit.

Ekblom, P. (1988). "Preventing Post Office Robberies in London: Effects and Side Effects." *Journal of Security Administration* 11:36-43.

—— H. Law and M. Sutton (1996). *Safer Cities and Domestic Burglary*. (Home Office Research Study, #164.) London, UK: Home Office.

—— and K. Pease (1995). "Evaluating Crime Prevention." In: M. Tonry and D.P. Farrington (eds.), *Building a Safer Society: Strategic Approaches to Crime Prevention*. (Crime and Justice, vol. 19.) Chicago, IL: University of Chicago Press.

Farrington, D.P. (1997). "Evaluating a Crime Prevention Program." *Evaluation* 31:157-173.

Fowler, F.J. and T.W. Mangione (1986). "A Three Pronged Effort to Reduce Crime and Fear of Crime: The Hartford Experiment." In: D. Rosenbaum (ed.), *Community Crime Prevention: Does it Work?* Beverly Hills, CA: Sage.

Gabor, T. (1983). "The Crime Displacement Hypothesis: An Empirical Examination." In: T. Fleming and L.A. Visano (eds.), *Deviant Designations: Crime, Law and Deviance in Canada*. Toronto, CAN: Butterworths.

—— (1990). "Crime Displacement and Situational Prevention: Toward the Development of Some Principles." *Canadian Journal of Criminology* 32:41-74.

Hesseling, R. (1994). "Displacement: A Review of the Empirical Literature." In: R.V. Clarke (ed.), *Crime Prevention Studies*, vol. 3. Monsey, NY: Criminal Justice Press.

Homel, R. (1993). "Drivers Who Drink and Rational Choice: Random Breath Testing and the Process of Deterrence." In: R.V. Clarke and M. Felson (eds.), *Routine Activity and Rational Choice.* (Advances in Criminological Theory, vol. 5.) New Brunswick, NJ: Transaction Publishers.

Jacobs, J. (1961). *The Death and Life of Great American Cities.* New York, NY: Random House.

Jeffery, C.R. (1971). *Crime Prevention Through Environmental Design.* Beverly Hills, CA: Sage.

Lavrakas, P.J. and J. Kushmuk (1986). "Evaluating Crime Prevention Through Environmental Design: The Portland Commercial Demonstration Project." In: D.P. Rosenbaum (ed.), *Community Crime Prevention: Does it Work?* Beverly Hills, CA: Sage.

Lowman, J. (1983). "Target Hardening, Burglary Prevention and the Problem of Displacement Phenomena." In: T. Fleming and L.A. Visano (eds.), *Deviant Designations: Crime, Law and Deviance in Canada.* Toronto, CAN: Butterworths.

Mayhew, P. (1998) Personal communication to the author from Home Office.

—— R.V. Clarke, J.N. Burrows, J.M. Hough and S.W.C. Winchester (1979). *Crime in Public View.* (Home Office Research Study, #40.) London, UK: Her Majesty's Stationery Office.

—— R.V. Clarke and D. Elliot (1989). "Motorcycle Theft, Helmet Legislation and Displacement." *Howard Journal of Criminal Justice* 28:108.

—— N.A. Maung and C. Mirrlees-Black (1993). *The 1992 British Crime Survey.* (Home Office Research Study, #132.) London, UK: Her Majesty's Stationery Office.

Miethe, T.D. (1991). "Citizen-based Crime Control Activity and Victimization Risks: An Examination of Displacement and Free Rider Effects." *Criminology* 29:419-440.

Miller, T.R., M. A. Cohen and B. Wiersema (1996). *Victim Costs and Consequences: A New Look.* Washington, DC: National Institute of Justice.

Mirrlees-Black, C., P. Mayhew and A. Percy (1996). *The 1996 British Crime Survey, England and Wales.* London, UK: Home Office.

Newman, O. (1972). *Defensible Space: Crime Prevention Through Urban Design.* New York, NY: Macmillan. Reprint. London, UK: Architectural Press.

Osborn, S. (1994). "Kirkholt Estate Burglary Prevention Scheme." In: Safe Neighbourhoods Unit (ed.), *Housing Safe Communities.* London, UK: Safe Neighbourhoods Unit.

Painter, K. (1991). *An Evaluation of Public Lighting as a Crime Prevention Strategy with Special Focus on Women and Elderly People.* Manchester, UK: University of Manchester.

—— (1994). "The Impact of Street Lighting on Crime, Fear and Pedestrian Use." *Security Journal* 5:116-124.

—— (1996). "Street Lighting, Crime and Fear of Crime: A Summary of Research." In: T. Bennett (ed.), *Preventing Crime and Disorder.* Cambridge, UK: Institute of Criminology.

—— and D.P. Farrington (1997). "The Crime Reducing Effect of Improved Street Lighting: The Dudley Project." In: R.V. Clarke (ed.), *Situational Crime Prevention: Successful Case Studies* (2nd ed.). Guilderland, NY: Harrow and Heston.

Pease, K. (1991). "The Kirkholt Project: Preventing Burglary on a British Public Housing Estate." *Security Journal* 2:73-77.

Poyner, B. (1991). "Situational Prevention in Two Car Parks." *Security Journal* 2:96-101.

—— (1992). "Video Cameras and Bus Vandalism." In: R.V. Clarke (ed.), *Situational Crime Prevention: Successful Case Studies.* Albany, NY: Harrow and Heston.

—— and B. Webb (1992). "Reducing Theft from Shopping Bags in City Centre Markets." In: R.V. Clarke (ed.), *Situational Crime Prevention: Successful Case Studies.* Albany, NY: Harrow and Heston.

Ramsey, R. and R. Newton (1991). *The Effect of Better Street Lighting on Crime and Fear: A Review.* (Crime Prevention Paper, # 29.) London, UK: Home Office.

Reppetto, T.A. (1976). "Crime Prevention and the Displacement Phenomenon." *Crime and Delinquency* 22:166-177.

Safe Neighbourhoods Unit (1993). *Crime Prevention on Council Estates.* London, UK: Her Majesty's Stationery Office.

—— (1994). *Housing Safe Communities.* London, UK: author.

Scherdin, M.J. (1986). "The Halo Effect: Psychological Deterrence of Electronic Security Systems." *Information Technology and Libraries* 5:232-235.

Sherman, L.W. (1990). "Police Crackdowns: Initial and Residual Deterrence." In: M. Tonry and N. Morris (eds.), *Crime and Justice*, vol. 12. Chicago, IL: University of Chicago Press.

Skogan, W.G. (1990). *Disorder and Decline: Crime and the Spiral of Decay in American Neighbourhoods.* New York, NY: Free Press.

Taub, R.P., D.G. Taylor and J.D. Dunham (1984). *Paths of Neighbourhood Change: Race and Crime in Urban America.* Chicago, IL: University of Chicago Press.

Taylor, R.B. and S. Gottfredson (1986). "Environmental Design, Crime and Crime Prevention: An Examination of Community Dynamics." In: A.J. Reiss and M. Tonry (eds.), *Communities and Crime.* (Crime and Justice, vol. 8.) Chicago, IL: University of Chicago Press.

Tien, J.M., V.F. O'Donnell, A. Barnett and P.B. Mirchandani (1979). *Phase I Report: Street Lighting Projects.* Washington, DC: U.S. Government Printing Office.

U.K. Home Office (1994). *Criminal Statistics, England and Wales, 1993.* London, UK: Her Majesty's Stationery Office.

Warr, M. (1990). "Dangerous Situations: Social Context and Fear of Victimization." *Social Forces* 68:891-907.

Welsh, B.C. and D.P. Farrington (1999). "Value for Money? A Review of the Costs and Benefits of Situational Crime Prevention." *British Journal of Criminology* 38:345-368.

Wilson, J.Q. and G.L. Kelling (1982). "Broken Windows." *Atlantic Monthly* (Mar):29-38.

Wright, R., M. Heilweil, P. Pelletier and K. Dickinson (1974). *The Impact of Street Lighting on Crime, Part I.* Washington, DC: National Institute of Law Enforcement and Criminal Justice.

A REVIEW OF CCTV EVALUATIONS: CRIME REDUCTION EFFECTS AND ATTITUDES TOWARDS ITS USE

by

Coretta Phillips
Home Office Policing and Reducing Crime Unit

Abstract: *This paper reviews studies that have evaluated the effectiveness of closed circuit television (CCTV) in reducing crime, disorder and fear of crime in a variety of sites. The guiding framework for the review is Tilley's (1993a) model for realist evaluation, which focuses on the mechanisms and contexts in which CCTV might operate. The paper concludes that CCTV can be effective in deterring property crime, but the findings are more mixed in relation to personal crime, public order offences, and fear of crime. Public attitudes towards the use of CCTV in public spaces are also considered, as is the issue of civil liberties and the targeting of marginalized groups.*

INTRODUCTION

In the last decade there has been a proliferation of closed circuit television (CCTV) installations, particularly in town centres, with Britain boasting the most extensive CCTV coverage in the world. This has, in part, been the result of proactive initiatives by central government whereby £38 million has been made available by the British Home Office to support over 585 local CCTV systems, with a further £170 million available for schemes over the next three years (Home Office, 1995, 1996, 1997, 1998). CCTV systems have been located in town centres, shops, shopping centres, banks, building societies, parking facilities, schools, colleges, hospitals, transport facilities, industrial estates, business centres, football grounds, police custody suites and, to a lesser extent, housing projects. The 1993 Commercial Victimization Survey revealed that 20% of retailers and 8% of manufacturers sampled in England and Wales had CCTV systems (Mirrlees-Black and Ross, 1995). In the public sector, Bulos (1994) reported that 43% of the councils surveyed had installed a CCTV system in a public place. In addition to funding by central government, the European community, local authorities, businesses, and extra charges on car park tickets have contributed to the financing of systems (Bulos and Sarno, 1996; Brown, 1995; Short and Ditton, 1996).

A common goal of most CCTV systems has been the prevention of crime and disorder through deterrence. It is also assumed that CCTV will aid detection through its surveillance capability and the opportunity it may afford to deploy security personnel or police officers appropriately. Claims are also made that CCTV provides public reassurance and therefore reduces fear of crime, which may, in turn, increase the use of public spaces (Bennett and Gelsthorpe, 1996; cf. Tilley, 1997 who suggests that CCTV may reduce crime as people are deterred from visiting CCTV-covered areas, believing them to be too dangerous). CCTV is also used as a site management tool, for example, to observe traffic patterns or for crowd control at football matches. CCTV may even indirectly increase trade and protect substantial property investments (Roberts and Goulette, 1996; Brown, 1995).

Alongside the expansion of the CCTV industry, there has been a wealth of information attesting to the effectiveness of CCTV in reducing and preventing crime and disorder, with little apparent scientific support for these claims (Groombridge and Murji, 1994a). Magazine articles abound that headline the success of CCTV, for example, "CCTV Works!" (*Security Installer*, 1998). Short and Ditton (1995) noted five types of problems with many of these claims. First, the time periods examined pre- and post-CCTV installation have been too short for adequate testing of the effects of the CCTV system, or they have not accounted for seasonal variations in crime. Second, crime is frequently considered as one category, thus obscuring increases or reductions in different types of crime. Third, in some cases there are no control areas, so there can be no assessment of crime patterns in other areas where crime may also be falling, indicating something other than a "CCTV effect." Fourth, little discussion of displacement or attendant publicity typifies these "self evaluations." Finally, the presentation of percentages only (without Ns) or inaccuracies in their calculation can also lead to erroneous claims of success. Bulos and Sarno (1996) report that very few CCTV schemes have been comprehensively evaluated by independent researchers. Indeed, it has most often been the case that those who have installed or commissioned CCTV systems are the ones who have come to these conclusions. Moreover, as Groombridge and Murji (1994b: 288) have warned "CCTV can only ever be a tool, it is not a panacea. But while there are powerful commercial and political interests behind its promotion, it seems that hype will continue to achieve prominence over the more prosaic series of questions that should be asked about CCTV before it is possible to evaluate its usefulness and whether it represents value for money." Even among staunch supporters of CCTV, it has been accepted that evaluative evidence of crime reduction effects must be provided to justify future investment (Speed et al., 1994; Farish, 1995; U.K. Home Office, 1998).

Evaluating the effectiveness of CCTV is the central theme of this chapter. The first section will introduce a framework for evaluating CCTV that recognizes the importance of studying its specific purposes and the contexts in which systems are put into place. This framework will then be used to assess evaluations of CCTV systems. Consideration will be given to both the impact of CCTV on reducing property, personal and public order crimes, and its effectiveness in reducing fear of crime. This will be followed by a discussion of the public's attitudes towards the use of CCTV in public spaces, since, despite its many advocates, the potential abuse of the surveillance capabilities of CCTV has led to concerns about civil liberties and the targeting of marginalized groups (Liberty Briefing, 1989). The social control and segregation of such groups through the use of CCTV in public spaces has also been criticized, where the pursuit of commerce overrides the free use of the space (Reeve, 1998; see also Armstrong and Giulianotti, 1998). The chapter will end with a discussion of the issues arising from this review of CCTV evaluations and further research needs.

A FRAMEWORK FOR EVALUATING CCTV

At the heart of all program evaluations, according to Tilley (1993a) and developed further by Pawson and Tilley (1994, 1997), is the relationship between the crime prevention measure (in this case, CCTV), the outcome (e.g., the reduction in crime and fear), the mechanism through which the outcome is produced, and the context in which it occurs. How CCTV can reduce crime and in what circumstances becomes the critical evaluative issue. Nine potential *mechanisms* identified by Pawson and Tilley (1994, 1997) through which CCTV can be expected to operate are summarized below. These are not mutually exclusive; more than one mechanism may be operating at one time.

- *Caught in the act* — CCTV could reduce crime by increasing the likelihood that present offenders will be caught, stopped, removed, punished and, therefore, deterred.
- *You've been framed* — CCTV could reduce crime by deterring potential offenders who will not want to be observed by CCTV operators or have evidence about them captured on camera.
- *Nosy parker* [1] — a reduction could take place because more natural surveillance is encouraged as more people use the area covered by CCTV. This may deter offenders who fear an increased risk of apprehension.
- *Effective deployment* — CCTV may facilitate the effective deployment of security staff and police officers to locations where suspicious behavior is occurring. Their presence may deter offenders or may mean they are caught in the act.
- *Publicity (general)* — this may assist in deterring offenders (but crime might be displaced by location or offence).
- *Publicity (specific)* — CCTV cameras and signs show people are taking crime seriously, and thus offenders may be deterred.
- *Time for crime* — CCTV may have less of an impact on crimes that can be done quickly as opposed to those that take a longer time, as offenders assume that they will have enough time to avoid the cameras or to escape from police officers or security staff.
- *Memory jogging* — publicity about CCTV encourages potential victims to be more security conscious and to take precautionary measures.
- *Appeal to the cautious* — those who are more security-minded use the areas with CCTV, driving out the more careless who may be vulnerable to crime elsewhere.

There are also a variety of *contexts* in which crime takes place, and these will influence the potential effect of the mechanisms specified above. Five such contexts identified by Pawson and Tilley (1994, 1997) are set out below.

- *Criminal clustering* — this depends on the offender-offence ratio. If it is one offender doing lots of crime, then the mechanism with the most potential is the *caught in the act* mechanism.
- *Style of usage* — if the area is always in use, then the *nosy parker* mechanism increases will have little effect on the pattern of

crime. If the area is little used, then any increases in usage and surveillance could increase the volume of incidents but reduce the number of people being victimized overall.

- *Lie of the land* — those in blind spots will be unaffected if it is presumed that CCTV will operate through increasing the likelihood of evidence being caught on camera (*you've been framed*), but not if it leads to people being more security-conscious (*memory jogging* mechanism) or increasing the likelihood that security-conscious people will use the area (*appeal to the cautious* mechanism).
- *Alternative targets* — regardless of a specific area's CCTV coverage, displacement may occur depending on the motivation of offenders and whether there are alternative targets.
- *Resources* — there may be few or no security staff to be deployed who can deter crime, as in the *effective deployment* mechanism.

To these can be added: the physical layout of the area, the cultural traditions and concerns of those within the area covered, the way the CCTV system is managed and operated, and attitudes towards its use (Tilley, 1997).

The utility of this framework for the current review is somewhat limited because most studies of CCTV schemes have tended to collect only data that can explore the *you've been framed* and *effective deployment* mechanisms, and sometimes the *publicity (general)*, *publicity (specific)* and *nosy parker* mechanisms. Less often have they included information on detections (*caught in the act*). Typically, researchers have been only able to speculate on the role of the *time for crime*, *memory jogging* and *appeal to the cautious* mechanisms. Indeed, as Pawson and Tilley (1997:80) note: "These hypotheses frame the requisite data and research strategies, and thus call upon a range of evidence entirely different from the standard comparisons." Thus, the extent to which the evaluations of CCTV lend themselves to the Tilley (1993a) framework is variable, but, where possible, it will be used to guide the understanding of how CCTV has operated in the sites under study.

Complicating the Picture Further: the Three Ds

In addition to the mechanisms and contexts through which CCTV operates, it is also necessary to explore the possibility that *displacement* has occurred following the installation of a CCTV system. The various types of displacement — functional, geographical, temporal, tactical, target and perpetrator [2] — may all be applicable in the CCTV context, and yet none of the evaluations reviewed below have been able to consider all of these; only some have examined functional, geographical and temporal displacement. An additional concern has been that the proliferation of CCTV in more affluent commercial and residential areas will lead to the displacement of crime to poorer areas, which has implications for the social ecology of such areas (Davies, 1995).

The flip side of displacement is *diffusion of benefits*. This occurs when the crime-reduction effects of CCTV are spread out and benefit surrounding areas beyond those targeted by CCTV (Clarke and Weisburd, 1994). This may understate the effect of the CCTV intervention, since when compared with so-called control areas, crime there will have also dropped (Clarke, 1995).

A third complication in evaluating the effects of CCTV is that increases in crime may actually reflect an increase in *detections* as a result of CCTV. There is also the possibility, as Groombridge and Murji (1994a) suggest, that CCTV could lead the public to feel a reduced responsibility for policing because they assume that this is the responsibility of the cameras. This may, in turn, reduce the likelihood that incidents are reported to the police as individuals may be less willing to report what they see if they assume they do not need to, and this would certainly affect crime rates for incidents not picked up. by CCTV operators. Conducting a pre- and post-installation victimization survey might be the only way to shed some light on whether or not changes in recorded crime rates are real, related to increased detections, or the result of underreporting by victims.

RESEARCH EVALUATIONS

The Impact of CCTV on Crime

Research evaluations of CCTV systems have attempted to assess whether any observed reductions in crime could be attributed to CCTV, general trends in local and national crime rates, other crime prevention activities, social and economic factors, or whether they are purely statistical artifacts.[3] To a lesser extent, studies have looked at the negative effects of CCTV, the use of CCTV by shop staff and the police, and its cost-effectiveness. The pretest posttest model that has guided much of the evaluative research has meant that researchers have typically collected police recorded crime figures or incident data to examine changes over time; sometimes this has extended to the collection of victimization, arrest and detection data. User surveys, offender interviews, and observations of offenders' behavior and risk perceptions have also been undertaken. The evaluations have been carried out in a variety of sites, including town centres, shopping centres, parking facilities, public housing, and small businesses, and on public transport. Although the operational requirements of CCTV systems may differ according to the site, for the purposes of this review the research evidence is evaluated according to the level of success in reducing crime. Since the majority of CCTV systems have targeted property crime, the results from these evaluations are considered first. This is followed by a discussion of the research findings with regard to personal crimes and public order offences. Table 2 on page 144 provides a summary of the findings from these evaluations.

Property Crime

(A) Promising Results

Using the Tilley model, Brown (1995) examined the effect of CCTV in Newcastle town centre, a northern English metropolitan area consisting mainly of commercial and entertainment establishments. Sixteen pan, tilt and zoom cameras were installed and continuously monitored at the police station. Operators were equipped with radio links to local retailers and police officers on patrol. Table 1 below presents the findings reported by Brown (1995) of average monthly totals for a 26-month pre-CCTV period, and for 15 months after installation. For all property crime types examined, there was a reduction in the number of incidents in the CCTV areas compared with the non-CCTV areas, and this was also true in the areas that had only two cameras. Incident and arrest data confirmed a deterrent effect (*you've been framed*), especially when the cameras were first installed and then were fully operational. This was sustained for burglary and criminal damage, but for some offences such as thefts of and from vehicles the effect seemed to fade over time. There was no evidence of displacement, but there was some evidence of diffusion of benefits to the neighboring area.

The potential of CCTV for reducing property crime was also demonstrated by the system installed in the English market town of Kings Lynn, also studied by Brown (1995). Nineteen pan, tilt and zoom cameras were installed to cover surface parking facilities and problem locations. The cameras were continuously monitored by security staff, with radio links to in-store security staff.

Table 1: Newcastle Town Centre: Difference in Monthly Incident Totals Pre- and Post-CCTV Installation

Crime	CCTV (14 cameras) %	No CCTV (2 cameras) %	Control (No cameras) residential %	Force Other %
Burglary	-57*	-39*	-3	-2
Criminal damage	-34*	-25*	+4	+8*
Theft of MV	-47*	-40*	-13*	-11*
Theft from MV	-50*	-39*	-11	-16*
Theft other	-11*	-18*	+1	-8

Notes:
1. Source: Brown (1995)
2. *=significant difference in the incidence of offences (p <.05)
3. MV=Motor Vehicle

A perennial problem in evaluating programs such as CCTV occurs when the original pre-installation crime rate is low, and this was the case in Kings Lynn. This made it difficult to discern any displacement effects following CCTV installation. The data for the period February 1991 to October 1993 showed that thefts from vehicles were reduced in the areas covered by CCTV, but this decline had started before the cameras were installed. Brown (1995) observed reductions in all areas for thefts of vehicles, but this was most dramatic in the CCTV areas. Burglary decreased in the CCTV area while increasing in the rest of the division and force, and this may have indicated geographical displacement. Importantly, as has been found with many crime prevention measures, the effect fades over time, and this was true in the case of criminal damage in Kings Lynn and to a lesser extent burglary, where the initial reduction effect faded 12 to 15 months after camera installation. It can be surmised that the crime-reduction effects were produced through the *you've been framed* and *caught in the act* mechanisms, since over 250 arrests resulted from the use of CCTV in the town centre.

The success of these two town centre systems can be viewed alongside that in Airdrie, Scotland (Short and Ditton, 1996). There, 12 cameras covering the town centre and one outlying area became operational in November 1992. The cameras were monitored by civilian operators based in the police control room. Recorded crime and offence data for two years pre- and post-installation showed a reduction of 21% or 772 incidents, and this effect did not seem to fade over time. Crimes of dishonesty (housebreaking, theft from and of motor vehicles, taking and driving away, fraud, shoplifting, etc.) dropped by 48%, while fire-raising and malicious mischief fell by 19%. Even after careful study, functional and geographical displacement seemed not to have occurred during this period. However, Short and Ditton (1998) noted that some offenders travelled to Glasgow to commit crime there, and some who came from Glasgow to Airdrie to shoplift probably went further afield following camera installation. There was no evidence of a diffusion of benefits to areas without CCTV. The 116% improvement in detections across the evaluation period does point to the influence of the *caught in the act* and *effective deployment* mechanisms, and it was probably the case that the *you've been framed* mechanism was also in operation.

Tilley's (1993a) post hoc evaluations of the use of CCTV in some parking facilities have also revealed crime reduction effects. In Hull, pan, tilt and zoom cameras linked to the police control room were monitored 24 hours a day. In addition to a reduction in car crime over the evaluation period, facility usage was up. Damage to vehicles was reduced by 45%, theft of vehicles was down 89%, and theft from vehicles declined by 76%. According to Tilley, this reduction was not associated with the operation of the *nosy parker* mechanism, because the increased usage was not large enough to have this effect. The same pattern of a reduction in theft of and from cars was observed in Bradford, although other crime prevention measures may have increased the perceived risk to offenders. The lack of arrests directly resulting from the monitoring of the cameras ruled out the influence of the *caught in the act* mechanism. In the Wolverhampton leisure centre parking facility, where car crime was slightly reduced, the CCTV effect may have been confounded by a decrease in the usage of the centre (Tilley, 1993a).

The success in the station parking facility in Lewisham, an inner London borough, demonstrated the crime-reduction benefits and cost-effectiveness[4] of CCTV under different operational circumstances. The CCTV installation consisted of three fixed-lens, and one dummy, cameras that were infrequently monitored and that did not permit accurate identification. The launch of the system was accompanied by both positive and negative publicity. Notwithstanding this, data available only for a short period post-installation did show a smaller number of car crimes being committed. Evidently CCTV can have an impact on crime even where the system is relatively unso-phisticated. The mechanisms through which the reduction occurred could have been *you've been framed* and *specific publicity* or possibly the *memory jogging* mechanism.

CCTV has also been responsible for reducing vandalism on buses in Cleveland, England (Poyner, 1992a). Following the success of the first bus program in which CCTV was installed (damage ceased al-most completely), a second bus was fitted with a CCTV system and three dummy cameras were installed on buses in August 1986. Poy-ner examined workshop seat repair data from the beginning of 1986 for the 80 buses operating out of the depot. These showed that there was a steady decline in damage to seat cushions on all buses over a nine-month period, to a third of what it was the previous year (which, in turn, led to a reduction in the number of cleaners required by the bus company). According to Poyner (1992a), the success could be attributed to coverage of the system by television and local newspa-pers, suggesting activation of the *general publicity* mechanism. Fur-thermore, the *Bus Watch* program (consisting of visits to local schools) showed children the likelihood of being caught on the cameras (the *you've been framed* mechanism). In addition, action was taken against some children in the first few months of the initiative, as a result of the *caught in the act* mechanism.

CCTV has also been shown to work effectively in public housing. Chatterton and Frenz (1994) evaluated the use of CCTV in a sheltered housing scheme where the elderly residents were frequently the vic-tims of burglary. Cameras were installed in 15 housing units, and prominent signs were displayed at entrances. Between one and five dummy cameras were placed where they would be seen by offenders to act as a deterrent, and some operational cameras were concealed to maximize their apprehension potential. The cameras were not monitored continuously, but the images were recorded 24 hours a day so that they could be used to identify offenders, most of whom were already known to the police, but had proved difficult to charge because of poor identification by elderly residents.

Across the evaluation period, completed and attempted burglaries decreased by 79%, from 4.25 to 0.9 offences per month, a statistically significant decrease. Before the implementation of CCTV, the police had arrested and charged 13 offenders compared with only three in the post-installation period. Despite the lower number of arrests, this represented an improvement in the arrest rate (number of arrests as a percentage of the number of offences), from 25% to 33%. The *you've been framed* and *specific publicity* mechanisms are likely to have generated this crime reduction effect.

Finally, CCTV appears to have assisted in reducing stock losses in a clothing store in Leeds, from almost £600 per week to £200 per week. Staff reported that CCTV gave them the confidence to approach customers who were acting suspiciously. CCTV images were used to detect two offenders during the study (Gill and Turbin, 1998).

(B) Mixed Impact

Other evaluations of CCTV systems have not reported the same unequivocal success documented above. For example, while theft of and from motor vehicles declined following the introduction of CCTV in Doncaster city centre, other crimes such as burglary, criminal damage, shoplifting, assault and other thefts did not (Skinns, 1998). Furthermore, although there was evidence of a diffusion of benefits to the areas immediately surrounding the town centre, displacement effects were also observed, with most offences increasing in outlying areas. Skinns calculated that there was an overall crime reduction effect from CCTV of 6%, once displacement and diffusion had been taken into account. Similarly, Squires (1998a) reported a reduction in criminal damage, robbery and theft-person offences following the installation of CCTV in Ilford town centre, but there was no associated drop in burglary, shoplifting, violence or drugs offences.

Tilley (1993a) found that CCTV had a mixed impact on car crime in Hartlepool and Coventry parking facilities. In Hartlepool, pan, tilt and zoom cameras were installed in April 1990, monitored by security officers with a link to the police control room. Over the evaluation period (1989-1992) there was a decline in theft of and from cars in the CCTV area, although this started to increase over time, suggesting a fading effect. There was also a strong indication that car crime was displaced to surrounding areas in Hartlepool when the cameras were first installed. Moreover, increased natural surveillance by shoppers and traffic wardens probably assisted the reduction in the CCTV-covered parking facilities. In Coventry, theft of cars fell over the period 1987 to 1992 (January-August); there was a similar reduction in Coventry as a whole, but this was followed by an increase. Across Coventry, theft from cars declined but the crime rate fluctuated, and the decline was most dramatic in the CCTV-covered parking facilities.

Poyner's (1992b) attempt to isolate the effects of CCTV in a university parking facility was frustrated by the implementation of a package of measures (improved lighting and the pruning of trees) introduced to reduce car crime. A CCTV camera (later fitted with a loud-speaker) was set up on a tower covering two adjacent parking facilities in March 1986. The analysis for the whole campus showed a reduction in theft from cars. This crime type stood at 61 in 1984 (pre-installation), increased to 92 crimes in 1985 (the year the crime prevention measures were introduced), and dropped to 31 crimes in 1986. Crime was also reduced in the facility that was not monitored by CCTV. Poyner suggested that this was because there was both *specific* and *general publicity* surrounding the use of CCTV, and this enabled the police to make a few arrests (cf. Tilley, 1993a). There were also two loudspeaker warnings. It is possible that functional displacement of thefts from cars occurred, since the number of offences of theft of cars increased over the same time period. There appeared to be little effect in reducing criminal damage offences.

Some evaluations, including those carried out in Ilkeston and Leicester town centres have shown reductions in property crime in the CCTV-covered areas and in those without CCTV (Charter Consultancy, 1997; Leicestershire Constabulary cited in Bone Wells Associates, 1998). This same pattern was observed in Sarno's (1996) evaluation of CCTV in parking facilities in Sutton (a town in southern England), although it is possible that improved lighting and overnight locking of the facilities were partially or wholly responsible for this crime reduction. Generally speaking, it has not been possible to ascertain whether such universal reductions are related to a general downward trend in crime or a diffusion of benefits (Clarke, 1995). In other cases, crime reduction has occurred but only in relation to one crime type. For example, Squires' (1998b,c,d) evaluations of CCTV in three small town centres in southern England (Sussex) reported reductions, over and above those in control areas, only for criminal damage.

(C) Negligible Impact

The final category of CCTV evaluations includes those where CCTV has failed to demonstrate an impact on crime, or has had only a small effect, perhaps in containing crime increases relative to areas not covered by CCTV. Brown (1995), for example, found this to be the case in Birmingham town centre. Nine pan, tilt and zoom cameras were installed at problem locations around the city centre. The system was controlled by the police and civilian operators based in the police control room who had links to officers on the beat, city centre officers and traders.

In the experimental zones covered by CCTV, Brown (1995) found that burglary from shops did not increase by as much as in the rest of the division, although this could not be attributed to the effect of CCTV (it may have occurred because of pedestrianization). Neither was Brown able to conclude that the decline in thefts of vehicles was the direct result of CCTV, since this may have been due instead to traffic-calming measures. Both criminal damage and thefts from vehicles increased in the areas covered by CCTV in Birmingham, whereas this was not the case in the rest of the division. Brown suggested that this may have been indicative of some functional displacement of offending into thefts from vehicles following the installation of the cameras, although there was no evidence of temporal displacement. Victimization survey data confirmed the pattern observed in the crime data.

Neither did the evaluation of CCTV in Sutton town centre replicate the crime reduction effects reviewed in the previous sections (Sarno, 1995; 1996). Notwithstanding this, success stories are frequently reported in CCTV evaluations, even where crime data do not support a crime reduction effect overall. For example, in Birmingham town centre, CCTV was used in 458 incidents, resulting in 173 arrests of suspected offenders (Brown, 1995).

One of the earliest studies of CCTV was undertaken by Musheno et al. (1978), and this too failed to find a crime reduction effect on a housing project, although some unusual features of this study make it rather difficult to generalize its findings. Cameras were placed in the lobby and elevator areas of three housing blocks in New York in August 1976. Images and sound were continuously transmitted to residents' TV screens. A victimization survey indicated that in four of eight crime types, there was an increase post-CCTV installation, while in the remaining four crime types there was only a tiny decline.

Musheno et al. (1978) concluded that CCTV failed to deter crime, although it is possible that their evaluation occurred too soon (before CCTV had had time to produce a deterrent effect). In addition, the *caught in the act* and *you've been framed* mechanisms were unlikely to have been exploited, since only 14% of residents interviewed said that they monitored the areas covered by CCTV at least once a day. Since it appeared that residents were often responsible for crime in the buildings, they would have been aware of the lack of monitoring. In addition, 33% said that they might not report crimes to the police because they feared retaliation from offenders.

In his study of the prevention of crime against small businesses, Tilley (1993b) looked at 10 businesses that, under the Salford Business Security Grant Scheme, had installed CCTV to protect them against crime. Of the three businesses with CCTV that responded to a questionnaire sent out to study the effect of the CCTV on break-ins, vandalism and other offences, all were victimized in the year before the security upgrade, and all were victimized in the year after the security upgrade. However, the number of incidents did drop from 35 to 30.

Personal Crime and Public Order Offences

Evaluations assessing the impact of CCTV on personal and public order crimes have also produced mixed results. Brown (1995) found that in Birmingham town centre there was a small increase in robbery, theft from the person and criminal damage, although this compared with a dramatic increase in these offences in the rest of the police division. Squires and Measor (1996) reported the same findings in relation to violence offences in Brighton town centre compared with the division as a whole. In Kings Lynn, post-CCTV decreases in assaults and wounding may have reflected the extent to which officers defused situations so they did not lead to an offence, rather than incidents not taking place at all (Brown, 1995). This explanation does not fit easily with the 24% drop in recorded violent crime comparing two-year periods pre- and post-CCTV in Rhyl town centre in Wales (Sivarajasingam and Shepherd, 1999). There, despite the drop according to police records, emergency room records showed an increase in assaults of 35%. A similar pattern was observed in Swansea city centre. Conversely, Sivarajasingam and Shepherd (1999) found increases in police recorded assaults (up to 20%) in Cardiff town centre following the introduction of CCTV, although emergency room records showed a decrease of 12% in the number of assault cases. The large discrepancy between police recorded crime and hospital records found in Rhyl and Cardiff in opposite directions, highlights the importance of using data other than that collected by the police to assess the effect of CCTV. Overall, Sivarajasingam and Shepherd concluded that CCTV had little effect on violent crime.

The effect of CCTV on public transport has not been clearly demonstrated either, in part because these studies have typically involved crime prevention initiatives, of which CCTV only formed a part. A study by Burrows (1978) followed the installation of CCTV cameras in four London Underground stations in November 1975, which occurred just after the deployment of targeted uniform and plainclothes police patrols. Recorded theft was nearly four times lower in the post-installation period, compared with only 1.4 times lower in the other

15 stations in the southern sector not covered by CCTV. There did, however, appear to be some geographical displacement. At the 15 stations in the southern sector without CCTV, thefts fell by 27%, whereas at other non-CCTV stations of the Underground they fell by 39%. This difference was statistically significant. Although there were only a small number of robbery offences, these did decline in the CCTV stations, with an increase in other southern-sector stations and in other stations in the London Underground network. A follow-up study by Webb and Laycock (1991) also seemed to indicate a CCTV effect in the reduction of robbery offences, although a range of other measures were also implemented around the same time as additional cameras were introduced.

In a second project at Oxford Circus station, CCTV and other crime prevention measures failed to reduce thefts and robbery, but passenger assaults did slightly decrease in the second year after their implementation. The absence of a "CCTV effect" was probably due to the large size and complexity of the station with its six platforms, eight entrances/exits and 14 escalators. Webb and Laycock (1991:23) concluded that "CCTV does not seem very useful in large, complex, and crowded environments to deal with more surreptitious behavior such as pick-pocketing or shoplifting."

The successful intervention of CCTV in relation to public order incidents has also been less evident. In Airdrie, crimes against public justice and drug offences climbed 1068% (180 more crimes) in the two years following the installation of cameras in the town centre. Public order offences (petty assault, drunkenness, breach of the peace, etc.) increased by 133% (Short and Ditton, 1996). Other crime prevention techniques, such as reducing the number of those intoxicated, improving the training of security personnel, and other management and legislative approaches, appear to have shown more success in reducing these type of crimes (see, for example, Homel et al., 1998; Ramsay, 1990).

The Offender's Perspective

Offenders themselves also offer a means for studying the effectiveness of CCTV, particularly displacement. Yet few studies have sought information on CCTV from offenders, and those that have, have utilized small samples. Butler (1994) carried out in-depth interviews with 27 offenders in England who had committed commercial burglary offences. Forty-one percent said they would be deterred by an external or internal CCTV system; the majority said that they would not be deterred from committing a crime. Survey research with offenders

(N=130) in Essex has suggested that CCTV can be effective in deterring crime, particularly among adults, although the offenders surveyed had not committed offences in areas where CCTV was installed (French, 1996). In contrast, Gill and Turbin (1998) found that most of the shop thieves they interviewed did not fear apprehension as a result of CCTV. Only two-fifths reported that they would sometimes or always be deterred by mobile cameras, and few offenders were influenced by *specific publicity* advertising the presence of cameras.

Short and Ditton (1998) found that most offenders they interviewed (n=30) were aware of the existence of CCTV in Airdrie town centre, and they had a reasonable idea of the areas that were covered by the cameras. Half of the offenders had been filmed engaging in illegal actions and were thus convinced of the evidential power of CCTV (Ditton and Short, 1998). Despite this, on the basis of the offender accounts, Ditton and Short (1998) concluded that CCTV appeared to only limit the extent of violence used in public order incidents or to deflect their location, rather than to prevent them altogether, mirroring the findings of Brown (1995) in Kings Lynn. Moreover, it seemed that CCTV acted as a deterrent for only some of those who were engaged in property crime. Offenders reported that the limits to the cameras' range of vision, their ability to dodge the cameras, and the speed with which many offences (especially car theft) could be undertaken meant that CCTV was not effective in increasing the risk of apprehension. For public order offences, the disinhibiting effects of alcohol also played a part.

The Impact of CCTV on Fear of Crime

In addition to claims about its effectiveness in reducing crime, CCTV has also been proposed as a way of reducing fear of crime. The few studies that have examined fear of crime pre- and post-CCTV installation have produced similar findings. Chatterton and Frenz's (1994) study of the impact of CCTV in sheltered housing for the elderly, for example, reported that 46% of the respondents were very or fairly worried that their flat would be burgled before the installation of CCTV. The post-installation interviews revealed that 74% of respondents were less worried about being a victim of burglary, and more respondents reported that it was difficult for strangers to get in. Similarly, although the CCTV system in a New York housing project did not deter crime, 41% of respondents felt unsafe at night after the installation of CCTV compared with 50% pre-installation (Musheno et al., 1978). This may have been related to the small reduction in robbery victimization. The town centre research in Birmingham and

Sutton has confirmed this picture, with reductions in fear of crime following the introduction of CCTV, even where there has not been an associated reduction in crime (Brown, 1995; Mahalingham, 1996; Sarno, 1996).

The fear-reduction potential of CCTV has also been noted in public attitude surveys. Bennett and Gelsthorpe (1996) found that 73% of Cambridge (England) residents who were sampled believed that CCTV was effective in reducing fear of crime. In contrast, Honess and Charman (1992) reported that 45% of town centre respondents felt that CCTV was not very effective or not effective in this respect. Notwithstanding this, the enhanced safety aspect of CCTV was greatest in parking facilities (around 60% said they felt safer), followed by shopping centres (48%) and streets (35% during the day and 48% at night). In contrast, Brown (1998) has noted that transport facilities monitored by CCTV are still regarded as high-risk spaces for women, and that CCTV is unlikely to make women feel safer in town centres that are dominated by men at night.

PUBLIC ATTITUDES TOWARDS THE USE OF CCTV

Generally speaking, the public's attitude towards CCTV has been favorable in the U.K. In the most comprehensive survey of public opinion regarding CCTV, Honess and Charman (1992) conducted surveys in streets, shopping centres and parking facilities. Over 85% of respondents said they would welcome a CCTV system (see also French, 1996). Studies have shown that offenders, too, are supportive of CCTV, perhaps because of their own vulnerability to personal victimization (French, 1996; Short and Ditton, 1998). Very few respondents (around 8%) surveyed by Honess and Charman expressed worries about the use of CCTV in public places (see also Beck and Willis, 1995; Gill and Turbin, 1998). Notwithstanding this, Ditton (1998) has demonstrated that the contextualizing questions preceding the key question on the acceptability of CCTV can lead to a margin of 35% difference in those who support CCTV, depending on whether the questions are pro-CCTV, anti-CCTV or neutral — a point that should be borne in mind when reviewing the findings from public attitude surveys.

Honess and Charman (1992) also convened focus groups with white, black and Asian youths, mixed-race groups and student activists. The survey and focus group data showed that those who did worry about CCTV were concerned about the excessive surveillance of, for example, young black men, and the abuse of the system by operators. In the survey of Cambridge residents, the civil liberties implications of CCTV concerned a larger proportion of the sample, although this did not mean they withdrew their support for CCTV in the city centre. Bennett and Gelsthorpe (1996) reported that 29% were very or fairly worried about civil liberties. In particular, respondents mentioned their dislike of being watched, their fear of greater state control, the possible abuse of recorded information, and a general erosion of civil liberties. Similar concerns were voiced in focus group discussions in Sutton among young people and ethnic minorities (Farish, 1995). In Brighton, opposition to CCTV led to a public demonstration against its use (Davies, 1998).

To some extent, fears about abuse and control may be alleviated by the regulation of CCTV. A study of 70 local authorities with CCTV systems in England, Scotland and Wales conducted by Bulos and Sarno (1996) showed that over 70% of those studied had codes of practice to govern their systems. However, these were not always operational and were principally concerned with protecting the public's civil liberties. A consideration of equal opportunities in relation to the use of CCTV was generally lacking, although in one local authority, consultation with minority groups had led to the cameras being directed towards a mosque entrance where graffiti and vandalism had occurred and to the route used by women students to get to residence halls. It was also recognized that operators needed training to overcome stereotypes that might be used to track and focus on certain individuals. The researchers, for example, found some examples of male controllers being more suspicious of black and Asian youths than of white youths.

DISCUSSION

To summarize the disparate findings on the impact of CCTV is a difficult task, not least because of the post hoc nature and limitations of some of the evaluations, the difficulties in establishing which causal mechanisms explained crime reduction effects, and contradictory findings. What does emerge from the review of CCTV evaluations, however, is that property crime has been reduced in certain settings where CCTV has been installed. This paper has noted examples of a reduction in burglary, thefts of and from motor vehicles (particularly the latter), and criminal damage in town centres, parking facilities, sheltered housing, and public transport facilities. Notwithstanding these successes, CCTV has had little effect in reducing property crime in other sites (e.g., Birmingham town centre). Similarly, where the logic behind the implementation of CCTV has been faulty (e.g., in the New York housing study that relied on residents to monitor activity) or oversimplified, (e.g., Oxford Circus station where its physical layout prevented it operating to its maximum potential), CCTV has had little impact on crime.

The picture in relation to personal crime, public order and fear of crime is less clear. Rather than deterring violence and public disorder incidents altogether, Brown (1995) argued that CCTV works to contain the seriousness of incidents by helping to ensure that the police or security officers are quickly deployed to the scene of incidents, thus minimizing the amount of harm. Any information recorded by the system can also assist the police in investigating the incident.

The Role of the Usual Suspects

Even where evaluations have demonstrated a "CCTV effect," this effect was found to sometimes fade over time, as has been found with other crime prevention measures (Berry and Carter, 1992). This waning of the deterrence effect was found in Newcastle and Kings Lynn town centres and in the Hartlepool parking facility. For this reason, both Tilley (1993a) and Brown (1995) have stressed the importance of continually demonstrating to offenders through publicity that the risk of apprehension with CCTV is high. This may be the only way to sustain any initial deterrent effects. The limited research on offenders' views about CCTV further supports this approach.

In addition, as Tilley (1993a) has observed, CCTV will most likely contribute to a reduction in property crime where other crime prevention measures are also implemented, even though from an evaluation point of view, it may be impossible to tease out the independent effect of CCTV when it is implemented at the same time as other situational measures.

Clearly important, too, is the role of crime displacement in assessing the crime reduction effects of CCTV; in the evaluations reviewed here there are examples of little or no displacement of crime. This was the case in Newcastle town centre, for example, and in Airdrie town centre where only a few offenders displaced their activities to another location. On the other hand, there was evidence of geographical displacement in Birmingham and Doncaster town centres. Displacement is also more likely where the layout of the area is complex and overcrowding obscures the view, providing a likely setting for pickpocketing and other types of theft, as at London Underground stations.

Alternatively, the opposite effect may also occur where the benefits of CCTV are diffused into a wider area than that covered by the system. A diffusion of benefits was found in the study of CCTV use on Cleveland buses. There, criminal damage to seats declined for all buses operating out of the same depot, even though the cameras were installed only on a few buses. Similarly, in Newcastle and Doncaster town centres, crime declined in the neighbouring areas that did not have camera coverage.

Ascertaining precisely the mechanisms through which CCTV operates is essential for determining whether it will be effective in other settings and contexts. To date, the evaluations demonstrating the success of CCTV have not been able to shed much light on the mechanisms through which it is effective. Where the evidence does exist, it can be concluded that the crime reduction effects of CCTV owe more to its deterrent value than its actual ability to apprehend criminals. This was exemplified in the Lewisham car park scheme, that utilized a rather unsophisticated system and was not able to deploy security personnel or police officers quickly. Particularly important in this regard is the use of *general* and *specific publicity* to highlight the perceived heightened risk to offenders, particularly since some offenders are skeptical about the capabilities of CCTV.

Future research will need to address the unanswered questions that remain. Directly examining the decision-making behaviour of offenders in a longitudinal study, particularly with regard to displacement and desistance offers promise (Short and Ditton, 1998). It will also be of interest to know whether CCTV affects surveillance by the public, their intervention in incidents, precautionary behavior, and the reporting of offences to the police. The role of CCTV evidence in getting offenders to admit an offence (offering criminal justice alternatives such as cautioning or sentence discounts for guilty pleas with reduced court costs) must also be examined. New research by Chenery et al. (forthcoming) has broached this subject from a different angle by examining the sentences imposed on offenders by magistrates where video evidence has been presented, compared with text-only presentations of the evidence. Following up on the work of Bulos and Sarno (1994) to assess the extent to which CCTV operators engage in abuses of privacy and the targeting of marginalized groups would also be an important step in examining the negative consequences of CCTV.

Finally, it is hoped that future evaluations will test and refine the framework proposed by Tilley (1993a) and by Pawson and Tilley (1994, 1997) by drawing on the expertise of practitioners and policymakers (Tilley, 1997). To empirically test which mechanisms are set in motion by CCTV in a given context, and to disentangle the cumulative or interactive effects of different mechanisms, will pose particular problems from an evaluation point of view (see also Gill and Turbin, 1998). Data on convictions resulting from CCTV, either through direct observation or taped evidence, will need to be collected. To assess the impact of the *appeal to the cautious, memory jogging* and *time for crime* mechanisms, data on the number of crimes, changes in the style of crime being committed, and security behaviour of potential victims must be gathered. Understanding the actions of undeterred offenders will assist in examining the *lie of the land* context, and will provide useful information for other CCTV schemes. Testing the influence of the *style of usage* context will mean collecting data on the time crimes occur alongside usage patterns. The effect of the *publicity* mechanisms and the *surveillance culture* context can only be examined by exploring the way individuals process publicity information about CCTV, once again highlighting the value of the offender's perspective.

Future developments in technology, such as license plate recognition, facial recognition, and algorithmic image interpretation to alert operators to unsanctioned events will also need to be monitored and evaluated, in terms of both their impact on reducing crime and their social control of citizens, particularly those who are already marginalized (Norris et al., 1998). It remains to be seen whether future evaluations — of which there should be many as funding agencies insist on this as a condition of funding — will meet these challenges.

Acknowledgements: This paper was written while the author was employed at the Loss Prevention Council, Melrose Avenue, Borehamwood, Hertfordshire WD6 2 BJ, UK. I would like to thank Marti Smith for her comments on an earlier draft of this paper. Thanks are also due to Paul Ekblom.

Address correspondence to: Dr Coretta Phillips, Home Office, Policing and Reducing Crime Unit, Clive House, Room 410, London SW1H 9HD, United Kingdom.

Table 2: Summary of Research Evaluations on the Effectiveness of CCTV

Site of CCTV/ Study	Evaluation Period	Measures	Findings[1]			Displacement/ Diffusion of Benefits	Notes
			Reduction	No Change	Increase		
City centres							
Sivarajsingam and Shepherd (1999) Swansea	24 months pre- 24 months post-	Recorded crime Emergency room records	Assaults (according to police records)		Assaults (according to ER records)	Geographical displacement to indoor locations, e.g., licensed premises?	
Rhyl	24 months pre- 24 months post-	Recorded crime Emergency room records	Assaults (according to police records)		Assaults (according to ER records)		
Cardiff	24 months pre- 24 months post-	Recorded crime Emergency room records	Assaults (according to ER records)		Assaults (according to police records)		

Site of CCTV/ Study	Evaluation Period	Measures	Findings[1]			Displacement/ Diffusion of Benefits	Notes
			Reduction	No Change	Increase		
Skinns (1998): Doncaster	12 months pre- 12 months post-	Recorded crime Victimization data Surveys of employees Young offender interviews	Theft of and from MV[2]	Burglary Criminal damage Shoplifting Other thefts Assault		Geographical displacement to outlying areas, although not indicated in interviews with offenders. Diffusion of benefits	Victimization data were consistent with recorded crime data. Changes in policing practices, parking arrangements in the town centre, and growth of out-of-town commercial and entertainment centres may have been influential in the reduction.
Squires (1998a): Ilford	6 months pre- 7 months post-	Recorded crime Incident data	Criminal damage Robbery Theft-person	Violence Burglary Shoplifting	Drugs	Geographical displacement	Dramatic reduction of MV crime in all areas.
Squires (1998b): East Grinstead	15 months pre- 8 months post-	Recorded crime Incident data	Criminal damage	Burglary	Violence Shoplifting	Diffusion of benefits	Very small sub-samples.
Squires (1998c): Burgess Hill	15 months pre- 8 months post-	Recorded crime Incident data	Criminal damage	Burglary Shoplifting Violence		Geographical and target displacement	Very small sub-samples. Several other crime prevention measures in place.
Squires (1998d): Crawley	18 months pre- 6 months post-	Recorded crime Incident data	Criminal damage	Violence Burglary Shoplifting		Diffusion of benefits	'Control' area included shopping parades also covered by newly installed CCTV cameras.

- 145 -

Site of CCTV/ Study	Evaluation Period	Measures	Findings[1]			Displacement/ Diffusion of Benefits	Notes
			Reduction	No Change	Increase		
Short and Ditton (1996): Airdrie	24 months pre- 24 months post-	Recorded crime Offence data Detections data	Crimes of dishonesty Fire-raising and vandalism		Drugs	No functional displacement Some geographical displacement [3]	The effect of CCTV on individual crime types not compared with control areas.
Squires and Measor (1996): Brighton	10 months pre- 13-17 months post-	Recorded crime Incident data	Selected offences combined[4]	Violence (but increasing in division)			
Brown (1995): Newcastle	26 months pre- 15 months post-	Final incident code data Arrest data	Burglary Criminal damage Theft of and from MV			No displacement Diffusion	
Brown (1995): Birmingham	12 months pre- 36 months post-	Recorded crime Victimization data	Theft of MV	Assault and wounding	Robbery, theft-person and burglary (but lower than in control areas) Criminal damage Theft from MV	Geographical and functional displacement	Other measures included pedestrianization and traffic-calming. Fear of crime decreased after dark only for those aware of the cameras.
Kings Lynn	9 months pre- 21 months post-	Incidents monitored by operators Recorded crime	Burglary Criminal damage Theft of and from MV Wounding and assaults				Low levels of crime. Decline in vehicle crime began before the installation of the cameras.

Site of CCTV/ Study	Evaluation Period	Measures	Findings[1]			Displacement/ Diffusion of Benefits	Notes
			Reduction	No Change	Increase		
Sarno (1996) and Mahalingham (1996): Sutton	12 months pre- 12 months post-	Recorded crime Public perception survey	Vehicle crime Assaults Criminal damage	Burglary Shoplifting	Theft Drugs Robbery		Recorded crime decreased by 13% in the CCTV area, and 30% in the borough as a whole. The effect of CCTV was not compared with control areas, except for vehicle crime, where it dropped in the facilities covered by CCTV and those without CCTV coverage. Increased feelings of safety.
Parking facilities							
Tilley (1993a): Hartlepool	12 months pre- 24 months post-	Recorded crime	Theft of MV	Theft from MV (gradual decline then increase)		Geographical displacement?	Increase in natural surveillance from traffic wardens and shoppers.
Hull	8 months pre- 8 months post-	Recorded crime	Criminal damage Theft of and from MV				Increased usage following CCTV installation.
Lewisham	4 months pre- 4 months post-	Recorded crime	Vehicle crimes				The effect of CCTV was not compared with a control area.

Site of CCTV/Study	Evaluation Period	Measures	Findings[1]			Displacement/Diffusion of Benefits	Notes
			Reduction	No Change	Increase		
Bradford	12 months pre- 12 months post-	Recorded crime	Theft of and from MV				Improved lighting and painting of walls.
Coventry	8 month-periods over 6 years	Recorded crime	Theft of and from MV				Variety of other crime prevention measures implemented.
Wolverhampton	12 months pre- 12 months post-	Recorded crime	Theft of and from MV				Usage of the leisure centre decreased by 28%. There was also a spate of thefts from cars.
Poyner (1992b): Surrey	27 months pre- 9 months post-	Recorded crime	Theft from MV	Theft of MV		Functional displacement? Diffusion	Foliage cut back and lighting improved.
Sarno (1996): Sutton	12 months pre- 12 months post-	Recorded crime	Criminal damage Theft of and from MV				Crime declined in almost all main car parks in the Sutton area. Improved lighting and overnight locking of the facility.
Public transport facilities							
Burrows (1978): London Underground	12 months pre- 12 months post-	Recorded crime	Theft-person Robbery			Geographical displacement	

Site of CCTV/ Study	Evaluation Period	Measures	Findings[1]			Displacement/ Diffusion of Benefits	Notes
			Reduction	No Change	Increase		
Webb and Laycock (1991): London Underground	47 months pre- 25 months post-	London Underground reports to the Department of Transport	Robbery				Variety of other crime prevention measures implemented.
Poyner (1992a): Cleveland buses	8 months pre- 8 months post-	Seat repair records	Vandalism			Diffusion of benefits	Bus Watch scheme also in operation.
Housing projects							
Chatterton and Frenz (1994)	12 months pre- 5-10 months post-[5]	Recorded crime Arrest and convictions data	Burglary				Reduction in fear of crime.
Musheno et al. (1978)	4 months pre- 3 months post-	Victimization survey	Robbery Att. robbery Purse-snatching and pick-pocketing Attempted burglary (small decline)		Aggravated assault Simple assault Burglary Vandalism		Reduction in feeling of being unsafe at night.

Notes:
1 Findings are based on comparisons with control areas, unless otherwise indicated in the *Notes* section.
2 MV = Motor Vehicle.
3 This was uncovered through interviews with offenders (see Short and Ditton, 1998).
4 The selected offences included: wounding and grievous bodily harm, assault and actual bodily harm, indecent assaults, violent disorder, affray (where two or more individuals engage in violence together causing fear), criminal damage (and endangering life), robbery and assault with intent to rob, aggravated vehicle taking, theft of and from motor vehicles, and supply of scheduled substances.
5 If the installation of the first CCTV camera is used, the pre-installation evaluation period was 10 months.

REFERENCES

Armstrong, G. and R. Giulianotti (1998). "From Another Angle: Police Surveillance and Football Supporters." In: C. Norris, J. Moran and G. Armstrong (eds.), *Surveillance, Closed Circuit Television and Social Control.* Aldershot, UK: Ashgate.

Barr, R. and K. Pease (1990). "Crime Placement, Displacement and Deflection." In: M. Tonry and N. Morris (eds.), *Crime and Justice: A Review of Research,* vol. 12. Chicago, IL: University of Chicago Press.

Beck, A. and A. Willis (1995). *Crime and Security: Managing the Risk to Safe Shopping.* Leicester, UK: Perpetuity Press.

Bennett, T. and L. Gelsthorpe (1996). "Public Attitudes Towards CCTV in Public Places." *Studies on Crime and Crime Prevention* 5(1):72-90.

Berry, G. and M. Carter (1992). *Assessing Crime Prevention Initiatives: The First Steps.* (Crime Prevention Unit Paper, #31.) London, UK: Home Office.

Bone Wells Associates (1998). "CCTV: Potential Crime Impact." (Unpublished report.) Bristol, UK: Bristol City Council.

British Department of Education and Science (1991). *Closed Circuit TV Surveillance Systems in Educational Buildings.* (Building Bulletin #75.) London, UK: Her Majesty's Stationery Office.

Brown, B. (1995). *CCTV in Town Centres: Three Case Studies.* (Police Research Group Crime Detection and Prevention Series Paper, #68.) London, UK: Home Office.

Brown, S. (1998). "What's the Problem, Girls? CCTV and the Gendering of Public Safety." In: C. Norris, J. Moran and G. Armstrong (eds.), *Surveillance, Closed Circuit Television and Social Control.* Aldershot, UK: Ashgate.

Bulos, M. (1994). *Closed Circuit Television and Local Authority Initiatives: The First National Survey.* (Research monograph.) London, UK: School of Land Management and Urban Policy, South Bank University.

—— and C. Sarno (1996). *Codes of Practice and Public Closed Circuit Television Systems.* London, UK: Local Government Information Unit.

Burrows, J. (1978). "The Impact of Closed Circuit Television on Crime in the London Underground." In: P. Mayhew, R.V.G. Clarke, J.N. Burrows, J.M. Hough and S.W.C. Winchester (eds.), *Crime in Public View.* (Home Office Research Study, #49.) London, UK: Her Majesty's Stationery Office.

—— (1991). *Making Crime Prevention Pay: Initiatives from Business.* (Home Office Crime Prevention Unit Paper, #27.) London, UK: Home Office.

Butler, G. (1994). "Shoplifters' Views on Security: Lessons for Crime Prevention." In: M. Gill (ed.), *Crime at Work: Studies in Security and Crime Prevention.* Leicester, UK: Perpetuity Press.

Chatterton, M.R. and S.J. Frenz (1994). "Closed Circuit Television: Its Role in Reducing Burglaries and the Fear of Crime in Sheltered Accommodation for the Elderly." *Security Journal* 5(3):133-139.

Chenery, S., C. Henshaw and K. Pease (forthcoming). "Does CCTV Evidence Increase Sentence Severity?" Unpublished report to the Nuffield Foundation, U.K.

Clarke, R.V. (1995). "Situational Crime Prevention." In: M. Tonry and D.P. Farrington (eds.), *Building a Safer Society: Strategic Approaches to Crime Prevention.* (Crime and Justice: A Review of Research, vol. 19.) Chicago, IL: University of Chicago Press.

—— and D. Weisburd (1994). "Diffusion of Crime Control Benefits: Observations on the Reverse of Displacement." In: R.V. Clarke (ed.), *Crime Prevention Studies*, vol. 2. Monsey, NY: Criminal Justice Press.

Davies, S. (1995). "Welcome Home Big Brother." *Wired* (May):58-62.

—— (1998). "CCTV: A New Battleground for Privacy." In: C. Norris, J. Moran and G. Armstrong (eds.), *Surveillance, Closed Circuit Television and Social Control.* Aldershot, UK: Ashgate.

Department of Education and Science (1991). "Closed Circuit TV Surveillance Systems in Educational Buildings." *Building Bulletin 75.* London, UK: Her Majesty's Stationery Office.

Ditton, J. (1998). "Public Support for Town Centre CCTV Schemes: Myth or Reality?" In: C. Norris, J. Moran and G. Armstrong (eds.), *Surveillance, Closed Circuit Television and Social Control.* Aldershot, UK: Ashgate.

—— and E. Short (1998). "When Open Street CCTV Appears to Reduce Crime: Does It Just Get Displaced Elsewhere?" *CCTV Today* 5(2):13-16.

Farish, M. (1995). "The Response of Special Interest Groups to CCTV." In: M. Bulos (ed.), *Towards a Safer Sutton? Impact of Closed Circuit Television on Sutton Town Centre.* London, UK: London Borough of Sutton.

French, P. (1996). "Inside the Offender's Mind." *CCTV Today* 3(3):16-19.

Gill, M. and V. Turbin (1998). "CCTV and Shop Theft: Towards a Realistic Evaluation." In: C. Norris, J. Moran and G. Armstrong (eds.), *Sur-*

veillance, Closed Circuit Television and Social Control. Aldershot, UK: Ashgate.

Groombridge, N. and K. Murji (1994a). "Obscured by Cameras?" *Criminal Justice Matters* 17(Autumn):9.

—— (1994b). "As Easy as AB and CCTV?" *Policing* 10(4):283-290.

Homel, R., M. Hauritz, G. McIlwain, R. Wortley and R. Carvolth (1998). "Preventing Drunkenness and Violence Around Nightclubs in a Tourist Resort." In: R.V. Clarke (ed.), *Situational Crime Prevention: Successful Case Studies* (2nd ed.). Guilderland, NY: Harrow and Heston.

Honess, T. and E. Charman (1992). *Closed Circuit Television in Public Places.* (Police Research Group Crime Prevention Unit Series Paper, #35.) London, UK: Home Office.

Liberty Briefing (1989). "Who's Watching You? Video Surveillance in Public Places." *Liberty Briefing* 16 (October):.

Mahalingham, V. (1996). "Sutton Town Centre Public Perception Survey." In: M. Bulos and D. Grant (eds.), *Towards a Safer Sutton? CCTV One Year On.* London, UK: London Borough of Sutton.

Mirrlees-Black, C. and A. Ross (1995). *Crime Against Retail and Manufacturing Premises: findings from the 1994 Commercial Victimisation Survey.* (Home Office Research Study, #146.) London, UK: Home Office.

Musheno, M.C, J.P. Levine and D.J. Palumbo (1978). "Television Surveillance and Crime Prevention: Evaluating An Attempt to Create Defensible Space in Public Housing." *Social Science Quarterly* 58(4):647-656.

Norris, C., J. Moran and G. Armstrong (1998). "Algorithmic Surveillance: The Future of Automated Visual Surveillance." In: C. Norris, J. Moran and G. Armstrong (eds.), *Surveillance, Closed Circuit Television and Social Control.* Aldershot, UK: Ashgate.

Pawson, R. and N. Tilley (1994). "What Works in Evaluation Research?" *British Journal of Criminology* 34(3):291-306.

—— (1997). *Realistic Evaluation.* London, UK: Sage.

Poyner, B. (1992a). "Video Cameras and Bus Vandalism." In: R.V. Clarke (ed.), *Situational Crime Prevention: Successful Case Studies.* Albany, NY: Harrow and Heston.

—— (1992b). "Situational Crime Prevention in Two Parking Facilities." In: R.V. Clarke (ed.), *Situational Crime Prevention: Successful Case Studies.* Albany, NY: Harrow and Heston.

Ramsay, M. (1990). *Lagerland Lost? An Experiment in Keeping Drinkers Off the Street in Central Coventry and Elsewhere.* (Police Research Group Crime Prevention Unit Paper, #42.) London, UK: Home Office.

Reeve, A. (1998). "Risk and the New Urban Space of Managed Town Centres." *International Journal of Risk, Security and Crime Prevention* 3(1):43-54.

Repetto, T.A. (1976). "Crime Prevention and the Displacement Phenomenon." *Crime and Delinquency* 22:166-177.

Roberts, A. and S. Goulette (1996). "CCTV Surveillance: The Local Authority's Role — A Review of Current Practice." *Proceedings of the Institute of Civil Engineers-Municipal Engineers* 1996, 115(2):61-67.

Sarno, C. (1995). "Impact of CCTV on Crime." In: M. Bulos (ed.), *Towards a Safer Sutton? Impact of Closed Circuit Television on Sutton Town Centre.* London, UK: London Borough of Sutton.

—— (1996). "The Impact of Closed Circuit Television on Crime in Sutton Town Centre." In: M. Bulos and D. Grant (eds.), *Towards a Safer Sutton? CCTV One Year On.* London, UK: London Borough of Sutton.

Short, E. and J. Ditton (1995). "Docs CCTV Affect Crime?" *CCTV Today* 2 (2):10-12.

—— (1996). *Does Closed Circuit Television Prevent Crime? An Evaluation of the Use of CCTV Surveillance in Airdrie Town Centre.* Edinburgh, SCOT: Scottish Office Central Research Unit.

—— (1998). "Seen and Now Heard: Talking to the Targets of Open Street CCTV." *British Journal of Criminology* 38(3):404-429.

Sivarajasingam, V. and J.P. Shepherd (1999). "Effect of Closed Circuit Television on Urban Violence." *Journal of Accident and Emergency Medicine* 26:225-257.

Skinns, D. (1998). "Crime Reduction, Diffusion and Displacement: Evaluating the Effectiveness of CCTV." In: C. Norris, J. Moran and G. Armstrong (eds.), *Surveillance, Closed Circuit Television and Social Control.* Aldershot, UK: Ashgate.

Speed, M., J. Burrows and J. Bamfield (1994). *Retail Crime Costs 1993/94 Survey: The Impact of Crime and the Retail Response.* London, UK: British Retail Consortium.

Squires, P. (1998a). *An Evaluation of the Ilford Town Centre CCTV Scheme.* Brighton, UK: Health and Social Policy Research Centre, University of Brighton.

—— (1998b). *The East Grinstead Town Centre CCTV Scheme: An Independent Evaluation.* Brighton, UK: Health and Social Policy Research Centre, University of Brighton.

—— (1998c). *CCTV and Crime Prevention in Burgess Hill Town Centre: An Independent Evaluation.* Brighton, UK: Health and Social Policy Research Centre, University of Brighton.

—— (1998d). *CCTV and Crime Reduction in Crawley: An Independent Evaluation of the Crawley CCTV System.* Brighton, UK: Health and Social Policy Research Centre, University of Brighton.

—— and L. Measor (1996). *CCTV Surveillance and Crime Prevention in Brighton: Follow-Up Analysis.* Brighton, UK: Health and Social Policy Research Centre, University of Brighton.

Tilley, N. (1993a). *Understanding Car Parks, Crime and CCTV: Evaluation Lessons from Safer Cities.* (Crime Prevention Unit Series Paper, #42.) London, UK: Home Office.

—— (1993b). *The Prevention of Crime Against Small Businesses: The Safer Cities Experience.* (Home Office Crime Prevention Unit Series Paper, #45.) London, UK: Home Office.

—— (1997). "Whys and Wherefores in Evaluating the Effectiveness of CCTV." *International Journal of Risk, Security and Crime Prevention* 2(3):175-185.

U.K. Home Office (1995). *CCTV: Winners by Government Regional Offices Round 1 1994/95.* London, UK: author.

—— (1996). *Closed Circuit ·Television Challenge Competition 1996/97 Successful Bids.* London, UK: author.

—— (1998). *Closed Circuit Television Challenge Competition (Round 4) 1998/99 Bidding Guidance.* London, UK: author.

U.K. Home Office Crime Prevention Agency (1997). *Closed Circuit Television Challenge 3 Competition 1997/98 Successful Bids.* London, UK: author.

Walker, A. (1998). "CCTV Works!" *Security Installer* (March):11-12.

Webb, B. and G. Laycock (1991). *Reducing Crime on the London Underground: An Evaluation of Three Pilot Projects.* (Crime Prevention Unit Paper, # 30.) London, UK: Home Office.

NOTES

1. Or "busybody."

2. See Repetto (1976) and Barr and Pease (1990).

3. For example, any reduction could reflect random fluctuations in local crime rates or "regression to the mean," where an effect will be achieved without any intervention simply because crime rates that are high will fall to the more normal rate (Tilley, 1997).

4. The cost-effectiveness of CCTV was assessed in a case study reported by the British Department of Education and Science (1991), although minimal information is provided for evaluative purposes. In the seven months prior to CCTV installation at a large secondary school in the Northeast of England (located close to a shopping center, bar, and near public footpaths) the estimated costs of vandalism were £8,700; in the first 12 months following the installation, £300 was spent on repairs. In this example, the cost of installing the system would have been recovered in less than two years. Burrows (1991), too, reported a reduction in losses following the installation of CCTV (as the key component in a security program) in nine large British supermarkets. Payback on the capital expenditure of the CCTV system was realised within six months in one store that was studied. Compare these findings with Tilley (1997), who argued that there is rarely enough data available to evaluators to determine which costs and benefits are directly associated with CCTV.

CCTV AND THE SOCIAL STRUCTURING OF SURVEILLANCE

by

Clive Norris
University of Hull

and

Gary Armstrong
University of Reading

Abstract: *The installation of Closed Circuit Television Cameras (CCTV) on British streets has been the crime prevention initiative of the century. However, little attention has been paid to who and what the cameras actually watch and how operators select their targets. This paper draws on a two-year study in the operation of CCTV control rooms to examine how target selection is socially differentiated by age, rage and gender and asks whether this leads to discrimination.*

INTRODUCTION

There is now a growing body of literature that has attempted to evaluate the effectiveness of closed circuit television (CCTV). These studies have shed considerable light on the complexity of measuring the impact of CCTV on the crime rate, and have led to a far more sober assessment of its reductionist potential (Tilley, 1993; Bulos and Grant, 1996; Short and Ditton, 1996; Squires and Measor, 1996; Ditton and Short, 1998; Skinns, 1998). However, one consequence of this concern with effectiveness has been to concentrate attention almost solely on outcomes rather than process. This is perhaps unsurprising: those who have commissioned evaluations have, to a large extent, been concerned with the bottom-line; i.e., does CCTV reduce crime? Evaluators have therefore concentrated their efforts on describing the correlation between the crime rate and the introduction of CCTV. They have then tried to isolate CCTV as the cause of the correlation by ruling out other factors. The time-consuming task of analysing trend data, displacement, and "halo effects" has left little time to explore the more general, but in our view, equally important question of how CCTV operates in practice. CCTV is about far more than just the reduction of crime. It is about the power to watch and potentially intervene in a variety situations, whether or not they be criminal. But who and what gets watched and the extent to which this is socially differentiated has largely been ignored by existing research.

This is important because CCTV has been portrayed, to use the words of one Home Office Minister, as a "Friendly Eye in the Sky" (*Guardian*, 1st January 1995) benignly and impartially watching over the whole population and targeting only those deemed as acting suspiciously. As one code of practice for a northern city centre system states, "CCTV is not a 'spy system.' There will be no interest shown or deliberate monitoring of people going about their daily business." Similarly, Graham (1998:99) writing of the North Shields system, states that the CCTV operators "have strict guidelines for the operation of the system. For example, guards are not permitted to 'track' people around the town unless they are acting suspiciously." However, what constitutes "suspicious behaviour" is not addressed by codes of conduct or by training, as Bulos and Sarno (1996:24) note: "The most neglected area of training consists of how to identify suspicious behaviour, when to track individuals or groups and when to take close-up views of incidents or people. This was either assumed to be self evident or common sense."

It is unpacking this "common sense" that is the aim of this paper: we want to know who and what gets targeted, and by what criteria they are selected. This issue of selectivity is central to any discussion of CCTV operational practice, because the sheer volume of information entering a CCTV system threatens to swamp the operators with information overload. Consider how much incoming information there is in a medium-sized 24-hour city centre system with 20 cameras.

The answer, as we can see from Table 1, is a quite staggering 43 million "pictures" per day. Inevitably, operators cannot focus their attention on every image from every camera — somehow they must narrow down the range of images to concentrate on. This problem could, of course, be solved entirely randomly, so that each person on the street has an equal chance of being selected for initial surveillance but only a small proportion have a chance of actually being sampled. However, this would still leave operators with the problem of whom to pay prolonged attention to once initial selection had taken place. For some the answer is obvious: those behaving suspiciously. But this begs the question as to what, in practice, constitutes suspicious behaviour?

Table 1: Incoming Information as Measured by Individual Frames of Video Footage in a 20-Camera, 24-Hour, City Centre System

25-frames per second per camera		25
x 20 cameras in system	Total number of frames entering the system per second	500
x 60 frames per minute	Total number of frames entering the system per minute	30,000
x 60 frames per hour	Total number of frames entering the system per hour	1,800,000
x 24 frames per day	Total number of frames entering the system per day	43,200,000

It is instructive here to draw on the writings of Harvey Sacks (1978) on the police construction of suspicion. For Sacks (1978:190), the key problem for a police patrol officer was how he or she could use a person's appearance as an indicator of their moral character and, thus, "maximise the likelihood that those who turn out to be criminal and pass into view are selected, while minimising the likelihood that those who do not turn out to be criminal and pass into view are not selected."

The problem is identical for the CCTV operator. Bombarded by a myriad of images from dozens of cameras, and faced with the possibility of tracking and zooming in on literally thousands of individuals, by what criteria can operators try to maximise the chance of choosing those with criminal intent? Camera operators and street patrol officers are at both an advantage and a disadvantage. Because the "presence" of operatives is remote and unobtrusive, there is less likelihood that people will orient their behaviour in the knowledge that they are being watched, and, by virtue of the elevated position and telescopic capacity of the camera, operators have a greater range of vision than the street-level patrol officer. However, these advantages must be offset against their remoteness, which means they are denied other sensory input — particularly sound —that can be essential in contextualising visual images. Unlike the patrol officer, the CCTV operative is both deaf and dumb: he simply cannot ask citizens on the street for information, nor can they hear what is being said.

Faced with such an avalanche of images, and a limited range of sensory data, how then does the CCTV operator selectively filter these images to decide what is worthy of more detailed attention? The problem is that operatives do not have prior knowledge that would enable them to determine which persons are going to engage in criminal activity. It is therefore an occupational necessity that they develop a set of working rules to narrow down the general population to the suspect population. To shed light on this, we now draw on our two-year study, funded by the Economic and Social Research Council, of the operation of CCTV control rooms, and we briefly outline our methodology below.

METHODOLOGY

Observations were carried out in three sites between May 1995 and April 1996. One was in the commercial centre of a major metropolitan city with a total population in excess of 500,000. During the day it was a bustling shopping and business district and as darkness fell supported a thriving night life based on clubs, pubs and eateries. Another site centred on the market square of an affluent county town with a population of nearly 200,000. It was thronged with shoppers during the day but at night was fairly quiet until the weekends, when it would attract revellers from the surrounding area for a night on the town. The third site focussed on a run down but busy high street in a poor inner-city borough with an ethnically diverse population of nearly 250,000. We have named these three sites Metro City, County Town, and Inner City, to reflect their contrasting features.

The systems also differed in other ways. Metro City, cost over £1 million to install, consisted of 32 cameras and had running costs of over £200,000 per annum. Although the system was located in the control room of the local police station, it was run by an independent trust responsible for all aspects of its day-to-day operation, including the staffing of the control room and maintenance of the system. In contrast, the County Town system cost around £500,000 to install and had annual running costs in the region of £120,000. It consisted of over 100 cameras, although the main monitors generally only displayed the pictures from the 25 or so cameras focused on the town centre. The Inner City system cost around £450,000 with annual running costs of about £100,000, and had 16 cameras focussing on the busy high street and surrounds. County Town and Inner City were run by their respective local authorities, were housed in purpose-built control rooms in local authority premises, and subcontracted the staffing of the controls rooms to private security firms. All three systems had 24-hour-a day monitoring. In County Town and Metro City this involved three eight-hour shifts; in Inner City, two 12-hour shifts.

In total, 592 hours of monitoring — the equivalent of 74 eight-hour shifts — were observed. All days of the week were covered, as were early, late and night shifts. On each shift the observer would "attach" himself to one operative and shadow that individual's work. In total, 25 different operatives were shadowed. A small notebook was used in the field when appropriate, and full field notes were written up at the end of each shift. These included full descriptions of any targeted surveillance. We defined targeted surveillance as one that lasted more than one minute on an individual or group of individuals, or where the surveillance was initiated from outside the system, for example, by police or private security, regardless of whether a target was identified. The field notes recorded key data for each targeted surveillance based on a checklist of salient features. Field notes were also recorded for general observations on the operation and control of the system, as well as operatives' beliefs and values, work tensions, interactions with visitors to the system, and included informal interviews with operators and managers.

The field notes of targeted surveillances also formed the basis for filling in the quantitative observation schedule. This recorded four types of data: (1) shift data, including the number of operatives on each shift, the time screens were left unattended, who visited the system, and whether and how many tapes were borrowed for inspection and for what purpose; (2) targeted suspicion data, including the reason for the suspicion, type of suspicion, how the surveillance was initiated, how many cameras were used, and whether the incident was brought to somebody else's attention; (3) person data, detailing the age, race sex and appearance of up to four people for each targeted surveillance; and (4) deployment data, recording all deployments initiated by the system operatives, how the system was used during the deployment and what the outcome was.

In total, this yielded data on 888 targeted surveillances. In 711 of these surveillances, a person was identified for whom basic demographic data (age, race, sex, and appearance) was recorded, as it was on another 966 people who were the second, third or fourth person in a group being surveilled.

THE SOCIAL STRUCTURING OF SURVEILLANCE

As Table 2 shows, selection for targeted surveillance appears, at the outset, to be differentiated by the classic sociological variables of age, race, and gender. Nine out of ten target surveillances were on men (93%), four out of ten on teenagers (39%) and three out of ten on black people (31%).

Table 2: Age and Sex of All People and Primary Person Surveilled

Sex		
Male	660	(93%)
Female	49	(7%)
Total	709	(100%)
Age		
Teenagers	270	(39%)
In their twenties	320	(46%)
Thirties plus	107	(15%)
Total	697	(100%)
Race		
White	483	(69%)
Black	210	(30%)
Asian	5	(0%)
Total	698	(99%)

In terms of the general population, men were nearly twice as likely to be targeted than their presence in the population would suggest. Similarly, teenagers — who account for less than 20% of the population — made up 40% of targeted surveillances. Of course, the street population (i.e., those available for targeting) is not the same as the general population. However, all three of our sites were busy commercial areas that during the day were populated by shoppers and workers, both male and female, many of whom were middle aged.

It is more difficult to estimate how a person's race affected the chance of being selected for targeting, since the proportion of ethnic minorities varied dramatically from site to site. However, we have calculated that black people were between one-and-a-half and two-and-a-half times more likely to be targeted for surveillance than their presence in the population would suggest (for further details, see Norris and Armstrong, 1997, 1999).

On their own, however, these findings do not indicate that CCTV operators are selecting targets for surveillance merely on the basis of observable social characteristics, since this distribution may relate to the behaviour of those targeted that initially prompted operator suspicion. To examine this we classified each surveillance as: "crime related," "order related," occurring for "no obvious reason," or "other." For instance, a youth crouching down by the side of a car would be classified as "crime related," a group of men involved in revelry at pub closing time as "order related," and surveying the scene of a traffic accident as "other." This "crime related" category does not imply that the person was involved in any criminal behaviour, merely that the operator had some explicit grounds for targeting the person or incident. A youth crouching by the side of a car is, in all probability, tying his or her shoelaces rather than removing hub caps, and the targeted surveillance may well confirm this. All the same, this action will still be coded as "crime related" since the operator is treating the behaviour as indicative of theft. Similarly, if the operator tracks a known shoplifter this would also be classified as crime related because the operator has explicit grounds for their suspicion. If there were no signs from a person's behaviour or he was not a "known offender," then we recorded the surveillance as for "no obvious reason."

Three out of ten people (30%) were surveilled for crime-related matters, two out of ten (22%) for forms of disorderly conduct, but the largest category — nearly four out of ten (36%) — were surveilled was for "no obvious reason." This was echoed when we examined the basis of suspicion, with one quarter (24%) of people subject to targeted surveillance because of their behaviour. But the most significant type of suspicion was categorical; one-third (31%) of people were surveilled merely on the basis of belonging to a particular social or subcultural group. The extent to which the reason for the surveillance was socially differentiated is shown in Table 3.

As Table 3 shows, the reason for the surveillance and the suspicion on which it was based was also found to be highly differentiated. Thus, we can see that two-thirds (65%) of teenagers — compared with only one in five (21%) of those aged over 30 — were surveilled for "no obvious reason." Similarly, black people were twice as likely (68%) to be surveilled for "no obvious reason" than whites (35%), and men three times (47%) more likely than women (16%). The young, the male and the black were systematically and disproportionately targeted, not because of their involvement in crime or disorder, but for "no obvious reason" and on the basis of categorical suspicion alone.

If we cannot explain the patterning of target selection on the basis of observable difference in behaviour, it is necessary to examine the influence of the values and attitudes of the operators and how they relate to age, race and gender.

Table 3: Reason for Surveillance by Age, Race and Gender in Numbers and Percentages

Age						
	Teenagers		In their twenties		Thirties plus	
Crime Related	59	(22%)	80	(26%)	17	(17%)
Public Order	30	(11%)	83	(27%)	46	(45%)
No Obvious	173	(65%)	115	(38%)	21	(21%)
Other	4	(2%)	29	(9%)	18	(18%)
Total	266	(100%)	307	(100%)	102	(101%)
Gender						
	Male		Female			
Crime Related	138	(22%)	19	(43%)		
Public Order	150	(24%)	12	(27%)		
No Obvious	302	(47%)	7	(16%)		
Other	49	(8%)	6	(14%)		
Total	639	(101%)	44	(100%)		
Race						
	White		Black			
Crime Related	115	(25%)	42	(20%)		
Public Order	148	(32%)	13	(6%)		
No Obvious	163	(35%)	141	(68%)		
Other	41	(9%)	12	(6%)		
Total	467	(101%)	208	(100%)		

Age

As we have seen, young men were the main targets of surveillance. This is not surprising given the attitudes that operators displayed towards youths in general and particularly those identified — by attire, location, or body language — as poor or belonging to the underclass. Further, like police, CCTV operators often referred to such categories as "toe-rags," "scumbags," "yobs," "scrotes," and "crapheads." As the following two examples illustrate, operatives need no special reason to ascribe malign intent merely on the basis of age, particularly if youths are in a group.

13.45: The operator sees and zooms in on four boys walking through a pedestrian precinct. Aged between 10 and 12 and casually, but fashionably, dressed, the four, — combining age, appearance, location and numbers — are suspects for a variety of possibilities. The four gather around in a form of "conference," and 30 seconds later walk a few yards to their left and enter a shop well known for selling toys. What the operator sees is not kids entering a shop meant for kids, but something else: they are all up to no good and, in his opinion, have probably just plotted to steal and will come running out any minute with stolen merchandise. In anticipation, he fixes a camera onto the shop door and tells the other operator to put the cameras onto the street he presumes they will run into.

Using two cameras and two operators, the surveillance lasts six minutes before the boys leave the shop — slowly and orderly and without any apparent stolen goods. Now, the operator informs me, he will zoom in on the four as they walk through town in a search for bulges under their clothing, particularly around the waistline — this according to him, is where stolen toys would be concealed. But the boys have jeans and T-shirts on and no bulges are apparent. Still, however, the four are followed by both operators to see if they will pull items out of their pockets; they don't. The four then disappear from view as they enter another department store. The operator looks elsewhere, but comments to his colleague, "They're definitely up to no good."

While youths are generally seen as suspicious and warranting of targeted surveillance, this would still leave CCTV operators with far too many candidates to choose from on the basis of the images alone. Two additional features — attire and posture — become salient for further subdividing youths into those who are worthy of more intensive surveillance and those who are not.

The following garments were thought by operatives to be indicative of the criminal intent of the wearer: "puffer" coats (ski-style fashion), track suit bottoms, designer training shoes, baseball caps (ponytail hairstyles only compounded suspicion), and anything that may conceal the head (a woolly hat, hood or cap) and football shirts or supporter paraphernalia. Any type of loose-fitting jacket could also provoke suspicion because in the operators' eyes it may conceal stolen items or weapons; a jacket or head gear worn in warm weather only compounded suspicion. The following field note extracts illustrate the manner in which a person's visual identity is used to further stigmatise and subclassify the youth population:

01.46: Surveilling the car park the operator finds a suspicious person. This is a white male in his early 20s, dressed casually but expensively. The object of suspicion is the sunglasses he wears. The operator asks himself why a man needs them on at night. Furthermore, the targeted person is leaning against a good (i.e., sporty) car talking to another male. The first male compounds his suspicion further by wearing a leather zip-up bomber jacket, designer trainers and a fashionable haircut. The camera is fixed on him and his colleague as they get into the car and drive away. As they do so, the vehicle registration number is zoomed in on and noted on a pad the operator has with him. The operator keeps his own dossier on "flash cars" and their occupants, and believes such people are all potential drug dealers. (2 minutes, 1 camera)

03.01: A male and a female are noted walking across the car park. Both are white and in their mid-20s. Whilst she is smartly dressed, it is her male companion who arouses the operator's suspicion. The companion has about him the stigmata of criminality — he has a coat on with a hood up. The operator knows it is not raining so cannot understand why (the possibility that it is because it is bitterly cold outside does not appear in his logic). The couple are carefully surveilled as they walk to the railway station, check a railway timetable board, and then retrace their steps and walk out of sight. (4 minutes, 4 cameras)

11.50: A black male, aged around 16, attracts the attention of the operator because of his white cloth cap. Followed and zoomed in on, he has no apparent criminal characteristics, but as the operator states, his attire makes him appear to be a "wide-boy " and therefore worth following. (2 minutes, 1 camera)

00.42: The operator follows two white males, aged 16, dressed casually but with hoods covering their heads on this cold winter night. The operator's suspicion is founded on two things: firstly, they have the ever-incriminating hood up, and secondly, they are walking through an open-air car park whilst apparently too young to drive. The operator sees in them a "result," and as they pass a cluster of parked cars mutters to the screen they are visible on "have a go, have a go". They disappoint him. Whilst followed, they merely walk out of the car park and towards a Council estate. (2 minutes, 1 camera)

There are two issues to note from these examples. First, suspicion is not unidimensional. The background assumptions concerning youths are refined by utilising other visual clues that can be inferred from the clothes of a potential suspect, and this is read in conjunction with temporal and spatial features of a locale. In the surveillance of the couple in the car park, attire is also compounded by place and time — a young man in a car park with his face obscured at three in the morning is unambiguously read as a potential car thief. In the first example, involving the young man with the sunglasses, attire was compounded by accoutrements — a flashy car, and the hour. Implicitly, this form of reasoning is based on a reading of the Protestant work ethic: who can afford to buy an expensive car by the fruits of an honest day's work if they are out enjoying themselves at nearly two o'clock in the morning?

The second point is that wearing headgear is particularly stigmatising in the view of CCTV operators. This has two components. First baseball caps, woolly hats, and hooded parkas were seen as indicative of subcultural affiliation, and thus helped to single out respectable from "deviant" youths. Indeed, sometimes the only distinguishing feature that could justify why one youth, as opposed to another, was targeted for extended surveillance was the presence of baseball caps, particularly if worn with the peak facing backwards. But, more importantly, operators know that hats can potentially deprive them of recording a clear image of a person's face. Knowing this, they act on the assumption that citizens do as well. Operators believe they have a right to surveille any person's face who appears in their territory. Anyone who supports a visible means of denying them this opportunity immediately places himself in the category of persons of questionable intent and worthy of extended surveillance. Moreover, in the eyes of the operator, moving the headgear to deliberately obscure the face merely compounds suspicion, as the following incident reveals:

> *13.13: Three youths are zoomed in on outside Santana's. One has a baseball cap on and elicits suspicion when, in the interpretation of the operator, he adjusts it so as to conceal his identity from the cameras. Whilst standing talking, the three are zoomed in on and when they walk down the street they are followed until out of sight. (3 minutes, 2 cameras).*

It is not just attire that provides a warrant for narrowing down the suspect population. In all sites operators believed in a practise known as the "scrote walk," which was a rather fluid concept reduced to a series of seemingly contradictory clichés:

- Too confident for their own good
- Head up, back straight, upper body moving too much
- Chin down, head down, shuffling along

- Swaggering, looking hard

Suspicion was compounded when a "scrote haircut" was evident. This could be very short, very long, or medium length with hair gel. But to make identification easier, "scrotes" generally could be identified because they hung around in groups.

> *21.45: The operator notices a character who has come to his attention before. Believed to be involved in all sorts of criminal activities, the suspect and his two mates are surveilled and zoomed in on as they stand outside McDonald's. The operators discuss with contempt the characteristics of these three males reserving particular venom for their "swaggering" and "scrote way of walking." However, they have done no wrong for the moment, bar offending the operator with their presence, and so are left alone after they walk through the town. (5 minutes, 1 camera)*

As Kenan Malik (1995:5) reported, in the March 3 edition of *Independent* on the operation of the CCTV in the West End of Newcastle, the selection of youth was also based on such categorisation. The operators told him: "... we keep an eye on them to see if they're up to something. They're the type you see...They're all scrotes round here — petty thieves, vandals, druggies, there's not much that you can do but keep an eye on them" (*Independent*, 9th March, 1995:5).

The selection of youths as potential candidates for targeting rests on the background assumption as to their overpropensity for criminality. This is then refined through the use of visual clues that enable some youths to be identified as belonging to commonsense categories of moral waywardness, and this then gives the warrant for targeted and extended surveillance.

This selective targeting of youth is not just a product of operator assumptions and values; it is also a consequence of operational policy. In Metro City, the police liaison officer informed us that the system was not to be used to target traffic offences or vehicle tax evasion, because this would mitigate against the "feel-good" factor that CCTV was supposed to promote amongst the town centre consumers. This was even echoed in the official codes of practice drafted for another scheme, which stated: "Police...may seek and take control of the system in respect of the following...to prevent or mitigate interruptions to traffic flow (not to enforce minor breaches of traffic law)." In this way, the underrepresentation of older, relatively affluent offenders is enshrined in the system's operating procedures, as they are protected from the full impact of the cameras' gaze. Thus, despite those over age 30 making up around half of the population, they represented only 15% of those subject to targeted surveillance. When they did become targets, in nearly two thirds (62%) of cases it was because of their overt behaviour directly indicating involvement in crime or disorder, and only 21% were targeted for "no obvious reason."

So far we have talked about the processes that make youths the disproportionate targets of surveillance. But, as we have seen, it is not only youths, but black youths in particular who are oversurveilled.

Race

Racist language was not unusual to hear among CCTV operators. Although only used by a minority, the terms "Pakis," "Jungle Bunnies" and "Sooties" when used by some operatives did not produce howls of protests from their colleagues or line managers. Stereotypical negative attitudes towards ethnic minorities and black youths in particular were more widespread. These attitudes ranged from more extreme beliefs, held by a few operators, about these groups' inherent criminality to more general agreement as to their being "work-shy," or "too lazy" to get a job, and in general, "trouble."

Given these assumptions, the sighting of a black face on the streets of either Metro City or County Town would almost automatically produce a targeted surveillance.

10.48: Whilst surfing the cameras and streets, the operator sees two young men standing in a pedestrian shopping precinct, both looking into a hold-all bag one of them is carrying. Whilst this scene is not remarkable, what is unusual is that one of the two is black — a rare sight in the city centre. The two are in their early 20s and smartly dressed. After a minute or so, one hands to the other a piece of paper that most onlookers would presume was an address or phone number. Finally, when going their separate ways, the two indulge in a fashionable "high-five" handshake. This alerts both operators.

To these two, the "high-five" is suspicious because it was not done with flat hands and it "wasn't firm enough." In fact, according to the second operator, one of the men had a distinctly cupped hand. Whilst this was explainable by his holding the piece of paper just given him by the other, the operators see only criminality — this could be a surreptitious yet overtly public exchange of drugs. The youth with the bag is surveilled closely as he continues his walk. He not only has a bag possibly containing the merchandise, but he is also black — a potential drug dealer. The suspect enters a men's fashion store, which means that the camera is now trained on the doors whilst the operator awaits a possible hasty reappearance complete with stolen items in shoulder bag. After a few minutes, the camera is zoomed into the store and the suspect is visible in a capacity the operators did not consider — he is a sales assistant.

As the next example demonstrates, this colour-coded suspicion was intensified when combined with cars or headgear, and when people were in places the operators presumed they should not be.

15.00: A black male with dreadlocks, wearing sports gear and in his mid-20s invites the operators' suspicion and surveillance because he is in the wrong place doing the wrong thing. He is, in fact, crouched by a bicycle rack fiddling about with a bike. Zooming in, the operator looks for evidence of a theft — is he looking around him as he fiddles? No. Is he forcing something that won't move? No. He gets something out of his back pocket that happens to be a bicycle rear lamp. Fitting it on, he rides the bicycle, which is obviously his, safely and legally. (4 minutes, 1 camera)

23.05: A group of 12 black youths, all in their late teens and casually dressed, is noted outside a fast-food outlet. Whilst doing nothing more than eating and talking to various youths — male and female, white and black — who approach them, the operator surveilles them. She is encouraged by the manager of the CCTV system, who instructs her to "watch that lot...our ethnic problem." So the operator follows them for the next 20 minutes as they move up the street. (20 minutes, 1 camera)

14.34: As a former police officer of 10 years' experience, the operator "knows" that young black men are "trouble." When she catches sight of a white escort convertible, complete with wheel trims/spoilers and with its hood down, driven by a black male aged in his mid to late 20s she is alerted enough to zoom in on him. The vehicle is parked and he is chatting to his passenger, a white girl with blonde hair aged in her early 20s. This combination of colour and technology is all too much for the operator. She phones the police controller, explaining that "men of that age and that colour only get their money one way and it's not through hard work," and puts the image onto his monitor. On suspicion of being a drug dealer the operator zooms in on the registration plate whilst police do a PNC [Police National Computer] on the vehicle. Whilst not disclosing fully what he did or is suspected of doing, the controller gets back to the operator to tell her that the driver is "of police interest." The suspect drives away out of sight, unaware of who has been watching and talking about him. (8 minutes, 2 cameras)

The overrepresentation of black youths cannot be simply understood as white operators selecting young black men on the basis of second hand stereotypes. However, as we have seen, some of the white operators targeted blacks with a relish that implied a deep prejudice. Black operators similarly targeted young blacks, but their comments directed at the screen were not usually so venomous. The following example goes some way towards illustrating the point.

19.20: The night shift has inherited a job from the day shift; namely, a group of 15 to 20 black males and females, all in their teens and casually/subculturally dressed, who are standing in a group outside an off-licence and general store called Santana's that is adjacent to a series of bus stops. Zooming in on this group the operator can see nine black males and four black females. The operator, Victor, a black man in his late 50s, is not impressed by this assortment, saying for my and the other operator's benefit that the police should round 'em up and get their mums and dads to come and fetch 'em and shame them. The group is generally standing, talking, and flirting, with the occasional bout of horseplay and dancing. The youths harass no one. Nearby are standing dozens of people awaiting one of the 12 bus routes that pick up at this point. Even so, the camera remains on the group for 30 minutes and then notices a group of eight black males in their early 20s who walk through the gathering and continue elsewhere. Two of this group then split off, and the operator decides to follow the remaining six but is thwarted when they walk out of range of the cameras. (51 minutes, 4 cameras)

02.00: Standing outside the all-night shop are three black males in their 30s. One has the stigma of being a Rastafarian and having a woolly hat balancing on long dreadlocks. The operator is confused and tells his co-operator of his dilemma: why are they still out at night and not buying anything? The answer: they don't work, they just sleep all day. With mutual disgust the two black operators watch these black men as they stand and talk and then drive away in a car. (5 minutes, 1 camera)

However, in Inner City, the selection of black youths was not just a matter of operator discretion but a deliberate matter of policy. The first weeks of operation saw the police officer responsible for setting up the scheme give advice to both shifts on where and what to watch. The priority target was stated to be black youths and the priority crimes drug dealing and street robbery. This effectively meant that the majority of the cameras were never really monitored, since they covered the more general shopping area. Instead, for the purposes of target selection, attention was focussed almost solely on a junction that housed a row of bus stops and a number of small shops that daily after school closing saw a congregation of black youths alighting from and awaiting buses to take them home.

Male youths, particularly if black or stereotypically associated with the underclass, represent the fodder of CCTV systems. But this overrepresentation is not justified on the basis of those subsequently arrested. While teenagers accounted for 39% of targeted surveillance, they only made up 18% of those arrested, whereas those in their 20s accounted for 46% of targeted surveillance but made up 82% of all arrests. Similarly, black people accounted for 32% of targeted surveillance but only 9% of those arrested.

Gender

While women make up 52% of the general population they only accounted for 7% of primary persons surveilled. Women were almost invisible to the cameras unless they were reported as known shoplifters by store detectives (33%) or because of overt disorderly conduct (31%). Nor were women more likely to became targets by virtue of a protectional gaze. Indeed, in nearly 600 hours of observation only one woman was targeted for protectional purposes — as she walked to and from a bank cash dispenser. Moreover, there was evidence that the same attitudes that have traditionally been associated with the police occupational culture surrounding domestic violence continue to inform the operation of CCTV.

Shortly after 01.00 a.m. the operator notices a couple in the street having an animated row. Both are white, in their late 20s and stylishly dressed as if returning from a night out. This quiet Monday night has produced nothing of interest, and these two arguing is the most interesting event of the past three hours. This and the fact that the woman in view is blond and good looking has added to the attraction. The operator tells the Comm Room staff (two men) to have a look at the event unfolding.

After a two-minute argument the woman storms off up the street, but does not go out of the man's sight and slumps against a wall looking miserable. The man, meanwhile, climbs into a nearby car, closes the door and waits in the driver's seat, lights off. The impasse lasts five minutes, the female walks slowly towards the car and begins to talk to the man via the driver's window, only to storm off again after a minute. This time the male follows her on foot to continue the row. The operators and police enter into a commentary urging the man not to chase after her. Having decided she is hot-tempered and sulky, the operator says aloud "You hit her and we'll be your witnesses."

The couple continue their debate and this time the female decides to walk off past the man. but as she does so he attempts to restrain her by holding her arm. She pulls back. In the stand-off further words are exchanged, and a blow is aimed from the male to the female that strikes her around the upper chest and causes her to stumble. The blow does not look to be a hard one and she picks herself up and walks away. Meanwhile the male returns to his car and once again sits and waits. This time the female walks down the street past the car and continues for 20 yards only to stop, walk back to the car and stand looking into it.

After a couple of minutes of her looking and him pretending not to notice the pair resume their chat, this time via the passenger door. The drama continues when she walks away again. This time the distance is only 10 yards. Then she does an about-turn and, returning to the car, opens the front passenger door. Whilst she sits in the car she leaves the door wide open. After a mutual silence (seen by zooming the camera into the car's windscreen), the pair decide to talk again. This time she lasts three minutes before getting out and storming off.

By now other personnel have appeared to watch this drama. Two other officers have entered the room so that six men can now, in pantomime mode, boo and cheer good moves and bad moves. One boo is reserved for the male when he starts up the car, does a three-point turn, drives up to where she is sulking, and, parking, tries to persuade her to get it. A cheer goes up when he has seemingly failed in this effort and so drives away. But cheers turn to boos when he reverses to resume his persuasion. His words work and, to boos, she climbs into the car. After a four-minute discussion, the stationary car drives away into the distance. (25 minutes, 2 cameras).

As this incident makes clear, there is no simple correspondence between the discovery of criminal activity and the resulting deployment and arrest. Lesser assaults, when perpetrated by men on men outside nightclubs, resulted in police officers being deployed and arrests being made. However, the images from the screen are filtered through an organisational lens that accords meaning, status, and priority to events. It will come as no surprise to critics of the police handling of domestic violence (Edwards, 1989; Stanko, 1985) that the existence of "objective" evidence led to neither a protective response in the first instance to prevent the assault from occurring nor, once it had occurred, a legalistic response to arrest the perpetrator. As Edwards has argued, the police have always concerned themselves more with public order than private violence, and this was deemed as essentially a private matter, albeit occurring in public space.

Moreover, this example gives credence to Brown's (1998) assertion that the essentially male gaze of CCTV has little relevance for the security of women in town centres, and may indeed undermine it by offering the rhetoric of security rather than providing the reality. CCTV also fosters a male gaze in the more conventional and voyeuristic sense: with its pan-tilt and zoom facilities, the thighs and cleavages of scantily clad women are an easy target for those male operators so motivated. Indeed, 10% of all targeted surveillances on women and 15% of operator-initiated surveillance on women were for voyeuristic reasons, which outnumbered protective surveillance by five to one. Moreover, the long-understood relationship between cars and sex provides operators and police with other chances for titillation, as illustrated by the following example.

01.00: On the first night shift the operator is keen to show me all his job entails. Eventually I am taken, via the camera, to "Shaggers Alley," an area of a car park near the railway station used by local prostitutes and their punters (customers). Whilst this location is out of the way to passers-by, many a punter and indeed a happy couple not involved in a financial transaction are unaware of the reach of the all-seeing camera, whose job is facilitated by a large and powerful car park light that does not leave much to the imagination of the observer.

Clearly visible on this night thanks to the cameras' ability to zoom in and look into cars, is a male in his late 20s sitting in the driver's seat with what can only be described as an expression of glee as a female, kneeling on the passenger seat performs fellatio on him. Her hair and head are noticeably bouncing up and down for around two minutes. When the performance is over the woman is clearly visible, topless, in the front seat. From beginning to end this scenario is put onto the police monitor, with the operator informing me that the police officers in the communications office enjoy such scenarios and, when bored, will sometimes phone to ask him to put the cameras on Shaggers Alley for their titillation. (11 minutes, 1 camera).

In one of our sites, the "appreciation" of such public displays was a regular feature of the night shift and not just confined to those with access to the monitors. Many such encounters could be found on the "Shaggers Alley greatest hits tape," which was compiled and replayed for the benefit of those who had missed the "entertainment."

DISCRETION, DIFFERENTIATION AND DISCRIMINATION

The power of CCTV operators is highly discretionary as they have extraordinary latitude in determining who will be watched, for how long and whether to initiate deployment. The sum total of these individual discretionary judgments produces, as we have shown, a highly differentiated pattern of surveillance leading to a massively disproportionate targeting of young males, particularly if they are black or visibly identifiable as having subcultural affiliations. As this differentiation is not based on objective behavioural and individualised criteria, but merely on being categorised as part of a particular social group, such practices are clearly discriminatory.

Of course, it may be argued that since those officially recorded as deviant — young, male, black, and working class — are disproportionately represented, targeting such groups merely reflects the underlying reality of the distribution of criminality. Such an argument is, however, circular: the production of the official statistics is also based on preconceived assumptions as to the distribution of criminality, which itself leads to the particular configuration of formal and informal operational police practice. As self-report studies of crime reveal, offending is, in fact, far more evenly distributed throughout the population than reflected in the official statistics (Coleman and Moynihan, 1996). Indeed, race and class differentials, so marked in the official statistics, disappear when self-reported offending behaviour of juveniles is examined (Bowling et al., 1994). Thus, McConville et al. (1991:35) argue, the convicted population "is a subset of the official suspect population. Whilst convicted criminals may be broadly representative of suspects, there is good reason to believe that they are very dissimilar to the 'real criminal population.' The make up of the convicted population is, therefore, like the make up of the suspect population: a police construction."

Another argument is that even if there is differentiation in target selection, it is irrelevant because it does not result in actual intervention and therefore no "real" discrimination occurs. As our own results clearly show, even though teenagers make up 39% of those targeted they constitute only 23% of those deployed against and 18% of the arrested population. Thus, we would respond that on effectiveness measures alone, such targeting is inefficient, but we would also challenge the notion that it is irrelevant. Just because no intervention or arrest results does not mean that a significant social interaction, albeit remote and technologically mediated, has not taken place. Imagine two youths who, on entering city centre space, are immediately picked up by the cameras. They notice the first camera moving to track them as they move through the streets and go out of range of one camera. At the same time, another camera is seen altering its position to bring them into view. In fact, wherever they go they can see cameras being repositioned to monitor their every movement. How do these youths feel? They have done nothing wrong, they have not drawn attention to themselves by their behaviour and they are not "known offenders." But they are being treated as a threat, as people who cannot be trusted, as persons who do not belong, as unwanted outsiders. The guarantee that such systems will show no interest or engage in deliberate monitoring of people going about their daily business is empty rhetoric.

This technologically mediated and distanced social interaction is, then, loaded with meaning. Moreover, for literally thousands of black and working-class youths, however law-abiding, it transmits a wholly negative message about their position in society. But it has wider consequences than just its impact on individual psychology. The central tenet of policing by consent — that policing is viewed as legitimate by those who experience it — is undermined. If social groups experience CCTV surveillance as an extension of discriminatory and unjust policing, the consequential loss of legitimacy may have disastrous consequences for social order. As Brogden et al. (1988:90) have argued, it was precisely this experience of unjust policing that was both the "underlying cause and the trigger of all the urban riots of the 1980s."

Acknowledgements: We gratefully acknowledge the support of the Economic and Social Research Council who gave substance to the first author's initial interest in CCTV by funding a project on CCTV, Surveillance and Social Control (Grant no: L210252023) under its Crime and Social Order Programme. This enabled the second author to work full-time studying the operation of CCTV control rooms. We would also like to thank the various colleagues who have helped in bringing this project to fruition, especially Keith Bottomley, Clive Coleman, Jason Ditton, Jade Moran, Nigel Norris and Malcolm Young.

Address correspondence to: Clive Norris, Centre for Criminology and Criminal Justice, University of Hull, Hull, HU6 7RX, United Kingdom.

REFERENCES

Bowling, B., J. Graham and A. Ross (1994). "Self-Reported Offending among Young People in England and Wales." In: J. Junger-Tas, G. J. Terlouw and M. Klein (eds.), *Delinquent Behaviour Among Young People in the Western World.* Amsterdam, NETH: Kugler.

Brogden, M., T. Jefferson and S. Walklate (1988). *Introducing Policework.* London, UK: Unwin Hyman.

Brown, S. (1998). "What's the Problem, Girls? CCTV and the Gendering of Public Safety." In: C. Norris, J. Moran and G. Armstrong (eds.), *Surveillance, Closed Circuit Television and Social Control.* Aldershot, UK: Ashgate.

Bulos, M. and D. Grant (1996). *Towards a Safer Sutton? CCTV One Year On.* London, UK: London Borough of Sutton.

—— and C. Sarno (1996). *Codes of Practice and Public Closed Circuit Television Systems.* London, UK: Local Government Information Unit.

Coleman, C. and J. Moynihan (1996). *Understanding Crime Data.* Milton Keynes, UK: Open University Press.

Ditton, J. and E. Short (1998). "Evaluating Scotland's First Town Centre CCTV Scheme." In: C. Norris, J. Moran, and G. Armstrong (eds.), *Surveillance, Closed Circuit Television and Social Control.* Aldershot, UK: Ashgate.

Edwards, S. (1989). *Policing "Domestic" Violence.* London, UK: Sage.

Graham, S. (1998). "Towards the Fifth Utility? On the Extension and Normalisation of Public CCTC." In: C. Norris, J. Moran and G. Armstrong (eds.), *Surveillance, Closed Circuit Television and Social Control.* Aldershot, UK: Ashgate.

McConville, M., A. Sanders and R. Leng (1991). *The Case for the Prosecution.* London, UK: Routledge.

Norris, C. and G. Armstrong (1997). *The Unforgiving Eye: CCTV Surveillance in Public Space.* Mimeo. Hull, UK: Centre for Criminology and Criminal Justice, University of Hull.

—— and G. Armstrong (1999). *The Maximum Surveillance Society.* Oxford, UK: Berg.

Sacks, H. (1978). "Notes on Police Assessment of Moral Character." In: J. Maanen and P.K. Manning (eds.), *Policing: A View from the Street.* New York, NY: Random House.

Short, E. and J. Ditton (1996). *Does Closed Circuit Television Prevent Crime?* Edinburgh, SCOT: Central Research Unit, Scottish Office.

Skinns, D. (1998). "Crime Reduction, Diffusion and Displacement: Evaluation of the Effectiveness of CCTV". In: C. Norris, J. Moran and G. Armstrong (eds.), *Surveillance, Closed Circuit Television and Social Control.* Aldershot, UK: Ashgate.

Squires, P. and L. Measor (1996). *Closed Circuit TV Surveillance and Crime Prevention in Brighton: Half Yearly Report.* Brighton, UK: University of Brighton.

Stanko, E. (1985). *Intimate Intrusions: Women's Experience of Male Violence.* London, UK: Routledge and Kegan Paul.

Tilley, N. (1993). *Understanding Car Parks, Crime and CCTV.* (Crime Prevention Unit Series Paper, #42.) London, UK: Home Office.

EVALUATING "REALISTIC EVALUATION": EVIDENCE FROM A STUDY OF CCTV

by

Martin Gill

and

Vicky Turbin
Scarman Centre, University of Leicester, UK

Abstract: *This paper examines a new evaluation methodology developed by Pawson and Tilley (1997) that they term "realistic evaluation." A small-scale evaluation of closed circuit television (CCTV) in two retail stores is used to illustrate the practical use of the methodology and to demonstrate the strengths and weaknesses of this approach. The study offers guidelines to other researchers about potential pitfalls in conducting a realistic evaluation. Some conclusions are presented about the possible impact of CCTV within a retail environment. The paper concludes that the Pawson and Tilley methodology shows great promise for future evaluations. It highlights the point that an apparent failure to affect crime levels (using statistical measures) may still generate other benefits if the research is designed within the realistic evaluation framework.*

INTRODUCTION

Evaluations of crime prevention measures have been characterised by an almost frantic search for what "works." This proliferation of research has examined all aspects of crime prevention, particularly measures such as closed circuit television (CCTV), electronic article surveillance (EAS), Neighbourhood Watch and so on (Bamfield, 1994; Beck and Willis, 1994, 1995; Brown, 1995; Gill, 1994, 1998; Handford, 1994; Husain, 1988; Laycock and Tilley, 1995; Short and Ditton, 1995). Over the last few years there have been growing calls for a change in the way evaluations are conducted (Ekblom and Pease, 1995; Tilley, 1993). This is partly a result of the disillusionment that accompanied evaluations of various high-profile crime prevention measures. Often these studies produce conflicting results (Davies, 1996; Graham et al., 1996; Horne, 1996; Short and Ditton, 1995; Tilley, 1997). Some studies conclude that a particular measure may have had an impact, whilst others are unable to corroborate such results. From the morass of conflicting results it has become all too easy to conclude that "nothing works."

Recently, a different approach to evaluation has been developed by Pawson and Tilley (1992, 1997) that they term "realistic evaluation." This approach differs from previous evaluations by stressing the need to evaluate crime prevention measures within their "context," and to ask what "mechanisms" are acting to produce which "outcomes." Previous evaluation methodologies have tended to focus primarily on the outcome of an evaluation to the detriment of the mechanism and context aspects. Few studies have as yet used this new approach, though it was used retrospectively to examine car parks and CCTV (Tilley, 1993) and has been used partially by other studies (e.g., Brown, 1995). This paper focuses on a small-scale evaluation of CCTV in two retail stores to illustrate how this methodology might be applied, and to demonstrate possible strengths and weaknesses of this new approach.[1]

Realistic Evaluation and Context

Evaluating any crime prevention measure is notoriously difficult. Policymakers and practitioners want quick decisions about whether a measure has been "effective" or has reduced crime, while academics stress the need to do things properly, which takes time. Over the last few years there has been a growing awareness that evaluations should attempt to determine *how* the crime prevention measure has had an impact. It is no longer enough just to say that it did have an impact. Hope (1991:242) touches on this point when he says "It is not sufficient merely to count crime; the value of crime pattern analysis for prevention lies in being able to examine the context in which incidents take place so as to make inferences about how such crime might have been prevented and how similar ones might be avoided in the future."

It was from this growing realisation of the importance of the context in which a crime prevention measure is placed that led to the development of the realistic approach. Realistic evaluation is really a consideration of how a measure affects something, rather than simply whether it works or not. Pawson and Tilley (1997) have broken this question down into three main investigative areas. First, is the context in which the system is expected to impact. This relates to the conditions needed to trigger mechanisms to produce particular outcome patterns. Second, is the 'mechanisms' through which the system might achieve its impact. This relates to what it is about the measure that might lead it to produce a particular result in a certain context. So, in the case of CCTV, one example of a mechanism could be that CCTV decreases criminal activity by helping staff to observe more offenders. Finally, the "outcome" of introducing the measure is explored. This relates to the observed result of introducing the measure, that is, what impact it has had. This is the one area that most previous evaluations have focused almost exclusively on by analysing crime or loss figures. Pawson and Tilley suggest that the three elements of context, mechanism and outcome should be related in the form of a pseudo equation — Context + Mechanism = Outcome — that they term a CMO configuration. This can then be tested by gathering data appropriate to each of the three elements.

The main strength of the realistic approach is its attempt to link specific contexts to mechanisms in a way that has perhaps not been considered quite so thoroughly before.[2] This has important implications for businesses. The ability to extrapolate accurately from one evaluation to decide matters of security policy on a company-wide basis is both important and costly for businesses. Sometimes, results from evaluations are used by managers to assess how appropriate a particular technology is to solve their crime problem. More often, there is no adequate evaluation before such a decision is made. Yet there is no guarantee that the results of one study will have any relevance for a different location or context. The commonsense observation that what has an impact in site A may not necessarily have an impact in site B has, to a large extent, been ignored by previous research that focuses largely on collecting figures to show whether the measure has worked at all. The main issue is not so much whether the measure worked but rather how it did so or, conversely, why it failed to work when logic indicated that it should, or as Pawson and Tilley (1997) state, "what works, for whom and in what circumstances." Eventually, of course, the result of conducting evaluations in a realistic manner should be that the contexts that do not trigger certain mechanisms (and, vice versa, those that do) are identified, providing a useful base of knowledge for crime prevention practitioners.

THE CCTV PROJECT

This research project had two aims. First, to examine the impact of introducing CCTV in two retail stores, and, second, to examine the practicalities of using realistic evaluation as an evaluation methodology. This paper focuses on the second of these two aims (for a discussion of the first, see Gill and Turbin, 1998). The research was conducted in a medium-sized jeans and casual clothing retailer over a 12-month period. The company has 10 stores and employs over 250 people in the U.K.

The research was designed to examine several mechanisms through which CCTV might be having an effect. However, the mechanisms chosen for testing were by necessity limited, and with hindsight some may not have been sufficiently well defined. The research has demonstrated that there is a need for flexibility during the data-gathering period so that new mechanisms can be explored as they arise. To gain consensus about which mechanisms were appropriate, suggestions were gathered from academics, retailers and installers, and by building upon Tilley's (1993) work on car parks and CCTV. Each of the mechanisms is explored in the following sections. Obviously, these mechanisms do not cover all the possible ways in which CCTV might have an impact in stores. Indeed, some of the mechanisms proved to be irrelevant, others were too difficult to obtain data on, whilst a new mechanism was proposed as a result of the research.

DATA COLLECTION

The two stores used for the study were located in Leeds and in Sheffield. The project involved collecting data, installing CCTV and collecting data, and removing CCTV and collecting data during a 12-month period. Four main sources provided data: customers, staff, shop thieves and regular stocktakes. A total of 480 customers were interviewed (120 customers at each store both before and during CCTV installation). In addition, staff at both stores were interviewed three times: before the CCTV was installed, whilst CCTV was in store and after CCTV was removed from the store. Interviews were also conducted with 38 shop thieves. Five were from the probation services while 31 were recruited via snowball sampling. The remaining two offenders were already participating in similar research with the retail company. Clearly, the shop thieves we interviewed are not a representative sample, though this would be impossible anyway since many are never caught or never admit all the offences they have carried out. But the aim was to gain an insight into the offenders' rationale regarding security measures. The offenders' views could then be related to the other data from customers, staff and stocktakes to obtain a broader picture of the potential impact of CCTV.[3]

The findings presented here provide only a brief summary of results, since the emphasis of this paper is on the evaluation methodology rather than the impact of CCTV. For a fuller description of general security issues, the reader is referred to the first paper (Gill and Turbin, 1998).

GENERAL CONTEXTUAL ISSUES

One of the most important aspects of the realistic approach is the emphasis it places on understanding the context in which mechanisms operate (or do not operate). Gaining evidence about contextual issues is not always easy. The copious amount of data available means that important aspects may be unintentionally missed. This study chose to examine general contextual issues by interviewing staff members in some depth. It is recognised that this narrow focus may miss locational or other contextual aspects, but with the time-frame and resources available this was felt to be the best approach to give useful background data.

Staff interviews were wide-ranging, covering attitudes towards various types of security measure and experiences of crimes at work. Interviews lasted about one hour per staff member and all were tape-recorded. In total, 25 staff were interviewed before CCTV was installed (i.e., all staff at that time), and this figure rose to 27 with the CCTV in stores. After CCTV was removed only nine staff were interviewed, but these had all been interviewed twice previously. This innovative approach was designed to examine changes in staff perceptions during the study period.

Two main issues arose from staff interviews and visits to the store. The first was that the two stores experienced similar crime problems but the frequency differed between Leeds and Sheffield. Shop theft was the biggest concern to all staff, greater than physical assault or verbal abuse, and this was linked to the frequency with which shop theft was perceived to occur. Unsurprisingly, there was a higher level of concern expressed by staff who dealt with more incidents of shop theft. Staff at Leeds, however, claimed to have apprehended more shoplifters and more frequently than those in Sheffield. Overall, shop theft was perceived to occur more than once a week by both Leeds and Sheffield staff.

The interviews also revealed that although shop theft is a common problem and one that caused considerable concern, some staff were choosing not to confront shop thieves. This was due to a variety of reasons, such as fear for personal safety, a general lack of awareness, or a belief that support was lacking from other staff (possibly due to low staffing levels). In addition, some staff mentioned their frustration at being unable to do anything about regular shop thieves, who often taunted them. Some blamed the company policy towards shop thieves for being too lenient. A comment included:

> The policy here is just to take the garments off them and ask them to leave, which to be quite honest, I think is really lame. It's not nearly enough of a slap on the wrist for them.

Staff recounted incidents of quite open intimidation, particularly when shop thieves were in groups. Indeed, staff at Leeds had even nicknamed one group the "Bash Street Kids" because they were such frequent visitors. It appears that some thieves were quite aware of the limitations of what staff could do and were willing to test authority to see how much they could get away with.

The second issue was that although staff on the whole welcomed the introduction of CCTV to the stores, there were some fears expressed that management would use the cameras to "spy" on them (a belief that was later justified by their subsequent use). This was predominantly a product of the Sheffield store, where over half the staff admitted to worries about the proposed installation of CCTV. However, despite these concerns, it is notable that staff had high expectations of the effectiveness of CCTV in reducing both violence towards staff and shop theft.

Finally, it is important to stress that the company had chosen the camera system to be a deterrent, rather than an aid to catch or prosecute offenders. Therefore, the monitors were larger than normal (28"), with good picture clarity, and were specially positioned to be clearly visible (by being hung down low in the shop). The camera output was recorded on tape but not constantly monitored. The company policy towards shoplifters was to approach and offer service in an attempt to deter them, and directly challenge them only if they exited with an unpaid-for item. Hence, it should be noted that the CCTV could not really be expected to have an impact on catching or prosecuting offenders, as this was not the outcome that the cameras were designed for or used to achieve.

The issue of context is obviously more complicated than the picture that emerged from our data collection. More could have been made of the context issue, and this is something for other researchers to be aware of. However, all evaluations should at least make some attempt to identify points about context that may be crucial to the setting in motion of particular mechanisms. In this case, staff attitudes towards the camera system and expectations about its effectiveness were shown to be potentially important contextual issues. It was noted that the system design will limit the mechanisms that are triggered, and this must also be recognised.

TESTING THE CMO CONFIGURATIONS

The following section describes the results of testing CMO configurations. While the mechanisms were proposed before the data collection began, they were not directly related to contexts or potential outcomes in the manner of CMO configurations. The CMO configurations were derived after the data were collected and analysed. This is perhaps one of the weaknesses of the realistic approach, namely, that you need a very good understanding of the processes involved in order to postulate appropriate mechanisms before the research begins. General CMO configurations can be quite easily identified, but the less obvious ones may well be missed or inadequate data collected to confirm or reject them because they were identified too late.

The following CMO configurations are presented either because the data strongly supported them or because they raise important points about the methodology. However, they are not exhaustive and the reader is referred to the original report for an examination of all the mechanisms tested.

(1) CONTEXT	+	MECHANISM	=	OUTCOME
Staff feel intimidated by shop thieves and lack confidence to challenge them		CCTV may give staff more confidence to approach suspects		By approaching shop thieves they are deterred from stealing and this reduces overall theft

This mechanism proposed that CCTV might give staff more confidence to approach offenders. The outcome of this would be that overall theft would decline as more shop thieves are deterred from stealing. The context in which this mechanism is triggered is one where staff feel intimidated and are not challenging known or suspected offenders. Evidence from interviews indicated that some staff did appear to gain confidence from the presence of in-store cameras. Staff reported feeling more comfortable with cameras there to back them up in confrontational situations. Some illustrative comments included:

> It's quite scary being on the shop floor on your own. If a big group of lads come in and you're on your own, at least you know you've got the cameras to back you up.

> The incident that I spoke about, I actually felt a lot safer with the camera being there, simply because if anything did happen then, I kept saying to him "Look, you wanna calm down, everything's being recorded and it's all on tape." Whether he'd have gone any further without the camera there I don't know, but I think personally I just felt a lot more comfortable with it being there.

> It makes me feel a lot more comfortable in doing my job.

> You know it's [CCTV] there if anything is going to happen. It just makes you feel, you know, more comfortable approaching the situation.

The cameras appeared to provide a backup in several ways. First, by indicating to the offender that they were on camera, staff felt that they had more control over the situation. This also provided them with the power to threaten suspects with taped evidence of their behaviour, irrespective of whether the cameras had recorded the incident — it was the immediate threat of taped evidence that was important. Even if staff were unsure or had not directly seen an act of shop theft, they had more confidence to challenge suspicious individuals. Though CCTV cannot in any physical way intervene to aid staff in a dispute, in psychological terms it may give staff more confidence. If CCTV acts as a reassurance to staff, it may positively affect their decision to approach shop thieves. Even if they are not being prosecuted the fact that they are challenged may, in itself, be a deterrent (particularly as many may not have been challenged before).

This mechanism is, of course, only activated when the context is appropriate. In this case it was apparent from the staff interviews that some staff did feel intimidated by shop thieves. However, the mechanism may not work in a store where staff are already confident in approaching suspects, or where it is not seen as their responsibility to do so (where there is a security guard or store detectives or perhaps where staff refuse to become involved for other reasons).

(2) CONTEXT	+ MECHANISM	= OUTCOME
Staff perceive CCTV, on its own, to be effective against shop theft	CCTV may decrease staff vigilance as they begin to rely on it	Theft levels increase as the surveillance by staff is reduced

The second CMO configuration proposed that if staff believe CCTV to be effective, then having cameras in the store may actually increase theft because staff rely on the system to deal with shop thieves. Theft then increases because staff surveillance and intervention is reduced. Interviews with staff both before and during the installation of CCTV demonstrated that they had very high expectations of its ability to reduce shop theft or violence towards staff. Though there was some degree of disillusionment once staff had experienced the cameras in action, the majority still felt that CCTV was effective at reducing shop theft.[4] Thus, the appropriate context was present for this mechanism to be triggered.

Evidence for this mechanism was qualitative. It highlights a potential problem with the realistic approach when attempting to link the theory to applying the approach in practice. While it is possible to propose a plausible CMO such as this one (and, indeed, proposing CMO configurations alone is an important development), the specificity of the proposition can make data collection problematic. So, for example, although it is not difficult to obtain data on staff perceptions of CCTV, it is far more difficult to assess whether staff vigilance actually begins to decrease. Of course, this is more a realisation of the limits of data collection than a criticism of the realistic approach. But, the approach does require far more stringent data collection if the theory is to be translated into confirmed results.

The approach taken in this project towards mechanism two was indirect. It relied on staff interviews to assess changing perceptions during the three interview phases (aided considerably by tape-recording all the interviews). We were looking to see if the staff used the CCTV system and if they provided any comments about reduced responsibilities after it was introduced. The findings suggested that before the cameras were introduced, some staff welcomed them because they felt they would no longer have to deal with shop thieves. But after they had experienced in-store CCTV and realised that no one would be constantly monitoring the system for them, staff seemed to come to accept that the cameras were an additional aid for them to tackle offenders. In addition, staff actively used the monitors to observe customers and suspicious individuals. Indeed, it is quite plausible that the reverse CMO configuration might be true — that staff vigilance increases with in-store cameras, at least initially.[5] Since the CCTV tapes were used for training purposes and were considered quite an exciting new feature, staff appeared to gain a heightened awareness of security issues during the time cameras were in the stores.

(3) CONTEXT +	MECHANISM =	OUTCOME
Customer satisfaction could be increased	CCTV is used as a management tool to increase customer satisfaction	More customers frequent the store as a result and provide natural surveillance

The third CMO configuration suggested that CCTV could be used as a management tool to increase customer satisfaction. More customers would then frequent the store as a result and therefore provide more natural surveillance.[6] This mechanism would be triggered only in a situation where customer satisfaction was low or could be increased by staff/customer care. Though concerned primarily with CCTV's impact on theft, the company was also understandably keen to ensure that the cameras did not deter genuine customers and result in lost sales. The evidence for this mechanism is not conclusive. Although the interviews suggested that CCTV was being managed in a way that was designed to increase customer satisfaction, there was no objective evidence to show if customer satisfaction did in fact increase.

Managers of both stores used the CCTV system to monitor how staff were dealing with customers (a fact that caused some initial friction in one of the stores and realised fears expressed by staff prior to the installation of CCTV). Many staff claimed to use the monitors to see where customers were in the store and to offer service if necessary. Some staff claimed that the monitors were particularly useful when the store was short-staffed, as they could monitor sections other than the one they were required to oversee. Management also used CCTV footage to identify times when more staff were required to manage particular sections. However, we do not know if customer satisfaction did increase. The ped-flow (number of customers entering) did not increase significantly while cameras were in the store. But as CMOs seven and eight show, most customers did not dislike the cameras and indeed the majority welcomed them. So, the results suggest that the proposed context and mechanism are probable, but there is little evidence to link the proposed outcome to these two elements. This CMO configuration is not proven and requires further analysis.

(4) CONTEXT	+ MECHANISM	= OUTCOME
Suspicious behaviour is not being observed by staff.	By observing the CCTV monitors, staff are effectively deployed to areas where suspicious behaviour is occurring.	Staff act as a visual deterrent and can apprehend offenders if necessary.

The fourth CMO configuration proposed that CCTV might allow the effective deployment of staff to areas where suspicious behaviour was occurring. They could then act as a visible deterrent and could help apprehend offenders. This mechanism would only work in a context where staff are not noticing suspicious behaviour because of observation problems. It was clear that staff did use the CCTV system to monitor suspected shop thieves, and most claimed to be able to identify either suspicious activity or known shop thieves. Staff tended to observe suspicious activities using the CCTV and then intervene if necessary by taking a service approach; by asking, "Can I help you?," for example. It is possible to conclude that CCTV did help staff to identify and deter individuals behaving suspiciously, but this was not necessarily linked to a particular location. Again, this demonstrates the need for flexibility with mechanisms so that they can be further refined in light of the evidence obtained. However, it is interesting to note how CCTV was used in an additional role of customer care and sales rather than simply in its crime prevention role.

(5) CONTEXT	+	MECHANISM	=	OUTCOME
In-store trouble spots are not well-known to staff		By viewing the CCTV monitors, the staff may be better able to identify trouble spots		Trouble spots can be monitored by staff to reduce losses from that area

The fifth CMO configuration takes a slightly different angle to the previous one. It suggests that CCTV might aid in the identification of in-store trouble spots. These could then be monitored by staff to reduce losses from that particular area. The context in which this mechanism would work is one where staff are not aware of trouble spots in the store. Again, the evidence for this CMO was not conclusive. Though staff did use the monitors to look at suspicious individuals, they did not relate this consciously to any particular area. This is because staff already knew where the trouble spots were (e.g., hidden corners, areas from which large amounts of stock had previously been stolen, etc.). Indeed, staff in both stores were very consistent about where the problem areas were. Thus, there was no incentive to try to use the monitors for this purpose. It is still open to testing to see if this mechanism might work in a different store where the context should facilitate it (i.e., where trouble spots are unidentified).

(6) CONTEXT	+	MECHANISM	=	OUTCOME
Prosecution of shop thieves is rarely sought because of lack of clear evidence		Recorded CCTV pictures may be used as evidence for the prosecution of offenders		CCTV evidence allows more successful convictions, and therefore reduces the number of active shop thieves and acts as a deterrent to others

The sixth CMO configuration considers whether CCTV works by providing evidence that can be used for the prosecution of offenders. It requires a context where shop thieves are not routinely prosecuted because there is a lack of clear evidence. The outcome is that more offenders would be prosecuted using CCTV evidence than before, thereby reducing their activity in the store, and that this might act as a deterrent to other shop thieves. The first point is obviously that the mechanism involves two factors. First, the system must record evidence of sufficient quality to be used for prosecution. Second, the incident must also have been observed by staff either at the time or on the tapes afterwards, so that the tapes are stored and used. It is also helpful if the thief is detained in store at the time, though not absolutely necessary as the following two incidents demonstrate.

During the time that cameras were in the stores, two individuals were prosecuted after taped evidence was taken by the police. The first incident involved a shop thief who was captured on CCTV but not detained at the time of the incident in the store. However, the tape was passed on to the police. The same offender was caught a few days later attempting to steal from a chemist's shop and was recognised by the police as the individual on the CCTV tape. When confronted with this evidence she admitted the theft and was subsequently prosecuted. The second incident involved a male shop thief who stole two jackets from the Leeds store. One of the sales assistants viewed the tape later, recognised the offender and was able to give the police his name.

(7) CONTEXT	+	MECHANISM	=	OUTCOME
Customers dislike store surveillance		Customers notice the CCTV monitors		CCTV may decrease sales if customers dislike the store surveillance. Fewer customers results in less natural surveillance

(8) CONTEXT	+	MECHANISM	=	OUTCOME
Customers like store surveillance		Customers notice the CCTV monitors		CCTV may increase sales if customers like the store surveillance and feel safer. More customers results in increased natural surveillance.

We cannot determine to what extent the CCTV tapes alone were responsible for these prosecutions. The two incidents suggest that taped evidence was useful in the offenders' detection but not necessarily in their prosecution. However, it should be noted that the company policy throughout the trial was to deter individuals rather than prosecute. Considering that most staff claimed that they could identify regular thieves, it remains open to conjecture how much impact could have been achieved if CCTV was actively managed to catch and prosecute such persistent offenders. We can conclude, however, that this CMO configuration is a viable path through which theft could be reduced, though it was not promoted in the trial stores.

The seventh CMO configuration suggested that sales might be decreased if customers disliked the store surveillance. This assumes a context in which the majority of customers dislike store surveillance and would alter their shopping behaviour if it were present in the store. The outcome is that customers will shop elsewhere, thereby reducing both sales and levels of natural surveillance. However, as we saw with CMO three, it is debatable whether this would actually increase or decrease theft levels. Although natural surveillance may be decreased with fewer customers, this may be balanced by the fact that staff are more able to monitor the remaining customers and to observe suspicious activity.[7] The eighth CMO configuration is really just a reversal of the seventh. It proposes that sales may increase if customers feel that the store is a safe and secure place to shop, which will in turn lead to an increased level of natural surveillance. Again, this only works if customers both notice the CCTV cameras in the store and find their presence reassuring.

There was strong evidence from interviews with 480 customers that, firstly, the majority do not notice security measures, and, secondly, they do not dislike them. Indeed, only 35% of the sampled shoppers noticed the CCTV (n=84), leaving 65% who did not. In terms of liking or disliking the cameras, of 480 customers interviewed the majority (70%, n=336) welcomed CCTV and expressed no worries about its presence. Only 4.8% (n=23) of the sample claimed to be worried by the presence of in-store CCTV, usually saying they would not like it in the changing rooms or that it made them feel uncomfortable. The remainder claimed to have "no opinion." The study found qualitative evidence that certain shoppers welcome CCTV in the store as it makes them feel safer, but this does not necessarily indicate that they would visit the store more often as a response.

Thus, the context proposed in the seventh CMO does not appear to be present. Rather, the context proposed in the eighth CMO appears to be true, as most customers do not dislike cameras or have a neutral opinion. However, the mechanism proposed in both CMOs seven and eight is unlikely to be triggered because almost two-thirds of customers did not notice the CCTV, so their behaviour could not be altered by the camera's presence. Hence, this CMO failed because the mechanism was not triggered for the majority of customers, even though there was a partly appropriate context for this to happen.

(9) CONTEXT +	MECHANISM =	OUTCOME
Shop thieves rationally weigh the costs or benefits of theft	The CCTV is positioned to be highly visible and the shop thieves notice the cameras/monitors	Shop thieves displace to another store, another time, or a different part of the store, or they cease theft activity due to an increased perception of risk

The final CMO configuration relates to the perception of shop thieves when faced with in-store cameras. This CMO used the hypothesis that CCTV might increase the offenders' perception of risk and therefore cause them to alter their normal behaviour. This relies on a context where offenders make a rational choice about the costs or benefits associated with stealing. Whilst evidence from offenders was obtained that gives interesting insights into how offenders perceive CCTV in-store in general, unfortunately they were not asked about the specific CCTV system in the store. The company was unwilling to allow known offenders in store, or to link the company name to specific questions during offender interviews. Thus we cannot use this evidence to assess the final CMO in a realistic manner. This is particularly pertinent because the CCTV system used was perhaps unusual, in having monitors that were larger than normal and positioned to be highly visible with good picture clarity. Indeed, the system was chosen following feedback from offenders who participated in previous research by the company. Our research was useful in confirming those general beliefs that, for example, picture quality would be poor, that there would always be blind spots, or that staff would not watch the system. Comments included:

> They can't pinpoint every area of the store. You can always hide behind the cameras. Especially if it's a busy shop, you can mingle in the background.

> To be honest, the pictures on those things [CCTV] are crap. They can't tell who it is.

Interestingly, a minority (two-fifths) of our sample replied that they would "sometimes" or "always" be deterred by mobile cameras.

Of course, we cannot say that if faced with the system used in the store that they would still hold that opinion, but it is interesting that such a relatively high percentage claim to be put off simply by the thought of cameras. Indeed it may be that some offenders have general perceptions about cameras that would not necessarily be overridden by seeing an actual system. To casual observation, one system is often very similar to another and, for example, it may not be apparent to the shop thief whether the cameras are real or dummy or are watched or simply recorded. However, this context may not be appropriate for all offenders. Indeed, some may not rationally weigh the risks associated with theft activity due to more pressing concerns (the need to fund a drug habit, for example). For other researchers who wish to retest this CMO configuration, it might be appropriate to conduct offender "walkabouts" in trial stores to see what aspects of security offenders notice without prompting. Obviously, if they do not notice the CCTV then the mechanism proposed here cannot be triggered. However, because the context and outcome depend entirely on individual offenders' beliefs, this type of CMO configuration may need considerable refinement before it can be used.

CONCLUSIONS

The Impact of In-Store CCTV

One important point that this study has highlighted is that the interaction among CCTV, staff and offenders deserves greater attention. Evaluators should begin breaking down the possible mechanisms (some of which have been raised here) in much greater detail. While it is acknowledged that this study was small in scale, the results appear to indicate that CCTV should perhaps be considered more a tool to help combat shop theft than a solution.

It is plausible to suggest that, in this context, CCTV encouraged staff to approach suspected shop thieves and that the system helped them to monitor suspicious individuals. Staff awareness of security issues may have increased with in-store cameras (at least initially), but fears that customers would be offended by CCTV and express dislike of the cameras were shown to be unfounded. It is notable that staff, however, are not only part of the mechanism through which CCTV achieves a result but can also be considered part of the context in which it is expected to work. Thus, staff attitudes and management involvement with the system become far more important than has previously been recognised. A system introduced to a store where staff welcome the CCTV and want to work with it may create the appropriate context for triggering crime-reducing mechanisms. Equally, a store where staff resent the system may trigger different mechanisms, with the potential to increase losses (by reducing staff vigilance or concern about shop theft). This may be an important aspect of context for both academic evaluators and practitioners to focus more closely upon.

For practitioners, therefore, a useful strategy might be to concentrate on issues of management and staff training to maximise the possible impact of CCTV. One way in which CCTV appears to work is by interacting with the staff, who then influence the shop thieves. Whether CCTV works by influencing shop thieves directly has yet to be shown. For businesses, the study also suggested that CCTV might have a useful but as yet underdeveloped role to play in customer care and service. Security managers need to look at their data in greater depth before installing CCTV if they are to avoid making expensive mistakes. Such "context-mechanism sensitivity" is important and can be guided by the greater understanding facilitated by this new approach.

Strengths and Weaknesses of the Methodology

This study has made only a modest start at using realistic evaluation to examine a specific crime prevention measure. Other researchers will need to refine the approach. There are both strengths and weaknesses to this method that deserve consideration. The theory on which the evaluation methodology is constructed is innovative and holistic, but there are some problems in translating this into practical research results (though these are not insurmountable). The requirements of data collection are far more specific using this methodology; notably, that each of the elements of context, mechanism and outcome require careful validation if they are to be proven. It is relatively easy to propose plausible CMO configurations but much harder to collect useful (or valid) data for all three, particularly where time and resources are limited. This project has demonstrated why issues of context should be examined in much greater depth before the main research phase begins. A good understanding of general contextual issues allows appropriate mechanisms to be proposed. Using CMO configurations is a useful method of teasing out how a measure might be working and in what circumstances it might not work. Indeed, as more research is conducted in this manner, it should be possible to identify common aspects of context that are important to trigger desired mechanisms. This is an important step in building up a body of useful data about what works in crime prevention.

Finally, a major lesson of realistic evaluation is that both academics and practitioners should not be too quick to dismiss evaluations where the loss figures show no significant decline. As with many branches of scientific investigation, a negative result does not mean that there is no result. One of the strengths of the realistic approach is its move away from an overreliance on simplified statistical data. By exploring the mechanisms through which the measure works and the context in which they are triggered, it is possible to identify specific situations that are inappropriate; i.e., those where crime figures do not fall. This area has great potential to help researchers avoid repeating failures.

◆

Acknowledgements: We would like to acknowledge the assistance and support given by Chris Chappill, Simon Reade and John Earnshaw in the retail company, and by the research students at the Scarman Centre; Charlotte Bilby and Steve Hearnshaw. We received extensive comments on an earlier draft of this paper from Martin Hemming, and we are grateful for his advice and also to the anonymous referee for his/her helpful suggestions.

Address correspondence to: Martin Gill, Scarman Centre for the Study of Public Order, University of Leicester, 154 Upper New Walk, Leicester LE1 7QA, United Kingdom. E-mail: <mg26@le.ac.uk>

REFERENCES

Bamfield, J. (1994). *National Survey of Retail Theft and Security*. Northampton, UK: Nene College.

Beck, A. and A. Willis (1994). "Customer and Staff Perceptions of the Role of Closed Circuit Television in Retail Security." In: M. Gill (ed.), *Crime at Work: Studies in Security and Crime Prevention*, vol. I. Leicester, UK: Perpetuity Press.

—— (1995). *Crime and Security: Managing the Risk to Safe Shopping.* Leicester, UK: Perpetuity Press.

Bennett, T. (1996). "What's New in Evaluation Research? A Note on the Pawson and Tilley Article." *British Journal of Criminology* 36(4):567-578.

Brown, B. (1995). *Closed Circuit Television in Town Centres: Three Case Studies.* (Crime Prevention and Detection Series Paper, #73.) London, UK: Home Office.

Davies, S. (1996). "The Case Against: CCTV Should Not be Introduced." *International Journal of Risk, Security and Crime Prevention* 1(4):327-335.

Ekblom, P. and K. Pease (1995). "Evaluating Crime Prevention." In: M. Tonry and D. Farrington (eds.), *Building a Safer Society.* (Crime and Justice: A Review of Research, vol. #19.) Chicago, IL: University of Chicago Press.

Gill, M. (ed.) (1994). *Crime at Work: Studies in Security and Crime Prevention.* Leicester, UK: Perpetuity Press.

—— (ed.) (1998). *Crime at Work: Increasing the Risk for Offenders,* vol. II. Leicester, UK: Perpetuity Press.

—— and V. Turbin (1998). "CCTV and Shop Theft: Towards a Realistic Evaluation." In: C. Norris, G. Armstrong and J. Moran (eds.), *Surveillance, Order and Social Control.* Aldershot, UK: Gower.

Graham, S., J. Brooks and D. Heery (1996). *Towns on the Television: Closed Circuit TV in British Towns and Cities.* Local Government Studies (August).

Handford, M. (1994). "Electronic Tagging in Action: A Case Study in Retailing." In: M. Gill (ed.), *Crime at Work: Studies in Security and Crime Prevention,* vol. I. Leicester, UK: Perpetuity Press.

Hope, T. (1991). "Crime Information in Retailing: Prevention through Analysis." *Security Journal* 2(4):240-245.

Horne, C. (1996). "The Case For: CCTV Should be Introduced." *International Journal of Risk, Security and Crime Prevention* 1(4):317-326.

Husain, S. (1988). *Neighbourhood Watch in England and Wales: A Locational Analysis.* (Crime Prevention Unit Paper, #12.) London, UK: Home Office.

Laycock, G. and N. Tilley (1995). *Policing and Neighbourhood Watch: Strategic Issues.* (Crime Prevention and Detection Series Paper, #74.) London, UK: Home Office.

Pawson, R. and N. Tilley (1992). "Re-Evaluation: Rethinking Research on Corrections and Crime." *Yearbook of Correctional Education:*1-31.

—— (1997). *Realistic Evaluation.* London, UK: Sage.

Short, E. and J. Ditton (1995). "Does CCTV Affect Crime?" *CCTV Today* 2(2):10-12.

Tilley, N. (1993). *Understanding Car Parks, Crime and CCTV.* (Crime Prevention Unit Paper, #42.) London, UK: Her Majesty's Stationery Office.

—— (1997). "Whys and Wherefores in Evaluating the Effectiveness of CCTV." *International Journal of Risk, Security and Crime Prevention* 2(3):175-186.

NOTES

1. Note that as the research strategy is still in the developmental stage, this enquiry may be said to incorporate many aspects of the realistic approach, but does not claim to be a strict realistic evaluation.

2. Though for a criticism of this approach, see Bennett (1996).

3. It is recognised that for a realistic evaluation, these data are limited. The offenders were not taken to the stores where CCTV was located, and, therefore, the data cannot be used to explore specific CMO configurations associated with the stores. Understandably, the company was not willing to allow in-store walkabouts with known offenders or to have interview questions refer to the company's name. Nevertheless, it was felt that offenders' general perceptions of CCTV could usefully be examined in this way. This represents our own adaptation of the realistic approach.

4. Interestingly, after staff had experienced cameras in the store, there was a strong shift in opinion about the ability of CCTV to reduce violence towards staff. Initially, most staff thought cameras would be "very effective" but once they were installed most changed their opinion to "ineffective" or "very ineffective." However, staff did claim that cameras gave them more confidence to deal with confrontations, even if they did not appear to reduce their frequency.

5. There are two issues here. First, staff vigilance may have increased because of the novelty of having cameras in the store. This may well have focused their attention on the problem of shop theft. Second, staff may have become more realistic about what CCTV could actually do and learnt how to use it to best effect.

6. There is, of course, the reverse argument that more customers in a store provide cover for shop thieves to operate. According to this position, staff will be more involved with genuine customers and less able to look for offenders.

7. Indeed, this problem could warrant a separate research project to investigate whether increasing natural surveillance provides more eyes to spot shoplifters or more cover for them to hide. It would be interesting to interview customers to see if they have ever observed shop theft activity and, if so, what they did about it. After all, natural surveillance is of little use if those observing the theft do nothing about it. This is perhaps a question that could be investigated in future offender-based research project to find out whether shop thieves consciously choose crowded shops or prefer quieter areas.

YES, IT WORKS, NO, IT DOESN'T: COMPARING THE EFFECTS OF OPEN-STREET CCTV IN TWO ADJACENT SCOTTISH TOWN CENTRES

by

Jason Ditton

and

Emma Short
Scottish Centre for Criminology

Abstract: This paper reports the evaluation of two contrasting open-street closed circuit television (CCTV) installations in Scotland. Twelve cameras were installed in a small town called Airdrie in 1992, and 32 cameras were installed in Glasgow, a large city, in 1994. After controlling for extraneous factors, it was discovered that, overall, recorded crime fell (and detections rose) in Airdrie after camera installation, but in Glasgow recorded crime rose (and detections fell). However, in both locations, some more specific types of recorded crimes fell and some others rose. It cannot simply be concluded that CCTV "works" in small towns, but not in large cities. In part this is because the goals of open-street CCTV installations are usually developed at a somewhat slower pace than are the systems themselves, and are often incompatible. For example, proponents claim that CCTV will both reduce crime (by deterring potential offenders) and increase it (by capturing more illegal acts on camera). Accordingly, in both locations studied, CCTV has been a different sort of success.

INTRODUCTION

There has been substantial investment in closed circuit television (CCTV) schemes in Britain since the early 1990s. Central and local government investment in open-street CCTV in the U.K. between the years 1994 and 1997 has been estimated to have been in excess of £100 million (Norris and Armstrong, 1998). Before this, some small-scale research had indicated that CCTV had had an impact in various closed locations, such as: in shops (Van Straelen, 1978; Burrows, 1991; Gill and Turbin, 1997); on buses (Poyner, 1988); in car parks (Poyner, 1991; Tilley, 1993); on the London Underground (Mayhew et al., 1979); and in small businesses (Hearnden, 1996). However, in general, instances of fully independent professional evaluation of open-street CCTV schemes has been rare,[1] a gap which the research reported here hopes partly to fill.

Scotland differs slightly from England and Wales insofar as, in the main, partially government-backed schemes were not introduced until slightly later, and not substantially before the results of independent professional evaluation were available. Flying in the face of its legendary fiscal caution, Scotland has since adopted town and city centre CCTV schemes with uncharacteristic abandon. There have been two distinctly different investment phases. Prior to 1996, the 12 schemes that were in operation in January 1996 were all the result of the handiwork of sharp-eyed solitary moral entrepreneurs working in different locations and occupying different roles.[2] Since 1996, funding has become institutionalised, with the Scottish Office playing a key role in encouraging the spread of CCTV by mounting two CCTV Challenge competitions. In the 1996-97 round, 32 additional schemes were partially funded by the Scottish Office (the total capital cost of the 32 successful schemes amounted to £4.859 million, of which the Scottish Office contributed £1.851 million). In the 1997-98 round, 30 more schemes were partially funded by the Scottish Office (the total capital cost of these schemes amounted to £4.953 million, of which the Scottish Office contributed £1.861 million).

Twelve open-street CCTV cameras were installed in Airdrie's town centre in 1992, and became operational in November of that year. This was the first multi-camera CCTV installation in Scotland. Almost exactly two years later, in November 1994, 32 cameras were installed in Glasgow's city centre. Glasgow is Scotland's biggest city, and Airdrie is a small town located some 15 miles east of Glasgow. We were responsible for the independent professional evaluation of both installations. Details of the governmental and other publications stemming from this endeavor are given at the end of this paper. This is the first time the effects of CCTV in the two places have been considered together.

THE EFFECT IN AIRDRIE

The area of the centre of Airdrie actually visible from one or more of the cameras represents parts of six separate police patrol beats. Crime and offence data were collected for the period November 1990 to October 1994. This represents exactly 24 months before installation of the cameras, and 24 months afterwards. Considerable care was taken to plot areas visible to the cameras, so as to be able to distinguish those crimes and offences recorded in areas visible to the cameras from those recorded in the remainder of the six beats.

Recorded crime and offence and detection data were also collected for six increasingly sized areas of comparison: the CCTV vision area, the rest of those six beats, the rest of the subdivision, the rest of the division, the rest of the police force area, and the rest of Scotland. These data were collected to allow both a comparison of rates of change in the commission of crimes and offences in the CCTV area and other comparable areas, and to allow a check to be made for possible displacement of criminal activity from the CCTV area to other areas, and/or for possible diffusion of benefits of CCTV to such areas.

Recorded Crime in Airdrie

The overall effect on recorded crime and offence rates of installing CCTV cameras in Airdrie can be seen in Figure 1.

The "before" segment represents the 24 months prior to installation, and the "after" segment, the two years following. The curved line represents the total recorded crime and offence rate derived from data that have been both seasonally adjusted and controlled for underlying trends.[3]

It is hard to determine visually a periodic trend from a curved line. To calculate the trend (in effect to straighten the line), the "line of best fit" (the regression line)[4] has been calculated separately for the before and after periods. For each line, the angle of slope indicates the trend (both before and after CCTV installation, recorded crimes were decreasing); and the position of the line from the baseline indicates the magnitude of the effect. The dashed line represents the line of best fit before installation, and the solid black one, the line of best fit afterwards.

Clearly, the installation of CCTV has had a beneficial effect. This is indicated in Figure 1 by the area between the dashed and solid sloped lines of best fit after CCTV installation. One way of looking at this area is to see it as representing 772 recorded crimes and offences that CCTV installation has prevented.

Figure 1: Recorded Crimes and Offences in Airdrie's CCTV Area, Lines of "Best Fit" Before and After Camera Installation November 1990 – October 1994

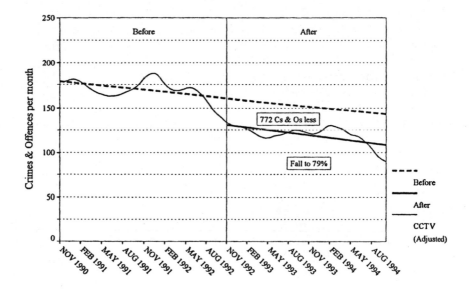

CCTV seems to have had a variable effect on the rates of different types of recorded crimes and offences. Recorded crimes and offences are divided into seven general groups by the Scottish Office, and it seems sensible to use identical aggregations. These groups vary in direction and the degree to which they are affected by the installation of CCTV. The first five groups are crimes; the last two, offences.[5]

It is not possible to analyse changes in recorded crimes from Group 1 (violence) and Group 2 (indecency), as too few were recorded.[6] Recorded crimes of dishonesty (Group 3 crimes) fell to 48% in the 24 months after installation of CCTV. This represents 1,231 fewer recorded crimes in the area of Airdrie covered by the cameras in the 24 months following installation (see Figure 2).

Figure 2: Fully Adjusted Recorded Crimes in Airdrie's CCTV Area, Group 3 (Crimes of Dishonesty) November, 1990 – October, 1994

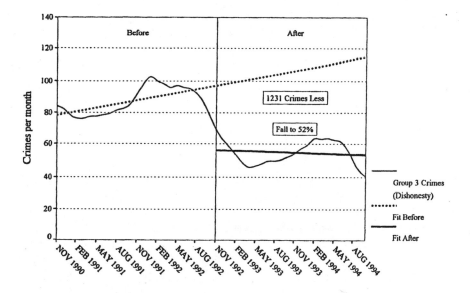

Group 4 crimes (fire-raising and vandalism) fell by 19% in the 24 months after installation of CCTV. This decrease is based on relatively small numbers of recorded crimes and translates into just 42 fewer crimes in the 24 months following CCTV installation. Recorded crimes in Group 5 (other) crimes rose by 1,068% (when compared to previously recorded levels) in the 24 months following installation. Again, the numbers are small in this group with this percentage representing 180 more crimes in the 24 months after CCTV was operational.

Similarly, 194 more Group 6 (miscellaneous) offences were recorded in the 24 months following CCTV installation — a rise to 133% of previously recorded levels in the 24 months. Finally, Group 7 offences (motor vehicle-related) increased by a total of 58, to 126% of previously recorded levels, in the 24 months following CCTV installation.[7]

Increases in recorded crimes in Group 5, and in recorded offences in Groups 6 and 7 are not necessarily indicative of the failure of CCTV. Within Group 5, an increase in drug offences may reflect well on the surveillance ability of CCTV to detect crimes that might otherwise have gone unnoticed. The same could be said of "breach of the peace" offences (Group 6) and minor traffic violations (Group 7).

Overall, crimes and offences fell to 79% of previously recorded levels in the two years following the installation of CCTV in Airdrie.

Detections in Airdrie

In the two years after CCTV installation, detections[8] improved to 116% of previously recorded levels. To put this another way, the clear-up rate improved from 50% to 58% of recorded crimes and offences. This is illustrated in Figure 3.

The improvement in detections varied by crime and offence group. Group 3 crimes of dishonesty did not play such a big role in the overall improvement in detections as they played in the reduction in recorded crimes, maintaining a 31% clearance rate both before and after CCTV installation. (Again, it is not possible to consider changes in detections for Group 1 and Group 2 crimes, as even fewer were recorded in each group than was the case for recorded crimes in these two groups.)

Most impressive were Group 4 crimes, which showed a detection improvement from a 20% to a 27% clear-up rate (itself, a 35% improvement). Detections in Group 5 crimes (from 95% to 97%), and Group 6 miscellaneous offences (from 82% to 87%) both show a slight

Figure 3: Adjusted Recorded Crimes, Offences and Detentions in Airdrie's CCTV Area, All Crimes and Offences November 1990 – October 1994

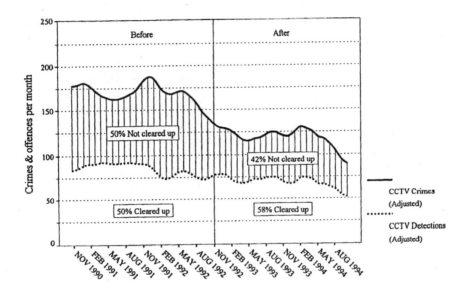

improvement. Group 7 motor vehicle offences saw a slight deterioration (from 98% to 94%). It should be recalled that Group 7 offences have a very high detection rate anyway, one that would be difficult to improve substantially.

Overall, detections improved to 116% of previously recorded levels in the two years following the installation of CCTV in Airdrie.

Displacement or Diffusion from Airdrie?

It is possible that at least some of the crimes and offences apparently prevented by the installation of CCTV were not prevented at all, but instead will have been "displaced" from that area and committed elsewhere or in other ways.

The areas surrounding the parts of Airdrie in camera vision generally saw an increase in recorded crimes. Much of this increase in criminal activity in adjacent areas was due to an increase in Group 5 (other) crimes, which include drug-related offences. These increased to 161% and 215%, respectively, of previously recorded levels in the 24 months after installation of CCTV in the rest of the CCTV visible beats and in the rest of the subdivision. This gives some sort of context to the finding that recorded Group 5 crimes also increased in the area covered by the cameras (to 145% of previously recorded levels in the 24 months after installation of CCTV).

A breakdown of Group 5 crimes in the CCTV area shows that Bail Act offences (something of a "phantom" crime)[9] and drug offences accounted for the majority of the increase. The same pattern holds in the potential displacement areas (both in the rest of the CCTV visible beats and in the rest of the subdivision). The best interpretation we can offer is that Bail Act offences and drug offences were increasing across the board and are relatively impervious to CCTV intervention.

There is no statistical evidence, therefore, to suggest that the crimes "prevented" in the CCTV area — mainly crimes of dishonesty (Group 3) — have been "geographically" displaced to either of the two immediately adjacent and larger areas. Nor is it likely that they have been displaced "functionally" to these areas, as displacement cannot explain the increase in Group 5 Bail Act and drug-related offences. Rather, as noted above, Bail Act and drug-related offences have increased in all areas.

This tentative conclusion seems to be borne out by attempting to "find" crimes apparently prevented in the CCTV area, in both the rest of the CCTV beats and the rest of the subdivision. Statistical evidence suggests that 772 crimes have been prevented in the CCTV area following installation of cameras. (This is calculated by projecting expected totals to the two years following camera installation in the CCTV area and then subtracting the actual adjusted recorded crime total). As it was not possible to trace any of these crimes to the immediately adjacent areas, it may be justifiable to treat them as having been prevented rather than merely displaced.

However, this cannot be treated as "proof" that displacement did not occur. Our check of geographical displacement was confined to adjacent areas; offenders may well be choosing to move very much further afield to continue offending. Various studies conducted in other countries have found that some burglars (Gabor, 1978) and some robbers (van Koppen and Jansen, 1998) will travel long distances and for many hours to reach their targets, while some, although not all, will be dissuaded from offending by such crime prevention measures (Bennett, 1986). Since conducting the main statistical study in Airdrie, we have piloted the idea of interviewing offenders in the area. This proved instructive, and these initial enquiries have been published as Short and Ditton,1998; and Ditton and Short, 1998a, 1998b. However, a full-scale study has not been undertaken.

THE EFFECT IN GLASGOW

Glasgow's city centre is covered by Strathclyde Police Force's "A" Division, which is itself divided into two subdivisions: "AB" and "AC." The CCTV cameras cover most, but not all of the beats in "AB" subdivision (21 of the 25), and some of the beats in "AC" subdivision (7 of the 24). Thus, the CCTV cameras cover, to some degree or other,[10] 28 separate beats in "A" Division.

Data were collected for the periods: 1st November, 1992 through 31st October, 1993; 1st November, 1993 through 31st October, 1994; and 1st November, 1994 through 31st October, 1995. This represents the first year after CCTV installation, compared with the identical calendar periods one year and two years before.

Equivalent data were also collected from: the beats in "A" Division that do not have any camera coverage (beats 1, 2, 5 and 6 from "AB" sub-division, and beats 26, 28-31, and 38-49 from "AC" subdivision, referred to henceforth as the rest of "A" Division); the surrounding police Divisions (Divisions "B," "C," "D," "E," "F," and "G"); and the rest of Strathclyde Police Force (Divisions "K," "L," "N," "P," "Q," "R," "U" and "X").

These additional data were collected, first, to establish a yardstick from which an underlying trend rate could be calculated. Then, after initial analysis ruled out alternative choices, the rest of "A" Division was chosen. In earlier work in Airdrie, a broadly similar aggregation (in that case, the rest of "N" Division) was chosen as the underlying trend yardstick.

Recorded Crime in Glasgow

The overall effect of installing CCTV cameras in Glasgow's city centre can be seen in Figure 4. The "before" segment represents the 24 months prior to installation, and the "after" segment the year following. The curved line represents the total recorded crime rate derived from data that have been both seasonally adjusted and controlled for underlying trends. A technical description of these processes is given in Annex Two of Ditton, et al. (1999). Apart from one slight but necessary modification, exactly the same analytic processes were used here as in the evaluation of the CCTV installation in Airdrie.[11]

Again, the line of best fit (the regression line) has been calculated separately for the before and after periods. For each line, the angle of slope indicates the trend (before CCTV installation, recorded crimes were decreasing); and the position of the line from the baseline indicates the magnitude of the effect. The dashed line represents the line of best fit before installation, and the solid black one, the line of best fit afterwards.

In Airdrie, it was calculated that recorded crimes and offences fell to 79% of previously recorded and adjusted totals. In Glasgow, contrarily, recorded crimes and offences rose to 109% of previously recorded and adjusted totals. CCTV seems to have had a variable effect on the rates of different types of recorded crimes and offences. The same Scottish Office groups that were used to aggregate data in Airdrie were used again in the Glasgow part of the study.

The pattern is by no means consistent, even if the overall effect is a slight rise. Recorded crimes in Groups 1 and 4, and recorded offences in Groups 6 and 7, all fell, but recorded crimes in Groups 2, 3 and 5 all rose.[12] Group 1 crimes fell to 78% of their previous amount (amounting to 230 fewer crimes); Group 2 crimes and offences rose to 117% (equivalent to 120 more crimes); Group 3 crimes rose to 123% (2,185 more crimes, as illustrated in Figure 5); Group 4 fell to 92% (57 fewer crimes); Group 5 rose to 132% (464 more crimes); Group 6 fell to 93% (272 fewer offences); and Group 7 fell to 88% (318 fewer offences).

Detections in Glasgow

Overall, the clearance rate (detections expressed as a percentage of recorded crimes and offences) fell slightly from 64% to 60% (Figure 6). In Airdrie, the clearance rate improved from 50% to 58% over all.

In Glasgow, crimes and offences in Groups 1, 4 and 6 fell, and those in Groups 2 and 3 rose. The clearance rates in Groups 5 and 7 remained virtually unchanged. Specifically, detections in Group 1 fell from 74% to 46%; in Group 2, they rose from 92% to 98%; in Group 3, they rose from 39% to 44%; in Group 4, they fell from 39% to 30%; in Group 5, they fell from 100% to 99%; in Group 6, they fell from 86% to 82%; and in Group 7, they rose from 99% to 100%.

Figure 4: Recorded Crimes and Offences in Glasgow's CCTV Area, Lines of "Best Fit" Before and After Camera Installation November 1992 – October 1995

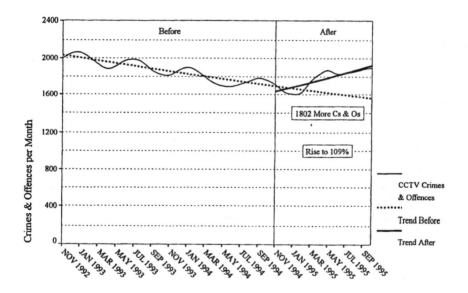

Complacency or Confusion in Glasgow?

It is only thus at an ambitious and unrealistic level (i.e., affecting *all* recorded crimes and offences positively) that CCTV in Glasgow can be said not to have "worked." Even after the undertaking of various statistical procedures (seasonal adjustment, smoothing, controlling for underlying trends) — each of which depressed the effect of CCTV when used on data from the first part of this study in Airdrie — there have been reductions in recorded instances of violence (Group 1), vandalism, etc. (Group 4), petty personal offences such as breach of the peace and petty assault (Group 6), and offences involving vehicles (Group 7). Because there was no recorded fall in the overall number of crimes and offences reported in Glasgow's CCTV area, no search for displacement could logically be undertaken.

DISCUSSION

Put at its starkest, after the installation of open-street CCTV in Airdrie, recorded crimes and offences fell to 79% of their previously recorded levels, and detections rose from 50% to 58%. Conversely, after the installation of open-street CCTV in Glasgow, recorded crimes and offences rose to 109% of their previously recorded levels, and detections fell from 64% to 60%.[13] Rather crudely, it could be concluded that CCTV worked in Airdrie, but not in Glasgow. This interpretation should be resisted firmly.

Why? Because there are a series of interrelated problems that preclude simplistic judgements like this. These may be grouped into concerns relating to the adequacy of the *test* of effectiveness; the *type* of situation in which CCTV was "tested," and the *timing* of the introduction of CCTV in different locations.

Adequacy of Tests of Effectiveness

First, then, concerns relating to the adequacy of the *test* of CCTV's effectiveness. A major difficulty here is confusion to the point of contradiction as to what, precisely, open-street CCTV cameras are supposed to do. From one point of view, their ability to see criminal events unfolding when there are no police officers physically present should increase logically the number of crimes and offences thus recorded. From another point of view, their sheer presence should deter offenders from offending, and should decrease the number of crimes and offences thus recorded. If such cameras prove better at the first goal than the second, then the crime rate should rise, and this would be counted as a "success." If, contrarily, they prove to be better at the second than at the first, then the crime rate should fall, and this would be counted as a "success."

We might, at this point, turn to the history of the two CCTV schemes to see what the goals of each actually were. In Airdrie, CCTV began as the imaginative response to a specific local crime problem (teenage shoplifters disappearing into the massed ranks of dancing teenagers at a local youth club). An energetic local police officer had confronted the youth club members, and at one point in these discussions, a young girl suggested to him, "you should put a camera in

Figure 5: Group 3 Recorded Crimes in Glasgow's CCTV Area, Lines of "Best Fit" Before and After Camera Installation November 1992 – October 1995

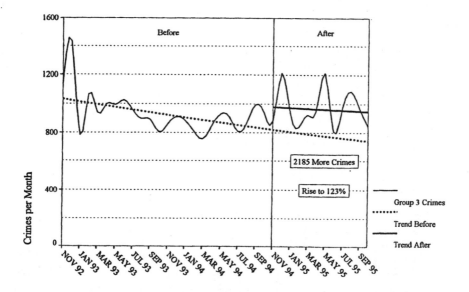

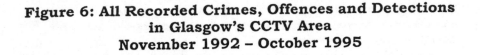

**Figure 6: All Recorded Crimes, Offences and Detections
in Glasgow's CCTV Area
November 1992 – October 1995**

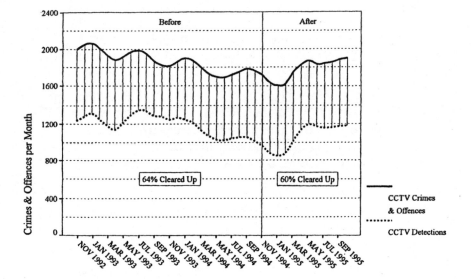

the youth club." Once germinated, the idea proliferated with speed: by the end of the week, he had planned the whole town centre network (Ditton & Short, 1998b).

In Glasgow, the CCTV scheme began life as an idea designed to have a positive impact on the erroneous image of the city as a "dangerous" place in the minds of inward investors based in other countries. In the early days, CCTV was actively promoted by the local development agency in terms that indicated that it was expected to increase inward investment to the city by £43 million per year, generate 1,500 new jobs, and bring an additional 225,000 visitors to the city every year. Within 18 months, CCTV was "about" reducing criminal victimisation to locally resident visitors to the city centre.

Indeed, there seem to have been a succession of goals, and with the benefit of hindsight, it is now clear that the original objectives have been regularly replaced to the point where, in a two-year period, current goals bear no resemblance to initial ones. However, by which goal achievement should Glasgow's cameras be judged?

In Airdrie, CCTV's "mission creep" (from policing a youth club to policing a town centre) was not self-contradictory. However, in Glasgow it was distinctly so. For example, the most famous piece of CCTV-captured offending is of two young men attacking, and finally jumping up and down on the head of, a third one. This has been widely shown on television (abroad, too), and photographic stills taken from it are frequently published in the British press.

No doubt this confirms the ability of CCTV to capture incidents on camera, and helps to justify the presence of the system, particularly in its endless search for annual running costs. It may also be good for employee morale. Indeed, the operators are justifiably proud of having noticed the incident unfold, of having alerted the police, and of having rushed medical assistance to the scene. But what has this publicity done to either calm the fears of foreign investors or reassure locally resident visitors that Glasgow is a safe place to visit?

These problems aside, a related issue is the vastly inflated expectations of the effect of open-street CCTV. It is really just some video cameras pointing either up or down a handful of city streets. Glasgow has 32 cameras, and Airdrie has 12, but each network has only two relatively untrained persons watching them at any one time. One person can really only watch one screen at a time, and our observation in the Glasgow control room indicated that there were occasions when nobody was watching anything. There were also many other occasions when operators were watching the screens, but nothing apparently was happening. Camera vision is impressive, yet occasionally obscured (by trees in leaf, by snow on the lens), and therefore ultimately limited. In addition, there is no sound.

Overall, in the first year of operation, Glasgow's CCTV system was linked to 290 arrests, although it is unclear how many of these would have been made without the cameras. Even if all 290 would not have occurred without the cameras in place, this is still a strike rate of one arrest per camera for every 967 hours of operation, or one every 40 days. Put another way, the cameras "saw" under 5% of the total number of crimes and offences that resulted in arrests in the area they surveilled during the first year of operation. Why, thus, should

CCTV there have more than a 5% effect in either reducing or increasing recorded offending?[14]

Types of Testing Situations

A second main concern relates to the *type* of situation into which open-street CCTV is being introduced. Glasgow has a "centre": so does Airdrie. There the similarity ends. Glasgow is a huge port city, and Airdrie is a sleepy little town. The people of Airdrie are very proud of their cameras. We have been told that when the control room first became operational there, thousands of local inhabitants queued for hours to get a quick glimpse of the monitors in the police station. A year or two later, when the budget was low and the survival of the whole installation under threat, these same local residents held coffee mornings to raise money to keep it going.

For Airdrionians, the middle of the town is "their" town centre. For Glaswegians, the middle of the city is "the" city centre. Only an insignificant number of people actually live in Glasgow's city centre, and most of those who visit it cannot get there on foot. More people actually live in the middle of Airdrie, and those who live in the rest of the town can easily walk to the centre. One year after camera installation in Glasgow (a year that saw frequent mentions of the cameras in the local media), only between a quarter and a third of the ambulatory population were even aware of their existence (Ditton et al., 1999). No satisfactory general population poll has been conducted in Airdrie, but when we interviewed a small group of offenders, most claimed to have first heard about the cameras from the local media.[15]

Timing of CCTV Introduction

Finally, and perhaps most crucially, the *timing* of the introduction of cameras in the two centres may well have had the biggest effect on relative success, when the latter is conceived narrowly in terms of reductions in the overall rate of recorded offending. It should be recalled — and this is unusual given the history of implementation of most crime prevention initiatives (see Campbell and Ross, 1968) — that CCTV was introduced into Glasgow's city centre at a point when recorded crime had been on the decline for at least two years. It is unclear why recorded crime rates oscillate over the long term. But, when they are on the rise, there is more inclination to experiment with ways of reversing this than when they are on the decline.

Had Glasgow's CCTV system been installed at a relative recorded crime zenith, it would have been a simple matter to predict an independent downturn thereafter. Being, as it was, installed at a nadir, an upturn thereafter was always the most likely consequence. Equally plausibly, had Airdrie's cameras been introduced two years later, then, after a probable period of decline in recorded offending, crime rates might well have begun to rise.

CONCLUSION

It should be noted that CCTV has had an impact very different in Glasgow than in Airdrie.[16] In both, some occasional yet noteworthy success was obtained in capturing emerging incidents on camera. Yet, in Airdrie recorded crime declined as a whole, and no displacement effect could be discovered. In Glasgow, on the other hand, recorded crime as a whole rose slightly (although it fell in some categories), and thus no search for displacement could be undertaken.

However, in Glasgow, the CCTV system seems gradually to be finding a different role for itself, particularly in the relatively recently developed reviewing of tapes to retrospectively investigate major crimes.[17] Here, rather than base the evaluated utility of the system on its ability to spot contemporary offending (or even prevent it), the videotape library is used as an archive. After the notification of a major criminal incident, tapes for the day and time in question are examined minutely, frame by frame, for anything that might help the police with their enquiries. Although this may be no more than a new and cost-effective way of conducting an age-old police activity, it is one job that police officers claim that CCTV can do well.[18] Given the alleged cost of conventional major criminal enquiries, and the apparent capability of CCTV networks to succeed at conducting them at little cost, this latterly discovered benefit may well be the real use of open-street CCTV systems in the centres of major cities. The use of the tape archive has been of great use in retrospectively investigating major crimes in Glasgow; but there has been little scope for this in Airdrie, which suffers few, if any, crimes of this seriousness.

It appears, then, that open-street CCTV works differently in different situations. Airdrie is a small town: Glasgow a major city. Many of those seen on screen in Airdrie were well-known to the local police as residents. In Glasgow, this was far less likely to be the case. For this and other reasons, instead of asking blandly "does CCTV work?" we need, following the advice of Tilley (1997), to ask what works, in what circumstances, and how.

We conclude: open-street CCTV can "work" in limited ways, but is not a universal panacea. It works in different ways in different situations, and future evaluation might choose wisely to concentrate on "how" rather than "if." In both locations studied, Airdrie and Glasgow, CCTV has been a different sort of success.

Address correspondence to: Jason Ditton, Scottish Centre for Criminology, Charing Cross Clinic, 8 Woodside Crescent, Glasgow, G3 7UY, United Kingdom.

REFERENCES

Bennett, T. (1986). "Situational Crime Prevention from the Offenders' Perspective." In: K. Heal and G. Laycock (eds.), *Situational Crime Prevention: From Theory to Practice*. London, UK: Her Majesty's Stationery Office.

Brown, B. (1995). *CCTV in Town Centres: Three Case Studies*. (Crime Detection and Prevention Series Paper, #68.) London, UK: Home Office.

Burrows, J. (1991). *Making Crime Prevention Pay: Initiatives from Business*. (Crime Prevention Unit Paper, #27.) London, UK: Home Office.

Campbell, D. and H. Ross (1968). "The Connecticut Crackdown on Speeding: Time-Series Data in Quasi-Experimental Analysis." *Law & Society Review* 3(1):33-53.

Ditton, J. and E. Short (1998a). "When Open Street CCTV Appears to Reduce Crime — Does it Just Get Displaced Elsewhere?" *CCTV Today* 5(2):13-16.

—— (1998b). "Evaluating Scotland's First Town Centre CCTV Scheme: Airdrie's Crime Data and Airdrie's Offenders." In: C. Norris and G. Armstrong (eds.), *Surveillance, CCTV and Social Control — The Rise of Closed Circuit Televisual Surveillance in Britain*. Avebury, UK: Gower.

—— S. Phillips, C. Norris and G. Armstrong (1999). *The Effect of the Introduction of Closed Circuit Television on Recorded Crime Rates and on Concern about Crime in Glasgow*. Edinburgh, SCOT: Central Research Unit, Scottish Office.

Gabor, T. (1978). "Crime Displacement: The Literature and Strategies for its Investigation." *Crime and Justice* 6(2):100-107.

Gill, M. and V. Turbin (1997). "CCTV and Shop Theft: Towards a Realistic Evaluation." Paper presented at the British Criminology Conference, Belfast, July.

Hearnden, K. (1996). "Small Businesses' Approach to Managing CCTV to Combat Crime." *International Journal of Risk, Security and Crime Prevention* 1(1):19-31.

Mayhew, P., R. Clarke, J. Burrows, J. Hough and S. Winchester (1979). *Crime in Public View.* (Home Office Research Study, #49.) London, UK: Home Office.

Norris, C. and G. Armstrong (1998). "CCTV and the Rise of the Mass Surveillance Society." In: R. Morgan and P. Carlen (eds.), *Crime Unlimited.* London, UK: Macmillan.

Poyner, B. (1988). "Video Cameras and Bus Vandalism." In: R.V. Clarke (ed.), *Situational Crime Prevention Successful Case Studies.* Albany, NY: Harrow and Heston.

—— (1992). "Situational Crime Prevention in Two Parking Facilities." In: R.V. Clarke (ed.), *Situational Crime Prevention Successful Case Studies (2nd ed.).* Albany, NY: Harrow and Heston.

Short, E. and J. Ditton (1996). *Does Closed Circuit Television Prevent Crime? An Evaluation of the Use of CCTV Surveillance Cameras in Airdrie Town Centre.* Edinburgh, SCOT: Central Research Unit, Scottish Office.

—— (1998) "Seen and Now Heard: Talking to the Targets of Open Street CCTV." *British Journal of Criminology* 38(3):404-428.

Skinns, D. (1997). *Annual Report of the Safety in Doncaster Evaluation Project.* Doncaster, UK: Doncaster Council and South Yorkshire Police Partnership.

Tilley, N. (1993). *Understanding Car Parks, Crime and CCTV: Evaluation Lessons from Safer Cities.* (Crime Prevention Unit Paper #42.) London, UK: Home Office.

—— (1997). "Whys and Wherefores in Evaluating the Effectiveness of CCTV." *International Journal of Risk, Security and Crime Prevention* 2(3):175-85.

van Koppen, P. and R. Jansen (1998). "The Road to the Robbery: Travel Patterns in Commercial Robberies." *British Journal of Criminology* 38(2):230-246.

Van Straelen, F. (1978). "Prevention and Technology." In: J. Brown (ed.), *Cranfield Papers.* London, UK: Peel Press.

NOTES

1. Brown (1995) is something of an exception, although it is more of an attempt professionally to reanalyse locally collected data from three very different areas.

2. These schemes are detailed in Annex A of Short & Ditton (1996). This report also contains a fuller analysis of the crime and offence and detection data discussed below. The collection and analysis of this statistical data was funded by the Scottish Office, to whom we are grateful.

3. Recorded crime and offence rates exhibit mostly inexplicable, but noticeable, seasonal patterns. These were extracted, in a formal sense, from the four years of data, and then deleted, leaving a seasonally adjusted residue. The underlying trend is the direction in which the recorded crime and offence "line" could have been expected to have gone if CCTV cameras had not been introduced. This underlying trend was calculated from trends in locally comparable areas where there were no cameras. This, too, was factored into the calculations.

4. These are standard regression lines, i.e., straight lines that minimise the *sums* of the *squared* vertical distances from the observed data points to the line.

5. Crimes are, generally speaking, more serious than offences. The groups are:

    Group 1: Crimes of violence, etc. This group contains the most serious crimes; for example, murder, attempted murder, serious assault, handling of offensive weapons and robbery. Group 1 crimes total about 1% of all crimes and offences recorded by the police in Scotland.

    Group 2: Crimes of indecency. This group contains sex crimes of violence (rape, attempted rape and indecent assault), lewd and libidinous practices, and prostitution. Group 2 crimes total about ½% of all crimes and offences recorded by the police in Scotland.

    Group 3: Crimes of dishonesty. This is the largest group, and contains housebreaking, theft of (and from) motor vehicles, etc., shoplifting, fraud, and other crimes of dishonesty. Group 3 crimes total about 38% of all crimes and offences recorded by the police in Scotland.

    Group 4: Fire-raising, malicious mischief, etc. Group 4 only includes fire-raising and vandalism. Group 4 crimes total about 9% of all crimes and offences recorded by the police in Scotland.

    Group 5: Other crimes. Group 5 includes crimes against public justice, drug-related offences, and other miscellaneous crimes. Group 5 crimes total about 5% of all crimes and offences recorded by the police in Scotland.

Group 6: Miscellaneous offences. Miscellaneous offences include petty assault, breach of the peace, and drunkenness. Group 6 crimes total about 12% of all crimes and offences recorded by the police in Scotland.

Group 7: Offences relating to motor vehicles. Motor vehicle offences include reckless and careless driving, drunk driving, speeding, unlawful use of vehicles, and various vehicle defect offences. Group 7 crimes total about 34% of all crimes and offences recorded by the police in Scotland.

6. One hundred eleven Group 1 crimes of violence were recorded in the 24 months prior to CCTV installation in the area surveyed by the cameras, with 99 being recorded in 24 months following installation. Six Group 2 crimes of indecency were recorded in the 24 months prior to CCTV installation in the area surveyed by the cameras, with 4 being recorded in 24 months following installation.

7. The net reduction in recorded crimes and offences is, calculating by this method, 841 fewer crimes and offences, which seems at odds with the reduction of 772 mentioned earlier. Of this difference of 69, 43 are accounted for procedurally, i.e., by one method totalling raw data and then adjusting for seasonality and controlling for underlying trends, and by the other method adjusting for seasonality and controlling for underlying trends and then totalling. This leaves 26 unaccounted for. These are probably accounted for by not including Groups 1 and 2 in the group totalling exercise. (Although both fell slightly in raw terms, this does not mean that adjusting and controlling might not have predicted increases.)

8. A crime or offence is detected, or, more properly, cleared up, "if one or more offenders is apprehended, cited, warned or traced for it."

9. If someone commits an offence while on bail, this is also recorded as a further offence of bail abuse.

10. Data for one test month (March 1994) were examined, and all crimes and offences recorded were classified in terms of whether or not they were in CCTV vision. There are two ways of looking at each beat: first, the degree of geographical camera coverage; and second, the percentage of recorded crime occurring in the areas in vision. Beats were classified in terms of the second into those with very low penetration (beats 3, 7, 8, 9, 11, 36 and 37), those with low penetration (beats, 4, 19, 25, 27, 32, 33, and 34), those with high penetration (beats 10, 16, 20, 22, 23, 24, and 35) and those with very high penetration (beats 12, 13, 14, 15, 17, 18 and 21). These four areas together are henceforth referred to as the

CCTV visibility area. On analysis, no relationship was found between degree of CCTV penetration and either changes in recorded crimes and offences, or detections. This offers slight confirmation of the overall finding that CCTV has not had a noticeable effect on crime in Glasgow.

11. See Short and Ditton (1996). The one exception relates to the fact that in Glasgow, only three rather than four years' data were available. This was dealt with by reverse-extrapolating data for a fictitious preliminary year, which were then used to construct a model for seasonal deconstruction before the fictitious year was dropped from all further calculations. In fact, two fictitious preliminary years were constructed (one maximising the level of recorded crime that might have occurred, the other minimising it). Both were used independently before being discarded. There was no significant difference in the results obtained whichever fictitious year was used.

12. When calculated as a single total, the trend effect for the CCTV visibility area is of 1,802 more recorded crimes and offences (a 9% increase). When calculated separately, the sum of the group changes amounts to 1,892 additional recorded crimes and offences. The difference of 90 additional recorded crimes and offences is a procedural artifact created by, in the first exercise, totalling raw data and then adjusting for seasonality and controlling for underlying trends; and in the second, adjusting for seasonality and controlling for underlying trends and then totalling.

13. To some degree, changes in recorded crimes and offences and changes in detections may not be independent measures. Given relatively fixed police manpower, a reduction in rates of offending presumably frees more time to concentrate upon detections. Conversely, an increase in rates of offending leaves less time to concentrate upon detections. This may in part explain the difference between the outcomes in Airdrie and Glasgow.

14. A separate query relating to the adequacy of the test of CCTV's effectiveness is the conventional analyst's lament: it is simply impossible to be sure that one has ever had all the relevant data at hand, and that analysis has not missed the operation of some ignored variable. An anecdote might suffice. Camera 12 in Glasgow (which saw more than three times as many arrests as any other camera) has been the success story of the whole installation. It is positioned overseeing a popular disco, which was a known trouble spot. Prior to installation, we have been told, a police van full of uniformed officers would be parked at the exit at the end of each evening. Nearby, an informal rank of taxis waited to take revellers home. After installation, the police van parked instead around the corner, and stayed in radio contact with the CCTV control room.

Thereafter, they could be alerted not only to any trouble, but also could be given descriptions of the offenders before appearing on the scene to arrest those thus implicated. Apparently to facilitate both recognition and tracking of offenders, the taxi rank was disbanded, allegedly on police advice. So, here, two simple crime and disorder prevention measures (the visible presence of police; and taxis in which the exuberant may leave peacefully) were discontinued, effectively encouraging offending for the camera to see. Is it any wonder that crime rates rose?

15. These interviews, reported in Short and Ditton (1998), were made possible by a small grant from the Nuffield Foundation, for which we are grateful.

16. Skinns (1997) suggests an impact somewhere between the two in his preliminary analysis of the effects of CCTV on crime in Doncaster. Doncaster is bigger than Airdrie and smaller than Glasgow. This suggests that town/city size may well affect the efficacy of open-street CCTV.

17. It is understood that this emerged relatively spontaneously in Glasgow. Apparently, an officer on light duties was given the task of searching for those attempting robberies at automated teller machines, with the expectation that any success, if any resulted, would take weeks to materialise. Again apparently, this officer identified those responsible in a day.

18. Glasgow's police have indicated that between April 1995 and June 1996, the CCTV archive has been used effectively in resolving 10 major incidents (including five murders and one attempted murder).

BURNLEY CCTV EVALUATION

by

Rachel Armitage
Huddersfield University

Graham Smyth
Burnley Borough Council

Ken Pease
Huddersfield University

Abstract: *This study examines the effectiveness of a closed circuit television (CCTV) system installed in Burnley, Lancashire in northwest England. It considers both the outcomes and mechanisms through which they were brought about. Three areas are identified: "focal" beats, within which the CCTV cameras were installed; "displacement" beats, which were continuous to the focal beats; and "other" beats, comprising the remainder in the police division. With regard to both overall recorded crime and separate types of offences, the research finds significant decreases in the focal area, no spatial displacement, and some diffusion of benefit to the displacement area. There was some dilution of impact over time. There was no evidence that the proportional effect of CCTV changes by time of day, according to periods when surveillance with cameras would be more or less difficult. Crime fell more steeply as the first cameras were installed, with diminishing increases in effect as more were put in place. These patterns suggest that the impact of cameras is not simply a result of surveillance effects per se. Other preventive mechanisms were also triggered.*

THE NATIONAL CONTEXT

CCTV is one of the fastest growing sectors of the security industry, estimated by the end of the century to account for close to 30% of all security system sales (Cully, 1996). The popularity of the method is very great, although the wisdom of many of the purchasing decisions may be called into question (Hearnden, 1996). The U.K. Home Office has actively promoted the use of CCTV for the surveillance of public areas, and expenditure on the tool has recently run at the astonishing level of *three-quarters* of *total* Home Office expenditure on crime prevention (Koch, 1997). Competitions for CCTV funding have survived the change of government, albeit with an apparently increased emphasis on mobile systems.

There is, at first sight, impressive evidence that CCTV may reduce crime. This has been brought together by Horne (1996), and his summary table is modified and presented below as Table 1. Whilst the figures are at first sight impressive, three points must be made. First, the comparisons tend to be of a simple before-after design, and there is emerging evidence — in Glasgow, Scotland at least — that such comparison obscures more complex trends. Second, the evaluations vary in their competence. Third, they are not helpful in suggesting *how* CCTV achieves its effects.

Short and Ditton (1995, 1996) are particularly critical of the standard of CCTV evaluation. The points they make include the following:

- The evaluations have often not been carried out by independent researchers.
- The before and after periods are not long enough, or else are not seasonally matched.
- Crimes are aggregated, masking contrary trends in different crime types
- Appropriate comparison areas are seldom used as a baseline.
- The nature of the attendant publicity is never mentioned.
- Percentage falls, rather than absolute numbers, are often reported.
- Displacement is rarely mentioned.

The second issue concerns why CCTV has the effect it does. Pawson and Tilley (1997) offer a number of possibilities, which the present writer has extended into the following list:

- *"Caught in the act"* — perpetrators will be detected, and possibly removed or deterred.

- *"You've been framed"* — CCTV deters potential offenders who perceive an elevated risk of apprehension.

- *"Nosy parker"* — CCTV may lead more people to feel able to frequent the surveilled places. This will increase the extent of natural surveillance by newcomers, which may deter potential offenders.

- *"Effective deployment"* — CCTV directs security personnel to ambiguous situations, which may head off their translation into crime.
- *"Publicity"* — CCTV could symbolise efforts to take crime seriously, and the perception of those efforts may both energise law-abiding citizens and/or deter others.
- *"Time for crime"* — CCTV may be perceived as reducing the time available to commit crime, preventing those crimes that require extended time and effort.
- *"Memory jogging"* — the presence of CCTV may induce people to take elementary security precautions, such as locking their car, by jogging their memory.
- *"Anticipated shaming"* — the presence of CCTV may induce people to take elementary security precautions, for fear that they will be shamed by being shown on CCTV.
- *"Appeal to the cautious"* — cautious people migrate to the areas with CCTV to shop, leave their cars, and so on. Their caution and security-mindedness reduce the risk.
- *"Reporting changes"* — people report (and/or police record) fewer of the crimes that occur, either because they wish to show the effects of CCTV or out of a belief that "the Council is doing its best" and nothing should be done to discourage it.

Is it academic self-indulgence to be concerned with the mechanism whereby something worked? Shouldn't one just be pleased that it apparently did? In fact, it is crucial to know the mechanism. Only knowing it will enable the reproduction of success in new schemes, the maintenance of success in existing schemes, and the cost-efficiency of CCTV operation generally.

In short, CCTV has a central place in current crime control technology; such evaluation as has been done suggests substantial effects. However, there is good reason for remaining cautious about the nature and extent of these effects, and, most important, for exploring more thoroughly why CCTV worked.

Table 1: The Success of CCTV?

Location	Crime	Reduction (%)	Evaluation Time Period (months)
Newcastle-upon-Tyne	Burglary Vandalism	56 34	unstated unstated
Glasgow	'Crime'	20	6
North Shields	Burglary Theft & damage	67 33	12 12
Stockton on Tees	Theft Burglary (non-dwelling) Assault	43 43 35	3 3 3
Kings Lynn (Industrial) (Car parks)	All	100 95	36 12
City of London	All	29	unstated
Birmingham	All	14	12
Airdrie	All 'Dishonesty'	21 48	24 24
Hull (Car Park)	Damage Theft of vehicle Theft from vehicle	45 89 76	7 7 7
Lewisham	Auto-crime	75	6
Bradford	Theft from vehicle Theft of vehicle	68 43	12 12

THE BURNLEY CONTEXT

All CCTV cameras installed to date in Burnley were placed in the three town centre beats, T1, T2 and T3. The present report will deal with matters *other than* the movement of crime *within* the beats covered by Burnley's CCTV. This point is of importance, since it looks at the very detailed relationship between camera coverage and crime, with its implications for camera siting and offender awareness, and the reason for its delay should be clarified. Such a study is under way.

While gross estimates of effect can be reached with a division of crime locations simply into beats, the more subtle effects require geocoding of the data very precisely. The Lancashire Police Service is currently moving towards routine geocoding of its crime data. That, of course, means that geocoding of the data other than in the very recent past did not happen. Even after retrospective geocoding was undertaken, upwards of one-third of even recent crime reports did not have a precise location attached. This can be improved by reference to text data but the process will be a hard manual grind. But it is worth going through this process. Otherwise, the data are vulnerable to the charge that non-geocoded events are somehow different from geocoded events, which makes any conclusions about the distribution of crime within the beats covered by CCTV unreliable.

This report concerns itself exclusively with recorded crime changes, comparing CCTV-covered and other areas. Also reported are time-trend data, examining changes of particular crime types alongside the number of cameras installed up to that point. The speed with which changes in different crime types occurred is also examined, as are the implications of those. An extended discussion section makes recommendations based on the data or upon problems and issues that are beginning to emerge in other areas of the country with which the writers are familiar.

We categorised areas of the Burnley police command into: beats with cameras (focal), beats having a common boundary with beats containing cameras (displacement), and other beats in the police division (other). The first group comprises beats in which crime should decline, insofar as CCTV has an effect. The second comprises areas into which crime would arguably be displaced from the beats covered by cameras. The last group operates as the baseline. Spatial displacement should not occur to these areas given that there are closer and equally promising areas to which CCTV may displace crime.

What follows are percentage changes in crime in the first two categories relative to the third, comparing each year with 1994 figures. Thus in Table 2 below are included all crimes. Also in the table is the number of crimes occurring in 1994 in the areas concerned, to get an idea of the relative scale of the areas' crime experience. To illustrate, total crime in 1996 was 28% lower in the focal areas than it had been in 1994. In the same year, total crime was 3% lower in displacement areas, and 9% higher in other areas. Figures for 1997 are grossed from crime occurring in the first eight months of the year, and are thus imprecise.

Table 2: Total Crime Changes Relative to 1994 (Pre-CCTV)

Area	95	96	97
Focal	-6	-28	-24
Displacement	+7	-1	+3
Other	+7	+9	+3

Note: N in 1994: 1,805 in focal areas, 6,242 in contiguous areas and 1,069 elsewhere. The numbers are greater than would be calculated from summing Ns from Tables 3-8, since some categories of crime do not feature in those tables.

Table 2 demonstrates that the areas in which cameras were installed showed a reduction of one-quarter in the crimes they suffered in 1996 and 1997 relative to 1994. The effect has held up quite well over time, suggesting that it was not solely the result of transient factors like additional publicity. Of great interest is the fact that the adjoining areas showed trends similar to those of the non-adjoining areas. This means that there is no evidence of displacement of crime to adjoining areas. In fact, in all three years, the change that occurred in displacement areas was intermediate in extent between those taking place in focal and other areas. If displacement had occurred, the displacement areas should have shown increases greater than those of other areas, since they would be experiencing their own crime increase *plus* crime displaced from the focal areas. If anything, the pattern shows diffusion of benefits rather than displacement. The concept of diffusion of benefits is crucial and will be briefly discussed.

When a crime prevention programme is put in place, the argument usually advanced by those sceptical of its worth is that crime is *displaced* to other areas. Research has suggested that displacement is seldom if ever total, so that there is virtually always a net benefit in crime reduction. Even more interestingly, research sometimes shows the opposite of displacement, namely, diffusion of benefits (see Hesseling, 1994). Diffusion of benefits occurs when the areas surrounding an area with a crime prevention programme also show a decline in crime. Intuitively, this makes sense, insofar as an offender does not think in terms of police beats or other administrative units, and will not be sure where a scheme's boundaries lie. Most volume crimes take place close to an offender's home base, and there is a limit beyond which most offenders do not typically travel to crime. The pattern of the Burnley data suggests a diffusion of benefits. Owing to CCTV, some crimes will become known to the police that would otherwise not have been recorded, so the observed reductions are almost certainly understatements of real reductions.

Having shown the change in crime generally, what does analysis of individual crime types show? Obviously, some crimes are so rare that analysis would not be meaningful. However, what is the picture for common crimes? Table 3 looks at all assaultive crimes combined (including robbery, attempted robbery and theft from the person). It will be seen that the reduction in the focal and displacement areas is greater for crimes of violence than for total crime, *in both focal and displacement areas.* The increase in other areas represents relatively few crimes. As in Table 2, the pattern is more consistent with diffusion of benefits than with displacement.

Table 3: Crimes of Violence: Changes Relative to 1994 (Pre-CCTV)

Area	95	96	97
Focal	-12	-35	-27
Displacement	-20	-20	-9
Other	-14	0	+46

Note: N in 1994: 117 in focal areas, 267 in contiguous areas, and 32 in other areas.

Turning to drug crime, the pattern is rather different, as Table 4 shows. All drug crimes are combined in Table 4, from cultivation (there are few opium poppy fields in Burnley town centre) and supply through possession and allowing premises to be used for drugs. Most of the crimes are simple possession. Drug crimes fell in the focal area. Although both displacement and other areas show increases, once again the displacement area shows less of a rise than other areas. The sharp increase in recorded drug crimes outside the CCTV area suggests a general trend that the focal area, by one means or another, was able to buck. Drug markets are particularly visual, and it may be that CCTV has been involved in the disruption of town centre drug markets. However, since the bulk of drug offences involve simple possession, this could not possibly be more than a contributory factor. More likely is a CCTV effect that is more complex than simple surveillance. This point will be returned to a little later.

Table 4: Drug Crimes: Changes Relative to 1994 (Pre-CCTV)

Area	95	96	97
Focal	+41	-44	-71
Displacement	+125	+134	+94
Other	+146	+146	+161

Note: N in 1994: 46 in focal areas, 78 in contiguous areas and 13 elsewhere

Another crime that will take place in large measure in public areas is theft of and from motor vehicles. Table 5 reveals the trends involved. Offences combined here are theft of and from motor vehicles, aggravated taking of motor vehicles, and interfering with a vehicle.

Table 5: Motor Vehicle Crimes: Changes Relative to 1994 (Pre-CCTV)

Area	95	96	97
Focal	-24	-48	-21
Displacement	0	-8	-6
Other	+10	-8	-9

Note: N in 1994: 375 in focal areas, 1842 in contiguous areas and 309 elsewhere

The familiar pattern recurs. Vehicle crime declines greatly in the target area, and the surrounding areas show trends that are intermediate between the focal areas and outlying areas, consistent with diffusion of benefits rather than displacement.

The next step is to look at burglaries, both domestic and other. The two are combined in Table 6. Roughly the same pattern is evident, with changes in displacement areas intermediate between CCTV and other areas.

Table 6: Burglary: Changes Relative to 1994 (Pre-CCTV)

Area	95	96	97
Focal	-22	-41	-32
Displacement	+15	+9	+5
Other	+11	+34	-7

Note: N in 1994: 143 in focal areas, 2,208 in contiguous areas and 366 elsewhere

As for criminal damage, shown in Table 7, there is a more modest decline in CCTV areas, and the displacement/diffusion-of-benefits story is unclear. Criminal damage is a poorly reported crime, so changes are especially difficult to interpret here.

Table 7: Criminal Damage: Changes Relative to 1994 (Pre-CCTV)

Area	95	96	97
Focal	-1	-23	-12
Displacement	+18	+20	+21
Other	+5	+42	+10

Note: N in 1994: 163 in focal areas, 643 in contiguous areas and 79 elsewhere

The next step is to look at a crime type on which CCTV should not have a direct, surveillance-based effect. Demonstrating a reduction for crimes not susceptible to visual scrutiny of public places would not suggest that the decline was spurious, just that its mechanism is a little more complex, within or beyond the mechanisms listed earlier. Table 8 combines fraud and handling of stolen goods, to generate numbers sufficiently large for analysis. These are crimes to which CCTV surveillance should not be directly relevant.

Although these crimes were aggregated so as to yield enough cases to make trend analysis feasible, there were still too few in out-lying areas for comfort, hence the proportionately huge increase in these offences in 1997. The cell to which attention should be drawn is the 1997 cell for focal areas. The decline in 1997 is greater than in

1996. The only other table for which this was true concerned drug crime. A more detailed analysis of trends is presented later in this report.

Table 8: Fraud and Handling Stolen Goods: Changes Relative to 1994 (Pre-CCTV)

Area	95	96	97
Focal	-2	-32	-53
Displacement	+21	-7	-12
Other	+57	-7	+586

Note: N in 1994: 117 in focal areas, 173 in contiguous areas and 14 elsewhere

Why do crimes not occurring in public and therefore not liable to CCTV surveillance show a decline? In particular, why do they show a decline that increases with time, rather than one that decreases, as with other crimes? Three explanations come to mind. All of these are testable by conducting more research, but are beyond the scope of the work presented here.

(1)   Criminals are versatile, and (with some exceptions) the most active offenders are the most versatile (see, for example, Tarling, 1993). By disrupting some types of offending, others are prevented directly (by the imprisonment or other control of perpetrators), or indirectly (by the generalisation of perpetrators' sense of the risks involved in offending). By either means, one would expect an *increasing* effect with time, whereas for direct effects, one would expect a diminishing effect with time. In short, CCTV has its effect by disrupting the general patterns of offending of *versatile* (and hence usually prolific) offenders. If this is true, it is important, because it would suggest that CCTV has its greatest effect on the people on whom one would most want it to impact, namely, versatile and prolific offenders. This could be tested by looking at detected crimes in the Burnley CCTV area. If this speculation is correct, then CCTV would coincide with a reduction in the proportion of cleared crimes attributable to the most prolific offenders. Thus, for example, if before CCTV the top 10% of offenders accounted for 50% of cleared crime, and afterwards the top 10% accounted for 25% of the cleared crime, that would support the notion advanced.

(2) CCTV either changes the way the police and local authority work, by knowing and logging the whereabouts of prolific offenders, or releases police time to deal with offences that take place in private and that require proactive policing. Offences like handling stolen goods, and drug possession, for example, are cleared as they become known. Of these two sub-options, the first is testable by interview with staff in the CCTV control room, and scrutiny of the logs insofar as they deal with recognised individuals. The second (which is believed implausible) would be testable by examination of the manner of clearance of a sample of cleared fraud cases in 1994 and 1997.

(3) By the memory jogging and reporting processes suggested by Pawson and Tilley, people become more crime conscious in private as well as public, so are more likely to become aware of these kinds of crime, and to report them. This is testable by examination of the number of crimes of these types cleared primarily through the public's supply of information to the police.

Time

The analysis of year-to-year trends, as presented in Tables 2 through 8, gives some partial insights into what happened in Burnley. However, this should be supplemented by examination of what happened over time, without breaking the time continuum into such crude slices. This is true for the important reason that the cameras were switched on at different times, so that the "active ingredient" — CCTV surveillance — grew in irregular steps. When time is broken down day by day, week by week or month by month in this way, the number of events occurring in each period quickly becomes too small to analyse. If the data are broken down into individual crime types, the numbers become too small to analyse very quickly indeed. This means either that the analysis must rely on aggregate crime, and/or that some method of smoothing the data statistically has to occur. For linking crime with camera deployment, the whole point of doing the analysis is to identify trends over short periods of time, so the second approach is unsatisfactory. Later, the trends of sub-aggregates of total crime are smoothed for a different purpose, namely the demonstration of which crime types decline quickly and which decline slowly.

For all its difficulties, time has to be incorporated in the analysis. Figure 1 presents monthly aggregate reported crimes for the CCTV area and the total for adjoining beats. The figure for January 1995 was set at 100 for both data sets, to enable easy comparison. Figure 1 confirms what we knew from the preceding analyses, namely, that crime in the CCTV areas declined relative to surrounding areas. Since we already have indications that there is some diffusion of benefits to surrounding areas, Figure 1 somewhat understates the extent of the reduction. While not designed as such, the figure is useful in depicting the CCTV-associated gross reduction, an area covered in the tables appearing earlier in the paper. What Figure 1 *is* important for is providing an indication of how CCTV worked.

Figure 1: Monthly Crime by CCTV Presence

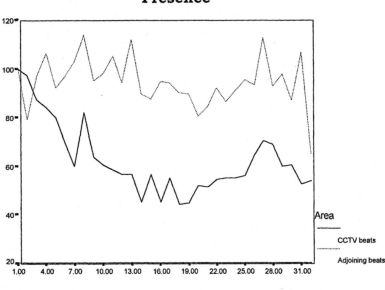

Months (1 = Jan 1995)

The decline seemed to begin in March 1995. The first CCTV camera went up in April 1995. This is not so bizarre as it may appear. In many cases, crime prevention measures work before they "should." Publicity, consciousness, and enthusiasm may all communicate themselves to people. What this trend suggests is that the CCTV mechanism may have more to do with a social climate change than changes in the processing of offenders, or changes in the perception that offenders have of situations in which they are taking a risk. The very simplest explanation may be that although the cameras were switched on in April, they may have had effects before that. It would be nice to know the schedule of installation work.

A better indication of the process may be gained from Figure 2, and from statistics associated with it. Figure 2 expresses the data of Figure 1 in a different way, and alongside some different data. One line in Figure 2 represents the proportionate reduction in crime in CCTV areas relative to surrounding areas. For example, in May 1995 (month 5) crime in the CCTV areas, at 80%, was 20% lower than crime in the surrounding areas, against a baseline of January 1995. The second line in Figure 2 represents the number of CCTV cameras installed by that month. To be precise, it represents the proportion of the eventually installed cameras that had *not* been installed by that month. For example, from July through September 1995, three-quarters of the CCTV units had yet to be installed. The reason for presenting the data in this apparently bizarre way is that the amount of crime should *decline* as the number of cameras *increases*. It is easier to see trends when the data series go in the same direction, and since the two ways of expressing the relationship are identical, the number of cameras installed was converted to the number of cameras yet to be installed. Sceptical readers should simply trace one of the lines and turn the tracing paper upside down.

The basic question here concerns whether the periods in which cameras increased in number were also those in which the number of crimes fell. It looks as though during the first installations, crime declined apace. In fact, the relationship was quite a close one up to September 1995. The large number of extra cameras installed during autumn 1995 was not associated with further large decreases in crime. The decline in crime continued until it bottomed out in mid-1996. Of course, we cannot tell whether the continuing decline in late 1995 and early 1996 was linked with the installation of extra cameras, or the working through of the effects of the first cameras. For example, it is unclear which of these might have incapacitated offenders detected through the deployment of the first cameras after the time it took for bail, court appearance and sentence.

The installation of the last few cameras was linked to a very slight increase in crime. Looking at the figures reinforces the view that the effect of CCTV is not the simple effect of increased surveillability. This is so because:

(1) The decline in crime began too early, i.e., it had started (perhaps through publicity) in the months before any camera was deployed.

(2)   There was no one-to-one relationship between the number of cameras deployed and either the absolute or the proportionate reduction in crime.

Oddly, this is good news. It may be that even quite a modest scheme, if appropriately presented and executed, may have a swift and disproportionately large effect upon rates of crime. However, it would be good to establish whether the later crime reduction was the immediate effect of extra cameras, or the delayed detection/incapacitation effect of the first cameras. A speculative attempt will be made to take this analysis further.

Figure 2: Crime and CCTV Cameras

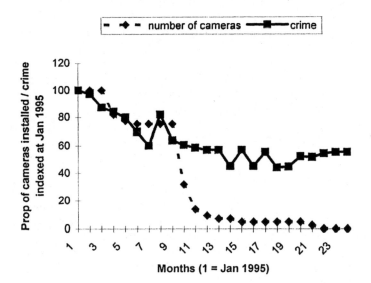

Crimes were aggregated into subtotals, for example, burglary, assaultive crime, sex crime and so on. Figure 3 shows those crimes that declined swiftly when (or even before) CCTV was installed. These were burglary, vehicle crime, and other property crime. The fact that these are the swiftly declining crimes gives confidence that CCTV is implicated in the declines, since they are among the crimes that may best be overseen.

Figure 4 shows those crimes whose decline was somewhat later. These are drug crime, fraud (including forgery and false accounting) and criminal damage. Violent and sex offences are intermediate between the crimes shown in Figure 3 and those shown in Figure 4. Sex crimes are quite rare, and a trend based on such small numbers is virtually meaningless.

What is different about the late-declining crimes? Fraud is a crime that typically occurs in private. Most drug crimes involve simple possession and are therefore not particularly conspicuous, so any effect of CCTV is likely to be indirect. Indeed, drug possession is entirely invisible unless one has a sackful of the stuff. Only when it is used is it visible, and even then the action is ambiguous in its interpretation.

Figure 3: Crimes that Fell Quickly with CCTV

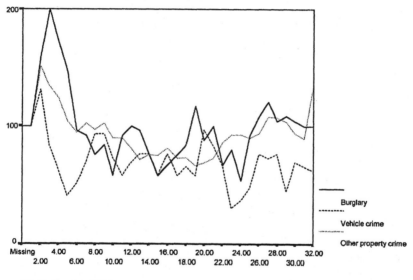

Month (1 = Jan 1995)

The decline in criminal damage may have been slow for a different reason; namely, that the cameras brought to attention damage that would otherwise have remained unreported, so that the real decline occurred earlier.

In short, all analysable crime types did decline. Two of the three types that declined later are crimes that typically occur in private. It is suggested, consistent with earlier data, that the CCTV effect is far from simple, and examination of the details of the offence should be undertaken to clarify this point.

An additional observation is that fraud and drug crime are crimes that are typically recorded at the point of detection. Unlike burglary and violence, for example, where victims suffer crimes and may or may not bring these to the attention of the police, fraud and drug crimes are typically only recorded when a police officer or other citizen identifies the offence as such. Those who possess drugs do not have a decision to make whether to report the crime to the police (or not a decision they would recognise as such). Thus the pattern observed is one that would be consistent with a more proactive policing style, perhaps made possible by the reduction in other types of town centre crime.

Figure 4: Crimes that Fell Slowly in CCTV Areas

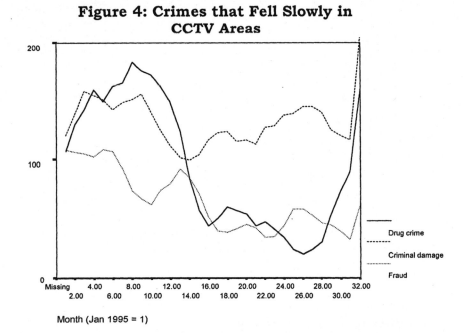

Month (Jan 1995 = 1)

Time trends may also be looked at to gain further information about displacement. Correlations reflect the degree of association between data sets, and may vary between +1 (which shows a perfect positive correlation, as, for example, between height and hand span) and -1 (which shows a perfect negative correlation, as, for example between individuals' enthusiasm for Burnley and Blackburn Rovers soccer teams). Month-by-month correlations between rates of crime in CCTV and adjacent areas can be used to show the association between these variables.

The correlations between rates of individual crimes in CCTV and adjoining areas were generally very low. They are presented as Table 9. None of these correlations is statistically significant. More important, only one is negative. If displacement were an important issue, these correlations *should* be negative, since the decline in CCTV areas should be associated with a simultaneous or quickly following increase in adjoining areas. For those interested in statistics, manipulating the data by lagging (i.e., linking a decline in one area with the change in the next month or the month after that) does not change the conclusion, so the data do not suggest that this month's crime prevented in the town centre moves to an adjacent area *next* month.

Table 9: Correlation between CCTV and Adjoining Areas: Monthly Data by Crime Type

Crime Type	Correlation
burglary	.002
drugs	.086
fraud	.444
other property	.354
sex	-.326
vandalism	.115
vehicle	.172
violence	.167

Time of Day

If CCTV works by direct surveillance, at what time of day should it work best? One possibility is that it should work best at those times when there is the least general bustle, because the signal/noise ratio is most favourable, i.e., these are times at which there is less movement other than that associated with the crime itself to distract the CCTV operator. This assumes one kind of mechanism by which the effect is achieved. Other mechanisms would imply different patterns. What do the data suggest?

It is surprisingly difficult and time-consuming to establish this, for two reasons. First, the meaning of morning and evening hours depends upon the season, and we do not have a whole year of pre-CCTV-timed data to make the appropriate seasonal adjustments. Second, crimes are not precisely timed, or precisely timeable, even by their victims. Particularly for crimes like car theft and burglary, much time may elapse before a crime is known to have occurred. In an extreme case, burglaries occurring when one is on holiday may have taken place at any time since one went away. These problems invite the question of how one allocates crimes to times without including meaningless time allocations but while retaining all the usable data for analysis.

This was done by selecting those crimes for which the first and last possible times were either on the same day or on successive days. Thus, a crime that could have occurred on February 2nd or 3rd was retained for further consideration. This included 91% of all crimes. However, allocating a time to a crime that may have taken place at any point between a minute after midnight on one day and a minute to midnight the next day is not especially helpful. For that reason, a time window was selected that did not reduce the data to meaninglessness. Then, those windows were selected that had a first and last possible time within six hours of each other. This comprised 68% of the remaining crimes (i.e., .91 * .68 of all crimes). The notional time was then set halfway between the first and last possible time, so that a crime that took place between 1 a.m. and 5 a.m. was timed at 3 a.m. The times were then classified into three-hour segments, as midnight but before 3 a.m. and so on. We thus ended up with each crime in one of eight time segments, as shown in Figures 5 and 6. Perhaps the first thing to say is the obvious point of how unequally crime is distributed across 24 hours, with very little crime occurring in the small hours. The writers' initial thought would be that CCTV would have its greatest proportional effect when particularly little was happening, because there would be few distractors at such times.

To allow for comparison of seasonally equivalent periods, the first three months of 1995, 1996 and 1997 were selected. These three-month periods are referred to below and in the figures as epochs.

The number of crimes in each of the three epochs — early 1995, early 1996 and early 1997 — is presented in Figure 5 for CCTV areas, and in Figure 6 for adjoining areas. The time distribution of crime in the adjoining areas remains fairly consistent. For CCTV areas, there is a reduction in crime in *each* of the time segments, and it is roughly

Figure 5: Changes in Crime by Time of Day: CCTV Areas

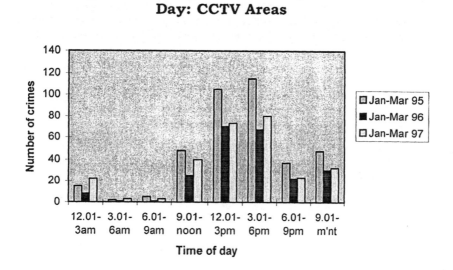

Figure 6: Changes in Crime by Time of Day: Adjacent Areas

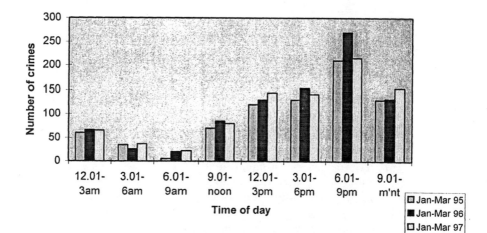

in proportion to the number of crimes at that time in the pre-CCTV period. In other words, the suspicion does not hold that the effect is greatest at times when there is little to distract the observer. Similarly, the notion that the reduction is related to daylight does not hold. This pattern seems to have less to do with the technicalities of CCTV and more to do with a general, more complex and subtle change in how people — including offenders — see CCTV operations.

CONCLUSIONS FROM THE DATA

(1)   The area covered by CCTV showed crime reductions of 25% in 1996 and 16% in 1997 relative to statistically expected levels. The real reductions are almost certainly greater than those shown because of additional crimes that came to police notice through CCTV.

(2)   Effects occurred across crime types rather than being specific to some crimes. There were declines even in the kinds of crime that are not usually carried out in public view. Such declines tended to come later than more visible crimes, suggesting an indirect effect beyond simple surveillance. This effect was also suggested by the changing relationship between the number of cameras deployed and the rates of crime. This is an important point in that it may suggest an optimum number of cameras per area to maximise effect at minimum total cost.

(3)   There was no evidence of spatial displacement. This conclusion was reached by correlational analysis and by comparison of CCTV areas with adjoining and other areas in Burnley. There was some evidence of diffusion of benefits whereby areas adjoining CCTV coverage also received some advantage. If any further research were undertaken locally it should perhaps be an examination of the subsequent criminal careers of those who are known to have committed crime in the CCTV areas before coverage began.

(4)   There was no suggestion that CCTV locates crime more precisely in time, nor that the proportional effect of CCTV is greater at some times of the day or night than others. This is intriguing, and again suggests effects that go beyond the simple efficacy of surveillance.

(5)   More sophisticated estimates of effects within target areas will provide information with greater practical implications.

(6) There are minor signs that crime is now beginning to increase in CCTV areas. It is suggested that some publicity be given to the final version of this report, complete with anecdotes of detections achieved via CCTV use. If we are right about how the effect is working, this may well induce a restoration of the full reduction.

SPECULATIONS AND RECOMMENDATIONS

There was a reduction in crime associated with the advent of CCTV, and it seems not to have been displaced. Indeed, the benefits of CCTV may have diffused to adjoining areas. Burnley has thus been successful in its CCTV work. What remains to be done is to clarify the means whereby the success was achieved and the ways available of maximising effects, both locally and nationally.

The reduction achieved seems to be more than a simple surveillance effect, and further research could clarify the mechanism further. However, what already exists is enough to speculate that even an unambitious scheme may have beneficial effects, and that extra camera coverage may not produce proportional extra reductions in crime.

Although what follows does not stem from the data analysis reported above, we would like to make some observations about emergent problems in CCTV usage elsewhere, and their relevance to the Burnley situation. CCTV has clearly been a success. To consolidate that success and to build upon it may be aided by an understanding of the dynamics of operating a system.

Control Room Operator Training

Two as yet unpublished studies of CCTV have concentrated on the performance of control room operators (see Norris and Armstrong, this volume). Both of these have yielded results that are controversial, and they will certainly stimulate debate. The criticism is that the choice of what is observed may be frivolous (with attractive women targeted), or may be stereotyped as to likely perpetrators (with young, minority-group males being observed more often than their frequency on the scene observed would justify). Obvious alternative responses to such charges could be found in training, and the requirement of awareness of the codes of practice that already exist. General principles that are not contentious can be enunciated to guide camera direction. These include targeting places in which more movement is found, places with recent crime experience, and places with incongruities like no light and single-person movement at night. In our view, this should go along with an investigation of logs to determine within-shift effects, e.g., fewer incidents observed per crime reported in surveilled areas as shifts proceed. It seems astonishing to us that the rich literature on radar operators' vigilance and efficiency, optimal rest breaks and the like have not been brought to bear on CCTV control room practice. These two issues — the ethics and the efficiency of control practice — go together. Practice is optimised by maximising the number of incidents reported by CCTV control room staff per incident in the surveilled area known to the police. Obvious attention to the efficiency of the process allied to a clear ethical stance stressed in training and enforced in practice is the clear answer to the emergent criticism.

Scheme Ownership

The next point concerns ownership of schemes. In essence, this is the problem of the free-rider — the individual who stands aside from contribution to an innovation that directly benefits him or her. The process is familiar in all crime contexts: the retailer or publican who does not contribute to ring-round schemes; the householder who does not join Neighbourhood Watch; the credit card company that does not join the Association of Payment Clearing Services.

The free-rider effect can operate at two levels in the CCTV context. First, shops in a mall that do not contribute to CCTV costs will benefit from CCTV equally with shops that do, through extra shoppers and fewer crime losses. Second, ostensibly collaborating organisations involved may become rivals rather than partners. The third author was first astonished by this latter process in the competition for drug investigations and arrests between police and Her Majesty's Customs, experienced in France, Belgium and the U.K. in remarkably similar forms. Similarly, there are all the ingredients for competition and rivalry between the police and the local authority in the Burnley context. Indeed, despite all the rhetoric about partnership and multi-agency cooperation that has been central to the current and previous administration's policies over the last decade, the reality has almost universally been tension and conflict between supposed partners (see, for example, Crawford 1997). First-time occurrences in Burnley would certainly include the acknowledgement of emerging tensions and the need to confront them to head off the breakdown of relationships that is common even in successful initiatives.

In our view, the same approach is important in addressing problems of both types. It has three elements.

(1) The attempt to improve the system is the only process in which all stakeholders have a common interest. It is suggested that there is periodic collaborative effort to advance the understanding of how CCTV works, shared with all involved. This sounds woolly, but it is necessary to stress the shared agenda positively, or the divisive factors will take over. For example, a summary of detections achieved through CCTV and how they happened would be informative. A study of retailer-CCTV-police interactions during incidents would be another. A study of store and street maintenance costs could easily be mounted by the stores. A study of indices of usage of the area by the Council by time of day may even help induce stores to increase opening hours.

(2) Shopkeepers, both those who do contribute and those who do not, should be explicitly and collectively consulted about the conflicts and tensions experienced by CCTV control staff that are inevitable in such an arrangement. This consultation would address issues like: whether cameras should point at contributing shops more than noncontributing shops, or just track developing incidents; who has responsibility for notifying the police for intrastore events; and whether control room notification should occur in the same way for both kinds of store.

(3) The police and the local authority should renegotiate their division of responsibilities now that practical experience of the scheme has been accrued. Elsewhere, there have been signs that unforseen turf wars jeopardise partnership for no better reason than an agreement made in ignorance was not reconsidered. Topics for such negotiation should include police powers to direct camera operation in emergencies, and, more generally, ownership and maintenance of tapes/disks, procedures for review and use as evidence of tapes; and even simple matters like rights of access to the control room and the police station.

A final point in which Burnley may wish to take a leadership role is the availability *and use* of CCTV evidence in sentencing decisions. CCTV data are currently used in inducing guilty pleas and the like. Other work carried out by the third author and his colleagues Sgt. Chris Henshaw and Sylvia Chenery shows that magistrates are keen to see available video evidence, and that the effect of such evidence is to increase the severity of sentences imposed. This evidence would both increase the efficacy of the process whereby offenders acknowledge their guilt and would make sentencing more commensurate with the act committed. Knowledge that such use of CCTV evidence was being promulgated in Burnley courts would almost certainly reinforce the publicity-driven effects of CCTV schemes.

Acknowledgements: The help of Bob Burns of Lancashire Police was invaluable and is immensely appreciated.

Address correspondence to: Ken Pease, Applied Criminology Group, University of Huddersfield, Queensgate, Huddersfield HD1 3DH, United Kingdom.

REFERENCES

Crawford, A. (1997). *The Local Governance of Crime*. Oxford, UK: Clarendon.

Cully, J. (1996). "CCTV — Where Does the Money Go?" *Professional Security* (6):23-26.

Hearnden, K. (1996). "Small Business Approach to Managing CCTV to Combat Crime." *International Journal of Risk, Security and Crime Prevention* 1(1):19-31.

Hesseling, R.B.P. (1994). "Displacement: A Review of the Empirical Literature." In: R.V. Clarke (ed.), *Crime Prevention Studies*, vol. 2. Monsey, NY: Willow Tree Press.

Horne, C.J. (1996). "The Case for: CCTV Should be Introduced." *International Journal of Risk, Security and Crime Prevention* 1:317-326.

Koch, B. (1997). *Crime Prevention Policy*. Aldershot, UK: Ashgate.

Pawson, R. and N. Tilley (1997). *Realistic Evaluation*. London, UK: Sage.

Short, E. and J. Ditton (1995). "Does CCTV Affect Crime?" *CCTV Today* 2:10-12.

—— (1996). *Does Closed Circuit Television Prevent Crime?* Edinburgh, SCOT: Central Research Unit, Scottish Office.

Tarling, R. (1993). *Analysing Offending.* London, UK: Her Majesty's Stationery Office.

CONTEXT-SPECIFIC MEASURES OF CCTV EFFECTIVENESS IN THE RETAIL SECTOR

by

Adrian Beck

and

Andrew Willis

Scarman Centre for the Study of Public Order
University of Leicester

Abstract: *This study reports a research project that explored the effectiveness of closed circuit television (CCTV) as a primary crime prevention measure directed against staff and customer theft in the retail clothing sector. It demonstrates the usefulness of a strong before-and-after research design, as well as the benefits of using different measures for different purposes, including loss measured as a percentage of sales, loss by number of units stolen and loss by value. The study also examines whether the costs of CCTV installations are offset by the benefits of reduced loss. It is concluded that robust measures that are "fit for a purpose" allow informed choices to be made about appropriate investment in crime prevention CCTV technology.*

RETAIL CRIME THREATS

The retail sector is one of the largest and most dynamic parts of the United Kingdom's economy (O'Brien and Harris, 1991; Cahill, 1994; Guy, 1994). By the mid-1990s the industry had a turnover of £187 billion, or 14% of the nation's gross domestic product, and it employed 2.4 million persons, or 10% of the British workforce, in some 328,000 retail outlets (Burrows and Speed, 1994; U.K. House of Commons, 1994; Beck and Willis, 1995; Wells and Dryer, 1997).

Growing concern about crime threats to retailing led to the establishment of the Retail Crime Initiative by the British Retail Consortium (BRC). From 1994 there has been an annual report on retail crime and its costs. The survey for the financial year 1995–96 was based on 48,000 U.K. retail outlets with a combined turnover of over one-half of all retail sales (Wells and Dryer, 1997).

The study revealed 5.3 million criminal incidents in the course of a year — the equivalent of 18 offences per outlet. The total annual costs of retail crime were estimated to be £1.9 billion — £1.4 billion sustained as a result of known or suspected criminal incidents, and a further £450 million of expenditure on security hardware and security services. Against annual sales of £187 billion, this was equivalent to 1.13% of total retail turnover. Crime costs amounted to an average loss of £85 from each household in the country.

Customer theft and staff dishonesty dominated retail crime figures. Retailers witnessed, or could quite clearly establish, 5 million instances of customer theft, with 1.6 million offenders apprehended and just over 1 million referred to the police. The gross loss due to customer theft was estimated to be £653 million — £211 million lost due to witnessed incidents and £442 million lost to unwitnessed crimes. The findings are similar to those of a 1993 U.K. Home Office study that identified 5.8 million instances of customer theft, with witnessed incidents accounting for losses of £200 million (Mirrlees-Black and Ross, 1995). The BRC survey also found over 31,000 recorded incidents of staff theft or fraud, involving nearly 20,000 staff of whom 40% were referred to the police. The value of staff theft recorded by stores was £386 million, £39 million derived from witnessed incidents (detected cases) and £347 million attributed to unwitnessed staff thefts (suspected cases).

Findings for the fashion retail sector reflected the broader picture. The BRC survey identified 30,000 outlets with an annual turnover of £19 billion that suffered criminal losses of £128 million, with a further £74 million spent on crime prevention measures. Against annual sales of £19.3 billion, this was equivalent to 1.05% of total clothing retail turnover. Over three-quarters of all losses were attributed to just two offence categories — customer theft at £53 million (41%) and staff theft at £47 million (37%). Earlier retail crime surveys pointed to near-identical findings (Bamfield, 1994; Burrows and Speed, 1994; Forum of Private Business, 1995; Mirrlees-Black and Ross, 1995; Speed et al., 1995), and related studies have also highlighted the extent and costs of retail crime (Ekblom, 1986; U.K. Home Office, 1986;

Ekblom and Simon, 1988; Touche Ross, 1989, 1992; Hibberd and Shapland, 1993; Beck and Willis, 1995).

The data are unequivocal — the criminal threat to the retailer in general, and the fashion retailer in particular, is substantial whether this is measured by the number of incidents or the direct costs of stock loss. There are also consequential costs caused by disruption to trade and taking remedial action, including instituting security measures. All of these costs have to be borne, either by retailers in the form of lowered profits, by the customers in the form of increased prices, or by both. Finally, most of this victimisation remains well outside the purview of the formal authorities; of the 5 million instances of retailer-identified thefts a year only 280,000 offences, or 6% of the total, are recorded as police crime statistics (U.K. Home Office, 1996a; Wells and Dryer, 1997). There is a crime detection deficit, and even when offenders are known, they are not necessarily passed on to the police. These shortfalls suggest that crime prevention initiatives need to be directed at the point where crimes are committed (individual stores) and focused on the problems of customer theft and staff dishonesty. It is at this point that CCTV commends itself as a suitable mechanism.

GROWTH OF CCTV

There is evidence that rising retail crime threats are increasingly being met by the installation and use of security surveillance equipment. All the indicators point towards substantial and continuing growth in the CCTV market. Surveillance cameras are now found in a "bewildering variety" of settings (Honess and Charman, 1992) and are seen as a common feature of public life. In a three-year period from 1994, government has provided £35 million for 350 CCTV installations, mostly in town centres (U.K. Home Office, 1996b). Beck and Willis (1995) estimate that over £300 million a year is spent on video surveillance equipment, with around 300,000 security cameras being sold, and that more than a million may be in use. More specifically, the retail sector accounts for the largest proportion of capital expenditure with over one-third of the total spend (36%), followed by the industrial sector (31%), the commercial sector (17%) and the public sector (16%).

The BRC survey confirms the prominent position of CCTV in the retail environment (Wells and Dryer, 1997). Total crime prevention costs in 1995-96 amounted to £450 million, of which £74 million or 16% was CCTV-related — £54 million capital expenditure on CCTV installations and £20 million on equipment maintenance and monitoring. Earlier sweeps of the survey showed even higher levels of spending — £133 million in 1993-94 and £119 million in 1994-95. In the three-year period from 1993-94 to 1995-96, a total of £326 million was spent on security surveillance in the retail sector. The prominent position of CCTV in retail crime prevention was confirmed by U.K. Home Office research (Mirrlees-Black and Ross, 1995). CCTV was found to be present in 20% of all retail outlets and 36% of the larger outlets; its installation being positively correlated with previous victimisation and a known crime problem. It is clearly being used as a principal weapon in the fight against shop crime.

This enthusiasm for CCTV is buttressed by a number of recurring themes (Beck and Willis, 1995). CCTV supposedly offers a technological equivalent to extensive police or security surveillance, a case of the officer on the beat or security guard being replaced by an omnipresent, near-infallible robot eye in the sky on duty 24 hours a day. It offers day-and-night surveillance, with an unparalleled capacity to deter or to detect the offender. Electronic surveillance promises comprehensive crime control in a neat, high-technology package — an off-the-shelf, state-of-the-art, electronic panacea for crime. There is a seductive appeal to what might be called the "high-tech fix." There is a danger, however, that commitment to (and expenditure on) CCTV, in both the public and private sectors, may be more a matter of "security wish fulfillment" than a judgement based on hard evidence and a reasoned assessment of its effectiveness. CCTV may be receiving a vote of confidence primarily because everyone wants to believe in its effectiveness rather than because its effectiveness has been demonstrated. It may be easier and more convenient to show blind faith in its supposed capabilities than to assess properly its contribution to crime control. To some extent the 'hunches' that inform decisions to install CCTV systems are largely a product of a needs-led belief that there is (at long last) a techno-fix solution that guarantees real-life, crime control benefits, but this is far from an evidence-led assessment of its contribution to crime prevention.

In its strongest form, an uncritical belief in CCTV's effectiveness could operate so as to preclude any formal assessment of its merits; and efficacy becomes a presumption that follows from installation. Equally, there can be technical reasons why CCTV remains under-researched or poorly researched (Ekblom and Pease, 1995; Tilley, 1997). Finally, Beck and Willis (1995) have pointed to a raft of unanswered questions about its impact in relation to: the detection of offenders; the deterrence of would-be offenders; the contribution to crime control of displacing criminal activities elsewhere; the relative usefulness of video recordings and real-time images; the ability of operators to monitor and make sense of multiple images; the impact on customers (who may be reassured even when there are no measurable benefits); and the effect on shop staff (who may become less vigilant about crime following its installation). These point to the need for high-quality data, which is seen to be in short supply (Edwards and Tilley, 1994).

Tilley (1997) goes rather further by suggesting that the question "Does CCTV work?" is not susceptible to any consistent answer either because of technically weak evaluations or because different systems will have differential impacts, which implies that the question itself is not "sensible, useful or intelligible" (p.179). This is too pessimistic, however, because the author promptly proceeds to offer a new approach, called realistic evaluation, that seeks to establish what works for whom and in what circumstances, where CCTV's effectiveness is seen as a "range of outcomes...generated through mechanisms triggered in context" (Tilley, 1997:183; see also Pawson and Tilley, 1994, 1997). What is really being asserted here is the need to establish how CCTV works in defined settings so as to produce particular outcomes.

These reasonable precepts can be applied to the evaluation of CCTV in the fashion retail sector, where outcomes or measures of effectiveness can be understood as the product of the deployment of CCTV in a specific context (fashion stores) for a particular purpose. The critical variable is the purpose for which CCTV is installed, and there are major differences here between the interests of the academic researcher and those of the retailer. The former may wish to explore subtle differences between CCTV's impact on detection or its deterrent effect, or its effect on customer confidence and the fear of crime. The latter has a more straightforward agenda — namely, the effect of CCTV on the store's ability to make money; under normal circumstances the "bottom line" is the "bottom line." This may be none too elegant but it reflects commercial realities. It is a solid enough imperative from the retailer's point of view, and it gives the researcher a clear enough agenda for evaluation, especially with the use of an experimental design.

The research question focuses, therefore, on whether CCTV is fit for the purpose of reducing loss to the point where its costs are more than offset by a reduction of loss due to its deployment. Again, this stands in contrast to Tilley's (1997) suggestion that there will "rarely if ever be sufficient data to assess the full costs and benefits that can be directly attributable to CCTV" (p.182), but this is to misunderstand the realities of business life. Where the prospect of maximising financial advantage is threatened by crime (stock loss caused by customer theft or staff theft) it is an absolute business imperative — and a straightforward empirical question — as to whether the costs of installing CCTV can be compensated for by reduced stock loss equal to (or greater than) the crime prevention initiative. This is an every-day commercial calculation of the same order as, for example, whether an investment in product advertisement generates additional sales over and above the costs of the publicity.

METHODOLOGY

The aim of the project was to measure the impact of different types of CCTV systems on levels of loss, including its performance over time, and to assess whether its costs were more than compensated for by crime control benefits. The project was carried out in 15 stores operated by a large U.K. fashion retailer with over 180 branches nationwide. All the stores were located in similar retailing environments. Three different types of CCTV systems were installed, each with varying degrees of sophistication. Three stores had a high-level system with between two and four pan, tilt and zoom colour cameras; between eight and 12 static colour cameras; public monitors positioned at all customer entrances; the facility to record; and security staff monitoring the system at all times. The average cost of installing a high-level system was £24,000. Six stores had a medium-level system with between six and 12 static colour cameras, public monitors at each customer entrance, the facility to record, but with monitoring carried out by the store manager from his or her office when time permitted. The average cost of installing a medium level system was £14,000. The remaining six stores had a low-level system with up to 12 dummy cameras, public monitors at all entrances but no facility to record. The average cost of installing a low-level system was £4,000. The terms high-level, medium-level and low-level are used below to refer to stores with these systems. Members of staff in all the stores were given training on how to use the system prior to the research, and all the equipment was in full working order throughout the study period.

The research used a before-and-after experimental design. Prior to the installation of CCTV, a stocktake was carried out in each of the stores to measure the amount lost as a percentage of sales, the number of units stolen and their value. This process was repeated 13 weeks after installation (3 months) and then again after 28 weeks (6 months). Whilst every effort was made to keep strict control over the way in which the stocktakes were carried out, the project had to rely upon the staff within the stores to perform the data collection process. Although the stocktake assessment of loss is an incomplete and imperfect indicator because it fails to discriminate between stock loss due to customer theft and staff theft, as well as failing to distinguish non-criminal, accidental shrinkage of product, it is the method of first choice throughout the retail sector. Although it could be argued that this approach needs refining, it is difficult to see how loss could be assessed other than by some means of checking stock held against stock sold.

EFFECTIVENESS OF CCTV

The primary mechanism for measuring loss is to calculate the value of goods lost expressed as a percentage of all goods sold, in this case before the installation of CCTV and then at a point some three and six months later (Table 1). Within three months of the installation of CCTV, the figures for loss to sales went down from 2.45% to 1.97% for all stores, with a reduction from 1.96% to 1.62% per cent in high-level stores, from 2.53% to 2.03% in medium-level stores, and from 3.08% to 2.38% in low-level stores. The percentage change in stock loss reduction over this three-month period was greatest for stores with low-level CCTV installations (23%), followed by those with medium-level systems (20%) and then those with a high-level specification (17%). The installation of CCTV had a dramatic effect on the levels of stock loss, showing an immediate improvement of 20% overall, with marginally greater improvements in low-level compared with high-level stores.

Findings from the second stocktake, six months after CCTV installation, were much more mixed. Using adjusted figures because only 10 stores completed the experiment in full, the figures for loss to sales over six months remained unchanged at 2.25% for all stores, with an increase from 1.96% to 2.70% in high-level stores, a reduction from 2.40% to 1.97% in medium-level stores, and a reduction from 2.63% to 1.93% in low-level stores.

The percentage change in stock loss reduction over the six-month period was greatest for stores with low-level CCTV installations (27%) followed by those with medium-level systems (18%), suggesting that the initial improvement was being maintained at or above the rates achieved after the three-month stocktake. In contrast, there was a substantial increase in the stock loss to sales figure over the six-month period for stores with high-level CCTV installations (38%). This had the effect of wiping out the initial impact of CCTV across all stores, and the overall percentage of loss to sales figure returned to the pre-installation level.

Table 1: Stock Loss to Sales Before and After CCTV Installation by Type of System

Type of system	Percent stock loss to sales				Percent stock loss reduction from installation	
	Pre-CCTV†	After 3 months	Pre-CCTV††	After 6 months	After 3 months	After 6 months
High	1.96	1.62	1.96	2.70	17.3	37.8
Medium	2.53	2.03	2.40	1.97	19.8	17.9
Low	3.08	2.38	2.63	1.93	22.7	26.6
All	2.45	1.97	2.25	2.25	19.6	0.0

† Base figure derived from 15 stores with complete stocktake.

†† Adjusted base figure derived from 10 stores with complete stocktake and 2 stores with partial stocktake.

Whilst the percentage of loss to sales is the usual way of measuring the rate of loss in retailing, another (widely used) option is to compare the number of units stolen, together with their value, before and after installation. Table 2 presents data covering the three-month experimental period, and Table 3 presents findings obtained over the six-month experimental period, in both cases using the average losses over a one-week period.

Within three months of the installation of CCTV the average number of units lost had fallen from 72 to 52 for all stores — with a reduction from 166 to 100 units in high-level stores, from 54 to 45 units in medium-level stores, and from 44 to 35 units in low-level stores. The corresponding figures for loss by value showed an overall reduction from £900 to £650 for all stores — with a reduction from £2,075 to £1,250 in high-level stores, from £675 to £562 in medium-level stores, and from £550 to £438 in low-level stores. The installation of CCTV had a dramatic effect on the level of stock loss, which was lowered by 28% for all stores — with a reduction of 40% in high-level stores, 17% in medium-level stores and 20% in low-level stores.

Table 2: Average Number and Value of Stock Units Lost Per Week Before CCTV Installation and After Three Months by Type of System

Type of System	Pre-CCTV		After 3 months		Percent reduction in loss
	Average number lost	Average value lost (£)†	Average number lost	Average value lost (£)†	
High	166	2,075	100	1,250	39.8
Medium	54	675	45	562	16.7
Low	44	550	35	438	20.4
All	72	900	52	650	27.7

†Following company procedures, the value of loss is calculated on the basis of £12.50 per unit lost.

Table 3: Average Number and Value of Stock Units Lost Per Week Before CCTV Installation and After Six Months by Type of System

Type of system	Pre-CCTV		After 6 months		Percent reduction in loss
	Average number lost	Average value lost (£)††	Average number lost	Average value lost (£)††	
High	123	1,538	91	1,138	26.0
Medium	44	550	58	725	31.8
Low	44	550	48	600	9.1
All	64	800	63	788	1.6

†Adjusted base figure derived from 9 stores with complete stocktake and 3 stores with partial stocktake.

††Following company procedures, the value of loss is calculated on the basis of £12.50 per unit lost.

Within six months of the installation of CCTV, the average number of units lost had fallen from 64 to just 63 for all stores — with a reduction from 123 to 91 units in high-level stores, together with a rise from 44 to 58 units in medium-level stores and a rise from 44 to 48 units in low-level stores. The corresponding figures for loss by value showed only a marginal reduction, from £800 to £788 for all stores — with a marked reduction from £1,538 to £1,138 in high-level stores, together with an increase from £550 to £725 in medium-level stores and an increase from £550 to £600 in low-level stores. The short-term impact of CCTV on the overall level of stock loss had all but disappeared, with a reduction of a little more than 1% for all stores. However, high-level stores showed an impressive reduction of 26%, whilst there was an increase of 32% in medium-level stores and an increase of 9% in low-level stores.

The decision to install CCTV in part reflects a commercial judgement about whether it offers value for the money, in this case, a calculation about the expected payback period or the time it would take to recover the cost of the equipment based upon the savings made in the amount that would have been lost to theft. Table 4 summarizes the data on the average weekly reduction in loss compared with the rate prior to installation, the cost of installing the equipment in the experimental stores, and the number of weeks required to pay back the initial cost of installation.

Table 4: Average Weekly Reduction in Stock Loss, Cost of CCTV Installation and Estimated PayBack Period by Type of System

Type of System	Average weekly reduction per store (£)		Cost of installation (£,000)	Estimated payback period (Years)	
	After 3 months	After 6 months		After 3 months	After 6 months
High	371	178	24	1.2	2.6
Medium	52	nil	14	5.2	Never
Low	53	nil	4	1.5	Never
All	116	4	12	2.0	57.6

Three months after the installation of CCTV the average weekly reduction in loss for all stores was £116, which, given average capital expenditure of £12,000 per CCTV system, would mean that it would take two years (103 weeks) to recoup the capital costs of its installation. There was considerable variation in the payback period for the different types of systems. For high-level systems with an average weekly reduction in loss of £371 set against a capital expenditure of

£24,000, the payback period was just over one year (65 weeks). For medium-level systems with an average weekly reduction in loss of only £52 set against capital expenditure of £14,000, the payback period was just over five years (269 weeks), Finally, for low-level systems with an average weekly reduction in loss of just £53 set against a capital expenditure of £4,000, the payback period was one and one-half years (75 weeks).

Like the other measures of loss outlined above, the impact of CCTV was reduced significantly by the time of the second stocktake. Six months after installation the average weekly reduction in loss for all stores was a near-insignificant £4, which, given average capital expenditure of £12,000 per CCTV system, would mean that it would take 58 years to recoup the capital costs of its installation. There was considerable variation in the payback period for the different types of systems. For high-level systems with an average weekly reduction in loss of £178 set against a capital expenditure of £24,000, the payback period was now 2.6 years (135 weeks). For medium and low-level systems, however, the payback period was nonexistent; it could not be calculated because the average weekly reduction in loss had disappeared altogether.

DISCUSSION

The pre-CCTV loss to sales figure of 2.45% was rather larger than that found in the 1995-96 BRC retail crime survey of 1.13% for the whole sector and 1.05% for the clothing sector (Wells and Dryer, 1997), but high-fashion stores may well be more at risk than other outlets. The change in the loss to sales figures over three months (from 2.45% to 1.97% for all stores) represented a 20% reduction in loss, although the low base rate makes extravagant claims about percentage change somewhat suspect. This initial success was maintained in low-level (27%) and medium-level (18%) stores, but high-level stores witnessed a 38% increase in the loss to sales figures over six months.

The corresponding three-month figures for losses by number were impressive, with the average number of units stolen in a week down from 72 to 52, together with a reduction by value from £900 to £650 — a decrease of 28% overall. The six-month figures for losses by number were altogether less impressive, with the average number of units stolen in a week barely changing from 64 to 63, together with a marginal reduction by value from £800 to £788 — a decrease of rather more than 1% overall. Within these figures there was continued success for CCTV in high-level stores with a 26% reduction, although medium-level stores showed an increase in loss of 32% and low-level stores showed an increase in loss of 9%.

The first observation is that the introduction of CCTV was associated with a significant short-term decrease in loss whether this was calculated as loss to sales, the number of units lost or their value. The three measures point towards the same conclusion, but they fail to explain the mechanism that accounts for the change (Tilley, 1997). However, it is most likely that the mechanism increases would-be offenders' fears that the system would lead to enhanced prospects for detection and apprehension, thereby acting as a deterrent to crime. One interpretation would view the theft of fashion items (which are small, easily portable and of relatively high value) as a classic case of opportunistic offending — something that is usually held to include one or more of three factors: high enticement to commit crime or the attraction of unpaid-for product; material conditions that are conducive to crime or ease of access; and benefits that can be obtained at minimal risk with low prospects of detection (see Clarke, 1980; Hough et al., 1980; Poyner, 1983; Felson, 1994, 1996; Lab, 1997).

Equally, even where shop theft is interpreted as the product of an instrumental and considered approach in making a rational choice to engage in offending behaviour (Wilson, 1975; Cornish and Clarke, 1986), the low rates of apprehension and referral to the police suggest that the shop-wise offender will readily calculate that the stealing-with-success odds are very much in his or her favour. Data from the BRC's crime survey show that of five million offences witnessed or experienced by retailers, only around one million were referred to the police and fewer than 276,000 were recorded by the police (Wells and Dryer, 1997). The large attrition between known offending and formal action suggests that theft is the product of a reasoned decision that the likely costs (detection) are more than compensated for by the likely benefits (the value of stolen product). Again, the introduction of CCTV would operate as a deterrent by increasing the potential offenders' perceptions of the likelihood of being detected. The findings over the three-month experimental period support the use of CCTV for deterrent purposes, whether shop theft is interpreted as a function of opportunity or rational choice. This reflects an earlier interpretation by Tilley (1993) that CCTV impinges more on risk-perception mechanisms than it does on rates of detection and conviction (see also Pawson and Tilley, 1997).

Critics will rightly suggest that the model of the all-knowing, fully informed and all-thinking offender, spending much of his or her time calculating the criminal odds, does not reflect the reality of offending behaviour. The concept of the "reasoning criminal" (Cornish and Clarke, 1986) can, however, be reconstituted in terms of a weaker form of rationality — something often referred to as "bounded rationality" or "limited rationality" (Newman, 1997; Opp, 1997). This approach recognises the complexity of factors (social, environmental and cognitive) that influence and shape behaviour. In the retail context, it is likely that the "decision" to offend or not is the product of an interaction between an overall setting that actively encourages criminal behaviour and features within it that act as disincentives to crime (see Wortley, 1997). The retail environment can be seen as a near-perfect example of a crime-encouraging situation, where ease of access to highly desirable product is deliberately engineered — a form of structured enticement, preferably to shop but possibly to steal. Against this, CCTV can be seen as a crime-discouraging behavioural prompt — a visible cue or reminder that "guardianship" is actively present. Although it is unlikely that would-be offenders constantly calculate the likely rewards of crime against its costs, it is highly plausible that CCTV (cameras, monitors and signage) acts as an occasional situational prompt that encourages rationality in coming to a decision about whether or not to commit crime.

The second major observation is that the effectiveness of CCTV had largely disappeared by the six-month point. Using the figures for the number of units lost and their value, although high-level stores showed a decrease in loss (26%) this was wiped out overall because of an increased loss in medium-level (32%) and low-level (9%) stores. In contrast, the figures for loss expressed as a percentage of sales showed an increase for high-level stores (38%), with decreases for medium-level (18%) and low-level (27%) stores. Although the data do not offer a consistent picture, it is worth exploring the possible reasons for success and failure. The explanation for continuing success (decreased loss) is straightforward: would-be offenders are inhibited by the potential that CCTV poses for increased detection, thereby securing a deterrent effect. The explanation for success not being sustained (decreased loss giving way to increased loss) is more problematic, but a likely mechanism is that would-be offenders become progressively inured or desensitised to CCTV's deterrent potential.

It is well-established that CCTV operators can be subject to so-called video blindness, wherein they fail to take in information from a number of screens in a way that allows them to analyse and react to images that give grounds for concern (Broadbent, 1958; Edwards and Tilley, 1994: Beck and Willis, 1995). It is equally possible that newly installed CCTV systems command the attention and respect of would-be offenders (with deterrent impact), but that familiarity over time leads to the equipment becoming a taken-for-granted, routinised part of the retail environment (with diminished deterrent impact). This is consistent with the "bounded" or "limited" perspective on rational choice in offending behaviour (see Newman et al., 1997) where long-term exposure to rationality-enhancing and crime-discouraging environmental prompts (such as CCTV) can lead to inhibition satiation — a case of over-familiarity breeding contempt. This is reflected by the data on loss by number of units and value (see Table 3), where there was continuing effectiveness for high-level systems, which had security staff monitoring the equipment at all times, and diminishing effectiveness for both medium-level systems with occasional monitoring and low-level systems with dummy cameras.

To the extent that the lack of long-term effectiveness is a product of familiarity over time leading to a reduction in deterrence, the crime prevention implications would appear to centre on giving CCTV a high profile and then on maintaining it. Just as retailers routinely redesign the shopping environment in the interests of keeping the honest shopper attracted to product, the security manager may need to consider a similar approach to CCTV in the interests of reminding potential offenders of the in-store security system. At a minimum, this would suggest that CCTV signage should be changed regularly, but it could also include moving the cameras and monitors themselves, or even taking them out and replacing them with new equipment. In each case, the emphasis would be on highlighting the presence of security hardware — and its operators — in order to maximise its deterrent effect. Pawson and Tilley (1997) refer to this as emphasising the "publicity" mechanism associated with CCTV.

Diminishing effectiveness over time could also be a product of an uncritical acceptance of the crime-control attributes of CCTV by in-store sales and security personnel, leading to a relaxation in staff vigilance. Staff may presume that CCTV is making a major contribution to the detection or deterrence of offenders, perhaps in the mistaken belief that it offers a technological panacea for the problem of crime. If they believe that security hardware is a primary factor in crime prevention, this could result in an overreliance on an impersonal, high-tech approach to security. There is some danger that staff could see themselves as being absolved from security responsibilities. As the authors have argued previously, CCTV may be "a double-edged sword where any crime control benefits need to be set against the possible costs of lower levels of staff vigilance" (Beck and Willis,

1995:190). A Home Office guide is also alert to the possibility of CCTV inadvertently producing an "exaggerated sense of security" (Edwards and Tilley, 1994:15). There is a possibility that the introduction of CCTV may cause feelings of security to go up but in the process cause staff feelings of responsibility for crime prevention to go down; a scenario with obvious implications for staff training. The ways in which the impact of security equipment is mediated by the person-centred activities of sales and security staff is a relatively under-explored area.

There is a interesting irony that where the introduction of CCTV can cause store staff to "switch off" leading to a reduction in security, its use may reassure members of the shopping public even where there are no measurable security advantages. There is some strength in the point that it does not matter a great deal whether CCTV is genuinely effective or whether members of the public merely believe that it offers real crime control benefits, even though this belief may be mistaken and unfounded. In one recent study, more than nine in ten members of the public held the view that surveillance cameras in the shopping environment were acceptable — 91% in town centres and 96% in shopping centres (Beck and Willis, 1995; see also Honess and Charman, 1992). The ever-present cameras were seen as a sym-bolic and reassuring affirmation that crime was under control, something that would have the consequence of alleviating fear and anxiety about possible victimisation (which is good in itself) but also operating so as to encourage customers to part with their money (which is good for the retailer). Paradoxically, the security manager may want to play down the effectiveness of CCTV to the store staff in the interests of promoting their vigilance, but emphasise (or even ex-aggerate) its effectiveness so far as the shopping public is concerned in the interests of promoting a safe and secure shopping environ-ment. The "reassurance" factor should not be underestimated be-cause promoting customer confidence could be seen as a sufficient justification for its installation, irrespective of genuine crime control benefits.

The third major observation relates to the way in which expendi-ture on CCTV installations can be set against the benefits of average weekly reductions in losses due to theft. Although Tilley (1997) is sceptical about the feasibility of an authoritative cost benefit analy-sis, on the grounds that there are so many potential variables to con-sider, it is possible — using the retailers' emphasis on the "bottom line" — to offer a robust and meaningful measure. Retailers argue that there is only one key consideration: whether or not the expenditure on security equipment is more than compensated for by savings attributable to reductions in loss due to crime. The relevant data are unequivocal: taking the six-month review as the longer-term (and stronger) measure, the payback period for a £24K high-level CCTV system is 65 weeks, whereas because there is no measurable impact on loss for a £14K medium-level and a £4K·low-level system, there is no prospect of these installations ever paying for themselves. Moreover, these figures represent the most optimistic payback scenarios because they include only the capital costs of CCTV installation and not the recurrent costs of manning the systems.

The hard-nosed retail manager will begin by wanting to know whether a given investment in CCTV will drive down the losses caused by crime, within a certain time frame, to a point that covers the expenditure on it. This is not only legitimate it is an inescapable feature of commercial life. Even where investment in CCTV cannot be justified in terms of a strict cost-benefit analysis, it could still be justified by wider social considerations such as reducing the fear of crime, or by sales and marketing considerations that use it to promote customers' perceptions of a safe and secure shopping environment. This is especially important because research shows that frightened customers who are concerned about crime and nuisance threats to safe shopping will relocate their shopping activities to locations deemed to be safe and secure rather than remain at those that are perceived to be intimidating and unsafe (Beck and Willis, 1995). Even here, the bottom-line analysis of costs against benefits is still crucial: it allows the company to be clear about the grounds for its decision making by articulating a reasoned departure from the bottom line of cost effectiveness.

CONCLUSION

A realistic and feasible evaluation of the impact of CCTV in the retail environment will need to move away from exploratory analysis (Ekblom, 1988) and focus on specific situational variables (Burrows and Speed, 1996) so as to indicate which context-specific mechanisms produce particular outcomes (Pawson and Tilley, 1997; Tilley, 1997). The study confirms that loss to sales figures, the number of units lost and their value all work as robust and "good enough" indicators of the likely impact of CCTV on theft. These may be imperfect but they are easy to collect routinely and they do reflect the private sector's emphasis on profit. The findings indicate that the most likely mechanism is that of deterrence, which is consistent with understanding crime either as the product of opportunity or as a function of rational choice. There is some evidence that the deterrent impact of CCTV diminishes over time, a fact that directs attention to the "publicity" given to it. But there is also a possibility that store staff become less security-conscious when the cameras are turned on. Finally, the cost-benefit analysis indicates that high-level systems alone "pay for themselves" in terms of reduced loss, which covers capital expenditure, although it is possible (and legitimate) to install CCTV for other reasons. The deployment of CCTV in the retail environment has measurable effects with particular explanations, which allows for more informed decision making about its future use and its contribution to crime prevention.

◆

Address correspondence to: Adrian Beck, Scarman Centre for the Study of Public Order, University of Leicester, 154 Upper New Walk, Leicester LE1 7QA, United Kingdom. E-mail: <bna@le.ac.uk>

REFERENCES

Bamfield, J. (1994). *National Survey of Retail Theft and Security 1994.* Northampton, UK: School of Business, Nene College.

Beck, A. and A. Willis (1995*). Crime and Security: Managing the Risk to Safe Shopping.* Leicester, UK: Perpetuity Press.

Broadbent, D. (1958). *Perception and Communication.* London, UK: Pergamon Press.

Burrows, J. and M. Speed (1994). *Retail Crime Costs 1992/93 Survey.* London, UK: British Retail Consortium.

—— (1996). "Crime Analysis: Lessons from the Retail Sector." *Security Journal* 7(1):53-60.

Cahill, M. (1994). *The New Social Policy.* Oxford, UK: Basil Blackwell.

Clarke, R.V.G. (1980). "Situational Crime Prevention: Theory and Practice." In: J. Muncie, E. McLaughlin and M. Langan (eds.), *Criminological Perspectives: A Reader.* London, UK: Sage.

Cornish, D. and R.V.G. Clarke (eds.) (1986). *The Reasoning Criminal.* New York, NY: Springer Verlag.

Edwards, P. and N. Tilley (1994). *Closed Circuit Television: Looking Out For You.* London, UK: Home Office.

Ekblom, P. (1986). *The Prevention of Shop Theft: An Approach Through Crime Analysis.* (Crime Prevention Unit Series Paper, #5.) London, UK: Home Office.

—— and K. Pease (1995). "Evaluating Crime Prevention." In: M. Tonry and D. Farrington (eds.), *Building a Safer Society,* (Crime and Justice, vol. 19.) Chicago, IL: University of Chicago Press.

—— and F. Simon (1988). *Crime Prevention and Racial Harassment in Asian-Run Small Shops: The Scope for Prevention.* (Crime Prevention Unit Series Paper, #15.) London, UK: Home Office.

Felson, M. (1994). *Crime and Everyday Life.* Thousand Oaks, CA.: Pine Forge.

—— (1996). "Preventing Retail Theft: An Application of Environmental Criminology." *Security Journal* 7(1):71-75.

Forum of Private Business (1995). *Crime and Small Business.* Knutsford, UK: Forum of Private Business.

Guy, C. (1994). *The Retail Development Process.* London, UK: Routledge.

Hibberd, M. and J. Shapland (1993). *Violent Crime in Small Shops.* London, UK: Police Foundation.

Honess, T. and E. Charman (1992). *Closed Circuit Television in Public Places: Its Acceptability and Perceived Effectiveness.* (Crime Prevention Unit Series Paper, #35.) London, UK: Home Office.

Hough, M., R.V.G. Clarke and P. Mayhew (1980). "Introduction." In: R.V.G. Clarke and P. Mayhew (eds.), *Designing Out Crime.* London, UK: Her Majesty's Stationery Office.

Lab, J. (1997). *Crime Prevention Approaches, Practices and Evaluations.* Cincinnati, OH: Anderson.

Mirrlees-Black, C and A. Ross (1995). *Crime Against Retail and Manufacturing Premises: Findings from the 1994 Commercial Victimisation Survey.* (Home Office Research Study, #146.) London, UK: Home Office.

Newman, G. (1997). "Introduction: Towards a Theory of Situational Crime Prevention." In: G. Newman, R. Clarke and S. Shoham (eds.), *Rational Choice and Situational Crime Prevention.* Aldershot, UK: Ashgate Dartmouth.

—— R. Clarke and S. Shoham (eds.) (1997). *Rational Choice and Situational Crime Prevention.* Aldershot, UK: Ashgate Dartmouth.

O'Brien, L. and F. Harris (1991). *Retailing: Shopping, Space, Society.* London, UK: David Fulton.

Opp, K. (1997). "Limited Rationality and Crime." In: G. Newman, R. Clarke and S. Shoham (eds.), *Rational Choice and Situational Crime Prevention.* Aldershot, UK: Ashgate Dartmouth.

Pawson, R. and N. Tilley (1994). "What Works in Evaluation Research." *British Journal of Criminology* 34(2):291-306.

—— (1997). *Realistic Evaluation.* London, UK: Sage.

Poyner, B. (1983). *Design Against Crime: Beyond Defensible Space.* London, UK: Butterworths.

Speed, M., J. Burrows and J. Bamfield (1995). *Retail Crime Costs 1993/94 Survey: The Impact of Crime and the Retail Response.* London, UK: British Retail Consortium.

Tilley, N. (1993). *Understanding Car Parks, Crime and CCTV.* (Crime Prevention Unit Paper, #42.) London, UK: Home Office.

—— (1997). "Whys and Wherefores in Evaluating the Effectiveness of CCTV." *International Journal of Risk, Security and Crime Prevention* 2(3):175-186.

Touche Ross (1989). *Survey into Retail Shrinkage and Other Stock Losses.* London, UK: author.

—— (1992). *Retail Shrinkage and Other Stock Losses: Results of the Second Retail Survey.* London, UK: author.

U.K. Home Office (1986). *Standing Conference on Crime Prevention Report of the Working Group on Shop Theft.* London, UK: author.

—— (1996a). *Home Office Statistical Bulletin Issue 18/96, Notifiable Offences England and Wales, July 1995 to June 1996.* London, UK: author.

—— (1996b). *Further Funding for CCTV, Home Office Press Release No. 258/96.* London, UK: author.

U.K. House of Commons (1994). *Environment Committee, Session 1993–94, Fourth Report, Shopping Centres and Their Future. Vol. I, Report.* London, UK: Her Majesty's Stationery Office.

Wells, C. and A. Dryer (1997). *Retail Crime Costs 1995/96 Survey.* London, UK: British Retail Consortium.

Wilson, J.Q. (1975). *Thinking About Crime.* New York, NY: Basic Books.

Wortley, R. (1997). "Reconsidering the Role of Opportunity in Situational Crime Prevention." In: G. Newman, R. Clarke and S. Shoham (eds.), *Rational Choice and Situational Crime Prevention.* Aldershot, UK: Ashgate Dartmouth.

DATE DUE			
MAR 0 1 2007			